'The most important book I read this year was *The Strange Death of Europe* by Douglas Murray, about why Europe is done for ... Balanced and compelling.'
Katie Law, *Evening Standard* Books of the Year, 2017

'Douglas Murray's introduction to this already destructive subject of Islamist hegemony is a distinguished attempt to clarify the origins of a storm. I found myself continually wishing that he wasn't making himself quite so clear.'
Clive James

'His overall thesis, that a guilt-driven and exhausted Europe is playing fast and loose with its precious modern values by embracing migration on such a scale, is hard to refute.'
Juliet Samuel, *Daily Telegraph*

'Every so often, something is published which slices through the fog of confusion, obfuscation and the sheer dishonesty of public debate to illuminate one key fact about the world. Such a work is Douglas Murray's tremendous and shattering book, *The Strange Death of Europe*.'
Melanie Phillips, *The Times*

'Breathtakingly gripping'
Michael Gove MP, *Standpoint*

'This is a brilliant, important and profoundly depressing book. That it is written with Douglas Murray's usual literary elegance and waspish humour does not make it any less depressing. That Murray will be vilified for it by the liberals who have created the appalling mess he describes does not make it any less brilliant and important ... Read it'
Rod Liddle, *Sunday Times*

'This is a vitally important book, the contents of which should be known to everyone who can influence the course of events, at this critical time in the history of Europe.'
Roger Scruton

'Douglas Murray glitters in the gloom. His pessimism about multiculturalism is so well constructed and written it is almost uplifting. Liberals will want to rebut him. I should warn them that they will need to argue harder than they have ever argued before.'
Nick Cohen

'A compelling, insightful and persuasively argued narrative ... a deeply humane book that touches on individual tragedy ... It may even prove to be the start of a conversation, and for such a dangerously politicised and neglected subject, that would be most welcome.'

Entertainment Focus

'A cogent summary of how, over three decades or more, elites across western Europe turned a blind eye to the failures of integration and the rise of Islamism ... Persuasive'

The Times

'Powerful and engaging ... Murray is at his strongest when lampooning the neurotic guilt of Western liberal elites ... Disagree passionately if you will, but you won't regret reading it.'

Literary Review

'By far the most compelling political book of the year was Douglas Murray's *The Strange Death of Europe* ... fearless, truth-telling, and masterfully organised ... Don't hold an opinion about this book if you have not read it.'

David Sexton, *Evening Standard* Books of the Year, 2017

'Powerfully argued'

Roland White, *Sunday Times* Political Books of the Year, 2017

'This is the most disturbing political book I've read this year. Based on travels through key European centers, Murray weaves a tale of uncontrolled immigration, failed multiculturalism, systemic self-doubt, cultural suicide and disingenuous political leadership. Accurate, insightful and devastating, with applicable lessons for countries on both sides of the Atlantic.'

Rabbi Lord Jonathan Sacks

THE STRANGE DEATH
OF EUROPE

THE STRANGE DEATH
OF EUROPE

Immigration, Identity, Islam

DOUGLAS MURRAY

BLOOMSBURY CONTINUUM
LONDON · OXFORD · NEW YORK · NEW DELHI · SYDNEY

BLOOMSBURY CONTINUUM
Bloomsbury Publishing Plc
50 Bedford Square, London, WC1B 3DP, UK
29 Earlsford Terrace, Dublin 2, Ireland

BLOOMSBURY, BLOOMSBURY CONTINUUM and the Diana logo are trademarks of
Bloomsbury Publishing Plc

First published in Great Britain 2017
This paperback edition published 2018

A catalogue record for this book is available from the British Library.

Library of Congress Cataloguing-in-Publication data has been applied for.

ISBN: HB: 978-1-4729-4224-1; PB: 978-1-4729-5800-6; US: 978-1-4729-5805-1;
EPUB: 978-1-4729-4225-8; EPDF: 978-1-4729-4222-7

10

Typeset by Integra Software Services Pvt. Ltd
Printed and bound in Great Britain by CPI Group (UK) Ltd, Croydon CR0 4YY

To find out more about our authors and books visit www.bloomsbury.com
and sign up for our newsletters.

CONTENTS

INTRODUCTION

Europe is committing suicide. Or at least its leaders have decided to commit suicide. Whether the European people choose to go along with this is, naturally, another matter.

When I say that Europe is in the process of killing itself I do not mean that the burden of European Commission regulation has become overbearing or that the European Convention on Human Rights has not done enough to satisfy the demands of a particular community. I mean that the civilisation we know as Europe is in the process of committing suicide and that neither Britain nor any other Western European country can avoid that fate because we all appear to suffer from the same symptoms and maladies. As a result, by the end of the lifespans of most people currently alive Europe will not be Europe and the peoples of Europe will have lost the only place in the world we had to call home.

It may be pointed out that proclamations of Europe's demise have been a staple throughout our history and that Europe would not be Europe without regular predictions of our mortality. Yet some have been more persuasively timed than others. In *Die Welt von Gestern* (*The World of Yesterday*), first published in 1942, Stefan Zweig wrote of his continent in the years leading up to the Second World War, 'I felt that Europe, in its state of derangement, had passed its own death sentence – our sacred home of Europe, both the cradle and the Parthenon of Western civilisation.'

One of the few things that gave Zweig any hope even then was that in the countries of South America to which he had finally fled he saw offshoots of his own culture. In Argentina and Brazil he witnessed how a culture can emigrate from one land to another so that even if the tree that gave the culture life has died it can still provide 'new blossom and new fruit'. Even had Europe at that moment destroyed

1

itself completely, Zweig felt the consolation that 'What generations had done before us was never entirely lost.'[1]

Today, largely because of the catastrophe Zweig described, the tree of Europe is finally lost. Europe today has little desire to reproduce itself, fight for itself or even take its own side in an argument. Those in power seem persuaded that it would not matter if the people and culture of Europe were lost to the world. Some have clearly decided (as Bertolt Brecht wrote in his 1953 poem 'The Solution') to dissolve the people and elect another because, as a recent Swedish conservative Prime Minister Fredrik Reinfeldt put it, only 'barbarism' comes from countries like his whereas only good things come from outside.

There is no single cause of the present sickness. The culture produced by the tributaries of Judaeo-Christian culture, the Ancient Greeks and Romans, and the discoveries of the Enlightenment has not been levelled by nothing. But the final act has come about because of two simultaneous concatenations from which it is now all but impossible to recover.

The first is the mass movement of peoples into Europe. In all Western European countries this process began after the Second World War due to labour shortages. Soon Europe got hooked on the migration and could not stop the flow even if it had wanted to. The result was that what had been Europe – the home of the European peoples – gradually became a home for the entire world. The places that had been European gradually became somewhere else. So places dominated by Pakistani immigrants resembled Pakistan in everything but their location, with the recent arrivals and their children eating the food of their place of origin, speaking the language of their place of origin and worshipping the religion of their place of origin. Streets in the cold and rainy northern towns of Europe filled with people dressed for the foothills of Pakistan or the sandstorms of Arabia. 'The Empire strikes back' noted some observers with a barely concealed smirk. Yet whereas the empires of Europe had been thrown off, these new colonies were obviously intended to be for good.

All the time Europeans found ways to pretend this could work. By insisting, for instance, that such immigration was normal. Or that if integration did not happen with the first generation then it might happen with their children, grandchildren or another generation yet to come. Or that it didn't matter whether people integrated or not. All the time we waved away the greater likelihood that it just wouldn't work. This is a conclusion that the migration crisis of recent years has simply accelerated.

Which brings me to the second concatenation. For even the mass movement of millions of people into Europe would not sound such a final note for the continent were it not for the fact that (coincidentally or otherwise) at the same time Europe lost faith in its beliefs, traditions and legitimacy. Countless factors have contributed to this development, but one is the way in which Western Europeans have lost what the Spanish philosopher Miguel de Unamuno famously called the 'tragic sense of life'. They have forgotten what Zweig and his generation so painfully learnt: that everything you love, even the greatest and most cultured civilisations in history, can be swept away by people who are unworthy of them. Other than simply ignoring it, one of the few ways to avoid this tragic sense of life is to push it away through a belief in the tide of human progress. That tactic remains for the time being the most popular approach.

Yet all the time we skate over, and sometimes fall into, terrible doubts of our own creation. More than any other continent or culture in the world today, Europe is now deeply weighed down with guilt for its past. Alongside this outgoing version of self-distrust runs a more introverted version of the same guilt. For there is also the problem in Europe of an existential tiredness and a feeling that perhaps for Europe the story has run out and a new story must be allowed to begin. Mass immigration – the replacement of large parts of the European populations by other people – is one way in which this new story has been imagined: a change, we seemed to think, was as good as a rest. Such existential civilisational tiredness is not a uniquely modern European phenomenon, but the fact that a society should feel like it has run out of steam at precisely the moment when a new society has begun to move in cannot help but lead to vast, epochal changes.

Had it been possible to discuss these matters some solution might have been reached. Yet even in 2015, at the height of the migration crisis, it was speech and thought that was constricted. At the peak of the crisis in September 2015 Chancellor Merkel of Germany asked the Facebook CEO, Mark Zuckerberg, what could be done to stop European citizens writing criticisms of her migration policy on Facebook. 'Are you working on this?' she asked him. He assured her that he was.[2] In fact the criticism, thought and discussion ought to have been boundless. Looking back, it is remarkable how restricted we made our discussion even whilst we opened our home to the world. A thousand years ago the peoples of Genoa and Florence were not as intermingled as they now are, but today they are all recognisably Italian and tribal differences have tended to lessen rather than grow with time. The current thinking appears to be that at some stage in the years ahead the peoples of Eritrea and Afghanistan too will be intermingled within Europe as the Genoans and Florentines are now melded into Italy. The skin colour of individuals from Eritrea and Afghanistan may be different, their ethnic origins may be from further afield, but Europe will still be Europe and its people will continue to mingle in the spirit of Voltaire and St Paul, Dante, Goethe and Bach.

As with so many popular delusions there is something in this. The nature of Europe has always shifted and – as trading cities like Venice show – has included a grand and uncommon receptiveness to foreign ideas and influence. From the Ancient Greeks and Romans onwards the peoples of Europe sent out ships to scour the world and report back on what they found. Rarely, if ever, did the rest of the world return their curiosity in kind, but nevertheless the ships went out and returned with tales and discoveries that melded into the air of Europe. The receptivity was prodigious: it was not, however, boundless.

The question of where the boundaries of the culture lay is endlessly argued over by anthropologists and cannot be solved. But there were boundaries. Europe was never, for instance, a continent of Islam. Yet the awareness that our culture is constantly, subtly changing has deep European roots. The philosophers of Ancient Greece understood the conundrum, summing it up most famously in the paradox of the Ship of Theseus. As recorded in Plutarch, the ship in which Theseus had sailed had been preserved by the Athenians who put in new timber when parts of the ship decayed. Yet was this not still the ship of Theseus even when it consisted of none of the materials in which he had sailed?

We know that the Greeks today are not the same people as the Ancient Greeks. We know that the English are not the same today as they were a millennium ago, nor the French the French. And yet they are recognisably Greek, English and French and all are European. In these and other identities we recognise a degree of cultural succession: a tradition that remains with certain qualities (positive as well as negative), customs and behaviours. We recognise the great movements of the Normans, Franks and Gauls brought about great changes. And we know from history that some movements affect a culture relatively little in the long term whereas others can change it irrevocably. The problem comes not with an acceptance of change, but with the knowledge that when those changes come too fast or are too different we become something else – including something we may never have wanted to be.

At the same time we are confused over how this is meant to work. While generally agreeing that it is possible for an individual to absorb a particular culture (given the right degree of enthusiasm both from the individual and the culture) whatever their skin colour, we know that we Europeans cannot become whatever we like. We cannot become Indian or Chinese, for instance. And yet we are expected to believe that anyone in the world can move to Europe and become European. If being 'European' is not about race – as we hope it is not – then it is even more imperative that it is about 'values'. This is what makes the question 'What are European values?' so important. Yet this is another debate about which we are wholly confused.

Are we, for instance, Christian? In the 2000s this debate had a focal point in the row over the wording of the new EU Constitution and the absence of any mention of the continent's Christian heritage. Pope John Paul II and his successor tried to rectify the omission. As the former wrote in 2003, 'While fully respecting the secular nature of the institutions I wish once more to appeal to those drawing up the future European constitutional treaty, so that it will include a reference to the religious and in particular the Christian heritage of Europe.'³ The debate did not only divide Europe geographically and politically, it also pointed to a glaring aspiration. For religion had not only retreated in Western Europe. In its wake there arose a desire to demonstrate that in the twenty-first century Europe had a self-supporting structure of rights, laws and institutions which could exist even without the source that had arguably given them life. Like Kant's dove we wondered whether we wouldn't be able to fly faster if we lived 'in free air' without the bother of the wind keeping us aloft. Much rested on the success of this dream. In the place of religion came the ever-inflating language of 'human rights' (itself a concept of Christian origin). We left unresolved the question of whether or not our acquired rights were reliant on beliefs that the continent had ceased to hold or whether they existed of their own accord. This was, at the very least, an extremely big question to have left unresolved while vast new populations were being expected to 'integrate'.

An equally significant question erupted at the same time around the position and purpose of the nation state. From the Treaty of Westphalia in 1648 up to the late twentieth century the nation state in Europe had generally been regarded not only as the best guarantor of constitutional order and liberal rights but the ultimate guarantor of peace. Yet this certainty also eroded. Central European figures like Chancellor Kohl of Germany in 1996 insisted that 'The nation state ... cannot solve the great problems of the twenty-first century.' Disintegration of the nation states of Europe into one large integrated political union was so important, Kohl insisted, that it was in fact 'a question of war and peace in the twenty-first century'.⁴ Others disagreed, and twenty years later just over half of the British people demonstrated at the ballot box that they were unpersuaded by Kohl's argument. But once again, whatever one's views on the matter, this was a huge question to leave unresolved at a time of vast population change.

While unsure of ourselves at home we made final efforts at extending our values abroad. Yet whenever our governments and armies got involved in anything in the name of these 'human rights' – Iraq in 2003, Libya in 2011 – we seemed to make things worse and ended up in the wrong. When the Syrian civil war began people cried for Western nations to intervene in the name of the human rights that were undoubtedly being violated. But there was no appetite to protect such rights because whether or not we believed in them at home, we had certainly lost faith in our ability to advance them abroad. At some stage it began to seem possible that what had been called 'the last utopia' – the first universal system that divorced the rights of man from the say of gods or tyrants – might comprise a final failed European aspiration.[5] If that is indeed the case then it leaves Europeans in the twenty-first century without any unifying idea capable of ordering the present or approaching the future.

At any time the loss of all unifying stories about our past or ideas about what to do with our present or future would be a serious conundrum. But during a time of momentous societal change and upheaval the results are proving fatal. The world is coming into Europe at precisely the moment that Europe has lost sight of what it is. And while the movement of millions of people from other cultures into a strong and assertive culture might have worked, the movement of millions of people into a guilty, jaded and dying culture cannot. Even now Europe's leaders talk of an invigorated effort to incorporate the millions of new arrivals.

These efforts too will fail. In order to incorporate as large and wide a number of people as possible it is necessary to come up with a definition of inclusion that is as wide and unobjectionable as possible. If Europe is going to become a home for the world it must search for a definition of itself that is wide enough to encompass the world. This means that in the period before this aspiration collapses our values become so wide as to become meaninglessly shallow. So whereas European identity in the past could be attributed to highly specific, not to mention philosophically and historically deep foundations (the rule of law, the ethics derived from the continent's history and philosophy), today the ethics and beliefs of Europe – indeed the identity and ideology of Europe – have become about 'respect', 'tolerance' and (most self-abnegating of all) 'diversity'. Such shallow self-definitions may get us through a few more years, but they have no chance at all of being able to call on the deeper loyalties that societies must be able to reach if they are going to survive for long.

This is just one reason why it is likely that our European culture, which has lasted all these centuries and shared with the world such heights of human achievement, will not survive. As recent elections in Austria and the rise of Alternative für Deutschland seem to prove, while the likelihood of cultural erosion remains irresistible the options for cultural defence continue to be unacceptable. Stefan Zweig was right to recognise the derangement, and right to recognise the death sentence that the cradle and Parthenon of Western civilisation had passed upon itself. Only his timing was out. It would take several more decades before that sentence was carried out – by ourselves on ourselves. Here, in the in-between years, instead of remaining a home for the European peoples we have decided to become a 'utopia' only in the original Greek sense of the word: to become 'no place'. This book is an account of that process.

***

The research and writing of this book have taken me across a continent I have travelled well for years, but often to parts I might otherwise not have visited. Over the course of several years I travelled from the most south-easterly islands of Greece and the southernmost outposts of Italy to the heart of northern Sweden and countless suburbs of France, Holland, Germany and more. During the writing I have had the opportunity to speak with many members of the public as well as politicians and policy-makers from across the political spectrum, border guards, intelligence agencies, NGO workers and many others on the front line. In many ways the most instructive part of my research has been speaking to Europe's newest arrivals – people who sometimes literally arrived yesterday. On the reception islands of southern Europe and across the places they stay or settle on their way north all have their own stories and many have their own tragedies. All see Europe as the place where they can best live their lives.

Those willing to talk and share their stories were necessarily a self-selecting group. There were times, lingering outside a camp in the evening, when people emerged or returned who seemed – to say the least – not to be approaching our continent in a spirit of generosity or gratitude. But many others were exceptionally friendly and grateful for an opportunity to get their stories out. Whatever my own views on the situations that had brought them here and our continent's response, our conversations always concluded with me saying the only thing to them that I honestly could say without caveat: 'Good luck.'

1

The beginning

To understand the scale and speed of the change that is happening in Europe it is worth going back just a few years, to before the latest migration crisis and to a period of what had become 'normal' immigration. And it is worth considering a country that was comparatively cut off from the latest turmoil.

In 2002 the latest census for England and Wales was published. Compiled the previous year, it showed the extent to which the country had changed in the decade since the last census was taken. Imagine somebody then, in 2002, deciding to extrapolate on the findings in that census and speculating on what the next ten years might bring. Imagine that they said: 'White Britons will become a minority in their own capital city by the end of this decade and the Muslim population will double in the next ten years.'

How would such statements have been greeted? The terms 'alarmist' and 'scaremongering' would certainly have been used, as most likely would 'racist' and (although the coinage was then in its infancy) the word 'Islamophobe'. Safe to say such extrapolations of the data would not have been greeted warmly. Anybody inclined to doubt this might recall just one representative incident, when in 2002 a *Times* journalist made far less startling comments about likely future immigration, which were denounced by the then Home Secretary David Blunkett – using parliamentary privilege – as 'bordering on fascism'.[1]

Yet however abused, anybody offering such analysis in 2002 would have been proved wholly and utterly right. The next census, compiled in 2011 and published at the end of 2012, revealed not just the facts mentioned above, but far more. It proved that the number of people living in England and Wales who had been born overseas had risen by nearly three million in the previous decade alone. It showed that only 44.9 per cent of London residents now identified themselves as 'white British'. And it revealed that nearly three million people in England and Wales were living in households where not one adult spoke English as their main language.

These were very major ethnic changes to a country at any point in time. But there were equally striking findings about the changing religious make-up of Britain. For instance they revealed that almost every belief was on the rise apart from Christianity. Only Britain's historic national religion was in free fall. Since the previous census, the number of people identifying themselves as Christian had dropped from 72 to 59 per cent. The number of Christians in England and Wales dropped by more than four million, and the number of Christians overall fell from 37 million to 33 million.

But while Christianity witnessed this collapse in its followers – a collapse that was only expected to continue precipitately – mass migration assisted a near-doubling in the size of the Muslim population. Between 2001 and 2011 the number of Muslims in England and Wales rose from 1.5 million to 2.7 million. While these were the official figures there was a widespread acceptance that illegal immigrations made all these numbers far higher. At least a million people were recognised to be in the country illegally, and thus unlikely to have filled in census forms, and the two local authorities which had already grown the fastest (over 20 per cent in ten years) were those that already had the highest Muslim populations in the UK (Tower Hamlets and Newham). These were also among the areas of the country with the largest non-response to the census, with around one in five households failing to return the census at all. All of which suggested that the census results, startling as they were, drastically under-represented the actual numbers. Nevertheless, the findings were striking.

Yet, despite being hard to digest in a year, the story of the census passed by within a couple of days – like any other ephemeral news story. But this was not an ephemeral story. It was an account of the country's recent past, its immediate present and a glimpse into its inevitable future. To study the results of that census was to stare at one particularly unalterable conclusion, which was that mass immigration was in the process of altering – indeed had already altered – the country completely. By 2011 Britain had already become a radically different place from the place it had been for centuries. But the response to facts such as that in 23 of London's 33 boroughs 'white Britons' were now in a minority was greeted with a response almost as telling as the results themselves.[2] A spokesman for the Office for National Statistics (ONS) hailed the results as a tremendous demonstration of 'diversity'.[3]

The political and media reaction, meanwhile, was striking for being conducted in only one tone of voice. When politicians of all the main parties addressed the census they greeted the results solely in a spirit of celebration. It had been the same for years. In 2007 the then Mayor of London, Ken Livingstone, spoke with pride about the fact that 35 per cent of people who worked in London had been born in a foreign country.[4] The question that lingered was whether there was any optimal limit to this or not? For years a sense of excitement and optimism about the changes to the country seemed the only tone appropriate to strike. Bolstered by the pretence that this was nothing new.

Throughout most of its history, and certainly for the previous millennium, Britain had retained an extraordinarily static population. Even the Norman Conquest in 1066 – perhaps the most important event in the islands' story – led to no more than 5 per cent of the population of England being Norman.[5] What movement there was in the years before and after was almost entirely movement between the island of Ireland and the countries that would eventually comprise the United Kingdom. Then in the post-1945 period Britain needed to fill particular gaps in the labour market, especially in the transport sector and the newly created National Health Service. And so the period of mass immigration began, though slowly at first. The 1948 British Nationality Act allowed immigration from the former Empire – now the Commonwealth – and by the early 1950s a few thousand people a year were taking advantage of the scheme. By the end of the decade the number of newcomers had gone into the tens of thousands, and by the 1960s the numbers had entered six figures. The vast majority of these arrivals came from the West Indies as well as India, Pakistan and Bangladesh, often entering Britain to do factory work and recommending others – often from their own families or clans – to follow and do similar work in their wake.

Despite some public concern about all this and what it meant for the country, neither the Labour nor Conservative governments that alternated in office were able to do much to stem the movement. As with countries on the continent such as France, Holland and Germany, there was little clarity and less consensus over what the arrival of these workers meant, or even whether they would stay. Only once it became clear that they would stay, and would use the opportunity to bring their extended families to join them, did some of the implications become clear.

During the years that followed there were highly specific Acts of Parliament to address, for instance, criminality among migrants. But there were few attempts to reverse the trend. Even when there was legislation attempting to satisfy growing public concern this had unexpected consequences. For instance the 1962 Commonwealth Immigrants Act, which ostensibly aimed to limit the flow of migrants and persuade some to return home, had the opposite effect, persuading many immigrants to bring their entire families into the United Kingdom while they – as they saw it – had the chance. The fact that Commonwealth immigrants no longer had to have a job to come to after 1962 caused another upsurge. It was not until the 1971 Immigration Act that there was any further attempt to stem the resultant flow. So despite the fact that there had never been any plan to allow migration on such a scale, governments of all stripes found themselves forced to deal with the consequences of the situation in which they and the British people found themselves. It was a situation no one had ever accurately predicted, but which had repercussions that every subsequent government would have to react to.

The repercussions did include some serious bouts of racial trouble. The Notting Hill riots of 1958 are still remembered for being a violent confrontation between West Indian immigrants and white Londoners. But such flashpoints are remembered precisely because they were the exception rather than the rule. While low-level suspicion and concern about outsiders undoubtedly existed, all efforts to capitalise on such unrest were a consistent and wholesale failure – notably those of Oswald Mosley, former leader of the British Union of Fascists and now head of the Union Movement. When Mosley tried to take electoral advantage of the Notting Hill riots and run for Parliament in the general election of 1959, his share of the vote did not even make it into double digits. The British people recognised that there were issues arising from large-scale immigration, but they also showed that they knew the answers did not lie with extremists who they had seen off before.

But troubles did arise, not least for some of those who had arrived in the country by invitation only to find themselves, once there, the target of discrimination. One response to these problems was Parliament's passing of the Race Relations Acts of 1965, 1968 and 1976, which made it illegal to discriminate against somebody on the grounds of 'colour, race or ethnic or national origins'. It is a mark of how little thought through the whole subject was that no such bills were ever considered in advance but only ever as a reaction once problems arose. No Race Relations Act was prepared in 1948, for example, precisely because nobody foresaw the numbers of people who would be coming to the United Kingdom in the future or the fact that there could be unpleasant implications as a result.

Throughout this period opinion polls showed that the British public were overwhelmingly opposed to the migration policies of their governments and believed that immigration into Britain was too high. An April 1968 poll by Gallup found that 75 per cent of the British public believed that controls on immigration were not strict enough. That figure would soon rise to 83 per cent.[6] At this point there arose the only moment when immigration briefly had the potential to become a major political issue. In that same month the then Conservative shadow cabinet minister Enoch Powell gave a speech to a Conservative association in Birmingham that opened out the debate and just as quickly closed it down. Although it didn't quite use the words by which it became known, the 'Rivers of Blood' speech was filled with prophetic foreboding about the future of Britain if immigration continued at its then current rate. 'Those whom the gods wish to destroy, they first make mad,' declared Powell. 'We must be mad, literally mad, as a nation to be permitting the annual inflow of some 50,000 dependents, who are for the most part the material of the future growth of the immigrant-descended population. It is like watching a nation busily engaged in heaping up its own funeral pyre.'[7] Although Powell's speech was about identity and his country's future, it was also about practical concerns – about constituents finding hospital places or school places for their children in a stretched public sector.

Powell was immediately relieved of his position in the shadow cabinet by his party's leader, Edward Heath, and any mainstream political support Powell might have garnered – not to mention his own political future – was over. Yet public support for his views was high – with opinion polls showing around three-quarters of the general public agreeing with his sentiments and 69 per cent believing that Heath had been wrong to sack him.[8] Many years later, one of Powell's Conservative Party opponents, Michael Heseltine, said that if Powell had stood for the leadership of the Conservative Party in the aftermath of that speech he would have won by a landslide and that if he had stood to be Prime Minister he would have won by a 'national landslide'.[9] But politically there was no way through for Powell, and his career did not merely falter but remained in the political wilderness for the remaining decades of his life.

Ever since the 'Rivers of Blood' speech, common wisdom in Britain has had it that Powell's intervention not only wrecked his own career but wrecked any possibility of a full or frank immigration debate in Britain for at least a generation. So lurid were Powell's terms and so dire his warnings that anybody concerned about immigration for evermore risked being tarred as a 'Powell-ite'. Certainly parts of Powell's speech made it too easy for his political opponents to attack him and gave far too much cover for people way to his political right. But among the things most striking when reading his speech – and the reactions to it – today are the portions for which he was lambasted that now seem almost understated: for instance, Powell's insistence that there was a street in Britain on which only one white woman was living. In subsequent interviews and discussions the case of this woman was widely dismissed as a fabrication because it was believed that no such street could exist. However, if anyone had suggested to Powell in 1968 that he should use his Birmingham speech to predict that within the lifespan of most people listening those who identified as 'white British' would be in a minority in their capital city, he would have dismissed such an advisor as a maniac. As was the case in each of the other European countries, even the most famous prophet of immigration doom in fact underestimated and understated the case.

The truth behind the claim that Powell's intervention made immigration an impossible discussion for a generation was that his intervention – and the heat it unleashed – allowed politicians to excuse themselves from addressing the implications of their policy. Many had clearly concluded that the trajectory the country was on was unalterable. During the 1960s there was still parliamentary debate over returning immigrants to their country of origin if, for instance, they committed a crime in Britain.[10] Later there was legislation to prevent the habit of 'marriages of convenience' carried out solely in order to gain citizenship.[11] But by the 1970s and 1980s the size of the immigrant community meant it was plain that any policy aimed at diminishing the size of that community was impossible even if it was deemed desirable. As with countries across the continent, Britain was in a position that it had not intended to be in and would have to improvise its reactions to whatever challenges and benefits this new reality produced. But it was a measure of the unspoken concern about what these challenges comprised that throughout this period even the most straightforward expressions of truth became impossible to voice.

In January 1984 the headmaster of a school in Bradford, Ray Honeyford, published a piece in a small-circulation magazine called *The Salisbury Review*, in which he reflected on some aspects of running a school in an area where 90 per cent of pupils were of immigrant parents. He mentioned the refusal of some Muslim fathers to permit their daughters to participate in dance classes, drama or sport, and the silence of the authorities on this and other cultural practices, such as taking children back to Pakistan during term time. He also argued for pupils to be encouraged to speak the language and understand the culture of the country they were living in and not to be encouraged to live – as Honeyford argued the race-relations leadership were trying to encourage them to do – parallel lives within society.

A campaign against Honeyford was swiftly organised by the race-relations industry he had used part of his article to criticise. The Muslim Mayor of Bradford demanded Honeyford be sacked, accusing him even years later of (among other things) 'cultural chauvinism'.[12] Amid protests and nationwide cries of 'Raycist', Honeyford was forced out of his job and never again worked in education. He had said in his offending article that thanks to a corruption of politics and even of language it was difficult to write honestly about these matters, and his own treatment more than proved that point. Why should a popular headmaster – about whom there were no other complaints – have been forced into retirement for making such an argument? The only explanation is that at the time even plain truths about these matters had not yet become palatable. A political and social paradigm – uncomfortably referred to as 'multiculturalism' – had begun, and in 1984 it was not yet possible to shatter the basis of that belief. Although it would have been scant consolation to Ray Honeyford, within a couple of decades of his article's publication many more people were saying that perhaps he had been onto something, and by the time of his death in 2012 the thrust of his argument had become widely accepted.

During the 1980s and 1990s, under the new rubric of 'multiculturalism', a steady stream of immigration into Britain continued from the Indian subcontinent and elsewhere. But an unspoken consensus existed whereby immigration – while always trending upwards – was quietly limited. What happened then, after the Labour Party's landslide election victory in 1997, was a breaking of that consensus. Although neither a manifesto commitment nor a stated aim, once in power Tony Blair's government oversaw an opening of the borders on a scale unparalleled even in the post-war decades. They abolished the 'primary purpose rule', which had attempted to filter out bogus marriage applications. They opened the borders to anyone deemed essential to the British economy – a definition so broad that it included restaurant workers as 'skilled labourers'. And as well as opening the door to the rest of the world, they opened the borders to the new EU member states of Eastern Europe. It was the effects of all of this, and more, that created the picture of the country revealed in the 2011 census.

Of course there are various claims as to how this post-1997 immigration surge occurred. One, famously made in 2009 by the former Labour speech-writer Andrew Neather, was that Tony Blair's government wilfully eased the immigration rules because they wanted to 'rub the Right's nose in diversity' and create what they unwisely took to be an electorate that would subsequently be loyal to the Labour Party.[13] After the outcry caused by his 2009 recollection Neather qualified this particular memory. Other Labour officials from those years began to say they had no idea who Neather was. But it is not hard to see how anyone, however junior, could have come away with such an impression of what was happening in those years.

For instance, it was clear from the moment of her appointment as Minister for Asylum and Immigration during Tony Blair's first term that Barbara Roche was seeking a complete rethink of Britain's immigration and asylum policies. While the Prime Minister was concentrating on other matters, Roche changed every aspect of the British government's policies. From here onwards all people claiming to be asylum seekers would be allowed to stay in Britain – whether they were genuine or not – because as she informed one official, 'Removal takes too long, and it's emotional.' Roche also thought the contemporary restraints on immigration were 'racist' and that the whole 'atmosphere' around the immigration debate 'was toxic'. Over her period in office she repeatedly stated her ambition to transform Britain. As one colleague said, 'Roche didn't see her job as controlling entry into Britain, but by looking at the wider picture "in a holistic way" she wanted us to see the benefit of a multicultural society.'

Neither the Prime Minister nor the Home Secretary, Jack Straw, were interested in questioning the new asylum policy, nor the fact that under Roche everyone entering Britain, whether he or she had a job to go to or not, was turned into an 'economic migrant'. Wherever there was any criticism of her policy, either internally or externally, Roche dismissed it as racist. Indeed Roche – who criticised colleagues for being too white – insisted that even the mention of immigration policy was racist.[14] What she and a few others around her sought was a wholesale change of British society. Roche – a descendant of East End Jews – believed that immigration was only ever a good thing. Ten years after the changes she had brought about she told an interviewer with satisfaction, 'I love the diversity of London. I just feel comfortable.'[15]

The activities of Roche and a few others in the 1997 Labour government backs up the idea that theirs was a deliberate policy of societal transformation: a culture war being waged against the British people using immigrants as some kind of battering ram. Another theory, not running entirely counter to this view, is that the whole thing was a bureaucratic cock-up that had already run out of control under successive governments, and only did so spectacularly under New Labour. The disparity between the figures of new arrivals into the country that the Labour government claimed to expect as compared to those who actually came is evidence for this case. For instance, when it allowed free entry to the United Kingdom for the new EU accession countries in 2004, the British government announced that it expected around 13,000 people a year to take advantage of the scheme. A study commissioned by the government claimed that it would be able to 'totally control' the flood once restrictions had been lifted. It did no such thing. Rules around work permits, among others, were reformed so that skilled and unskilled immigrants could enter the country and stay under the guise of being 'foreign workers'. Most would stay. Entirely predictably the numbers soon ran away even from the estimates of the greatest advocates of mass migration. The numbers of non-EU nationals were expected only to double between 100,000 a year in 1997 and 170,000 in 2004. In fact over five years the government's predictions for the number of new arrivals would be off by almost a million people.[16] Among other things the government's experts wholly failed to anticipate that the UK might be an especially attractive destination for people from countries with significantly lower average income levels or without a minimum wage. In the event, because of these policies the number of Eastern Europeans living in Britain rose from 170,000 in 2004 to 1.24 million in 2013.[17]

Such massive underestimations of the scale of migration were of course predictable to anybody with any knowledge of the history of post-war immigration – a history that had been replete with vast underestimates of the numbers expected to come. But it did also partly demonstrate that detailed attention to immigration control was simply not a priority in those early Labour years. Most importantly, the impression that all immigration restriction was 'racist' (even restriction of 'white' Eastern Europeans) made any internal and external opposition hard to voice. Whether the policy of a surge in migration was unnoticed or officially approved, it was certainly not opposed within the British government.

Whatever the cause, or motive, what is rarely remarked upon is that the public response to the massive upsurge in immigration and to the swift transformation of parts of Britain was exceptionally tolerant. There were no significant or sustained outbreaks of racist sentiment or violence over the following decade, and the country's only racist political party – the British National Party – was subsequently destroyed at the polls. Opinion surveys and the simple evidence of living in the country showed that most people continued to feel zero personal animosity towards immigrants or people of a different ethnic background. But poll after poll did show that a majority were deeply worried about what all this meant for the country and its future. In spite of this, even the mildest attempts by the political class to raise these issues (such as a 2005 Conservative election campaign poster suggesting 'limits' on immigration) were condemned by the rest of the political class, with the result that there was still no serious public discussion.

Perhaps successive governments of all stripes had spent decades putting off any real discussion of this issue because they suspected not only that the public disagreed with them but that it was a matter on which control had slipped away. The Conservative Party that formed a coalition government with the Liberal Democrats in 2010 had promised to cut immigration from hundreds of thousands a year to tens of thousands, a promise they repeated in office. But they never got anywhere near that target. Neither did the successor Conservative majority government, despite mooring itself to the same promise. Indeed, after five years of a coalition government and the start of a Conservative government, both of which were committed to reducing immigration, not only had immigration not gone down, it had actually risen to another record net immigration high of 330,000 a year.[18]

2

How we got hooked on immigration

With slight variations, during these decades almost exactly the same story had occurred everywhere across Western Europe. After the Second World War each country had allowed and then encouraged workers to come into their countries. During the 1950s and 1960s West Germany, Sweden, Holland and Belgium, among other countries, all instituted a 'guest-workers' scheme to fill gaps in their labour supply. Across the continent this 'gastarbeiter' scheme, as it was known in Germany, drew from similar countries. In Germany the influx of workers came largely from Turkey, seeing a huge swell in numbers after the German-Turkish labour agreement of 1961. In Holland and Belgium they came from Turkey, but also from North Africa and other countries that were once their colonies. While part of this influx of workers would serve to address labour shortages, especially in the low-skilled areas of the industrial sector, part of it was also a result of decolonisation. In the nineteenth century, France had gone into North Africa and colonised portions of it, while Britain had colonised the Indian subcontinent. After the process of decolonisation, to varying degrees these former citizens, actually French citizens in the case of Algerians, were felt to be owed something, or at least to be given priority in the guest-workers' schemes. The 'Empire strikes back' concept suggests that it was inevitable and perhaps even just that in the twentieth century people from these former colonies should return the favour, albeit coming as citizens rather than conquerors.

In each European country's case the authorities laboured under precisely the same misapprehensions as the British authorities, not least in believing that the first guest-workers might prove a temporary phenomenon, returning to their home countries once their work was done. Across the continent it seemed to come as a surprise to governments that most of these workers would put down roots in the country they had entered – that they would seek to bring in their families, that their families would need assistance, and that their children would need to go to school. Once such roots had been put down there was ever less likelihood that they would be torn up again. And even if the lure of home remained great, the standard of living these workers were able to enjoy in the West meant far more people stayed than returned to their country of origin. Although Europe had opened up its borders at a time of need, the continent seemed to have no idea how attractive it was to much of the world, even in its diminished state.

Even when the guest-worker arrangements ended – as they did between Germany and Turkey in 1973 – still the people came. And the people who had begun as 'guest-workers' became part of the countries they were in. Some gained citizenship. Others enjoyed dual citizenship. Within five decades of this process beginning – in 2010 – there were at least four million people in Germany of Turkish origin alone. Some countries – notably France – took subtly different approaches to this. For instance, when France opened itself up to immigration from Algeria it did so honouring the idea that, as Charles de Gaulle said in Algeria on 4 June 1958, 'In the whole of Algeria there is only one category of inhabitant – there are only fully French people with the same rights and the same duties.' Nevertheless, when the movement from North Africa into France began in earnest, even de Gaulle privately conceded that France could only be open to other races so long as these people remained a 'small minority' in France. De Gaulle's confidants allege that he himself was deeply uncertain that France could absorb many millions of incomers from other backgrounds.[1]

Yet although there were differences in post-war immigration, each European country had the similar experience of a short-term policy creating the longest possible repercussions. Each country found itself playing endless catch-up – the result of the need to make up major policy decisions on the hoof. And in each country the debate similarly shifted with the decades. As the predictions of the 1950s were shown to be wrong, so were those of the subsequent decades. Expectations of the numbers that would come, as opposed to the numbers that actually did come, saw endless disparities in every country. And while government statistics told one story, the eyes of the European publics told another.

In response to public concern, governments and mainstream parties of all political stripes talked about controlling immigration – sometimes even getting stuck in a competition to sound tougher than each other on the matter. But as the years went on it began to seem as though this might merely be an electoral trick. The gap between public opinion and political reality began to look like a gap caused by other factors than a lack of will or deafness to public concerns. Perhaps nothing was done to reverse the trend because no one in power believed anything could be done. If this was a political truth then it remained wholly unmentionable. Nobody could get elected on such a platform, and so a continent-wide tradition arose of politicians saying things and making promises that they knew to be unachievable.

Perhaps it is because of this that the principal reaction to the developing reality began to be to turn on those who expressed any concern about it, even when they reflected the views of the general public. Instead of addressing concerns, politicians and press began to throw accusations back at the public. This was done not just through charges of 'racism' and 'bigotry', but in a series of deflecting tactics that became a replacement for action. All of these were identifiable in the wake of Britain's 2011 census, including the demand that the public should just 'get over it'.

In a column titled 'Let's not dwell on immigration but sow the seeds of integration', the then Conservative Mayor of London, Boris Johnson, responded to that census by saying, 'We need to stop moaning about the dam-burst. It's happened. There is nothing we can now do except make the process of absorption as eupeptic as possible.'² Sunder Katwala from the left-wing think tank 'British Future' responded to the census in a similar tone, saying, 'The question of do you want this to happen or don't you want this to happen implies that you've got a choice and you could say "let's not have any diversity".' But this was not possible, he insisted, 'This is who we are – it's inevitable.'³

Perhaps both were right and simply saying what any politician surveying the situation would have to say. But there is something cold about the tone of such remarks. Not least the absence of any sense that there may be other people out there not willing to simply 'get over it', who dislike the alteration of their society and never asked for it. Indeed, it seemed to have struck neither Johnson nor Katwala that there are those who may sustain a degree of anger about the fact that all the main parties had for years taken a decision so wholly at variance with public opinion. At the very least it seemed to occur to neither that there is something profoundly politically disenfranchising about such talk. Not only because it suggests a finality to a story that is in fact ongoing, but because it adopts a tone more ordinarily directed at some revanchist minority rather than towards a majority of the voting public.

In the same month that these insistences that people 'get over it' emerged, a poll by YouGov found 67 per cent of the British public believed that immigration over the previous decade had been 'a bad thing for Britain'. Only 11 per cent believed it had been 'a good thing'.⁴ This included majorities among voters for every one of the three major parties. Poll after poll both before and since have found the same thing. As well as routinely prioritising immigration as their number one concern, a majority of voters in Britain regularly described immigration as having had a negative impact on their public services and housing through overcrowding, as well as harming the nation's sense of identity.

Of course, the political impetus to 'draw a line' and not get into 'blame games' raises the possibility that having got away with their mistakes to date the politicians may feel ready – after such suitable imprecations – to repeat precisely the same mistakes in the future.

By 2012 the leaders of every one of the major parties in Britain had conceded that immigration was too high, but even whilst doing so all had also insisted that the public should 'get over it'. None had any clear – nor, as it would turn out, successful – policy on how to change course. Public opinion surveys suggest that a failure to do anything about immigration even while talking about it is one of the key causes of the breakdown in trust between the electorate and their political representatives.

Yet it is not only the political class who cannot speak to the concerns of the majority of the general public. On the night that the 2011 census results were announced the BBC's flagship discussion show 'Newsnight' held a discussion of the news on which three-quarters of the participants expressed themselves perfectly delighted with the census and could see no cause for concern in the results. On that occasion the philosopher A. C. Grayling, himself a hugely successful immigrant from Zambia (then Northern Rhodesia), said of the findings of the census, 'I think on the whole it's a very positive thing, a thing to be celebrated.' The critic and playwright Bonnie Greer, also a highly successful immigrant (from America), agreed that it was a positive thing and said, like Boris Johnson, 'It cannot be stopped.'[5] Over the whole discussion the allure of this 'get with the beat' attitude prevailed. Perhaps the temptation to 'go with the flow' is so strong in this argument because the price for stepping outside the consensus is so uniquely high. Get a studio discussion about the budget wrong and you might be accused of financial ignorance or poor interpretation of the public mood. But nod to the overwhelming public mood, let alone speak for it, on immigration and reputations, careers and livelihoods are on the line.

Yet somewhere, lost in the middle of all the hip consensus of that Central London studio, what was almost entirely absent were the views of most people sitting at home, a world that few people ever appear to want to put their finger on in public. The upsides of migration have become easy to talk about: to simply nod to them is to express values of openness, tolerance and broad-mindedness. Yet to nod to, let alone express, the downsides of immigration is to invite accusations of closed-mindedness and intolerance, xenophobia and barely disguised racism. All of which leaves the attitude of the major-ity of the public almost impossible to express.

For even if you believe – as most people do – that some immigra-tion is a good thing and makes a country a more interesting place, it does not follow that the more immigration the better. Nor does it mean – however many upsides there are – that there are not down-sides which should be equally easy to state without accusations of malice. For mass immigration does not continue bringing the same level of benefits to a society the more people who come in. If it is possible to praise mass immigration for making us richer as a whole, it should also be possible to explain that the process has made us poorer in some ways, not least in introducing or re-introducing cultural problems that we might have hoped never to see.

The January before the release of the 2011 census results a gang of nine Muslim men — seven of Pakistani origin, two from North Africa — were convicted and sentenced at the Old Bailey in London for the sex trafficking of children between the ages of 11 and 15. On that occasion one of the victims sold into a form of modern-day slavery was a girl of 11 who was branded with the initial of her 'owner' abuser: 'M' for Mohammed. The court heard that Mohammed 'branded her to make her his property and to ensure others knew about it'. This did not happen in a Saudi or Pakistani backwater, nor even in one of the northern towns that so much of the country had forgotten about and which had seen many similar cases over the same period. This happened in Oxfordshire between 2004 and 2012.

Nobody could argue that gang rape or child abuse are the preserve of immigrants, but the development of particular types of child-rape gangs revealed – and a subsequent government-commissioned inquiry confirmed[6] – specific cultural ideas and attitudes that were clearly held by some immigrants. These include views about women, specifically non-Muslim women, other religions, races and sexual minorities that were pre-medieval. Fear of accusations of 'racism' for pointing out such facts, and the small but salutary number of careers like Ray Honeyford's that had been publicly wrecked for saying far less, meant that it took years even for such facts as these to come out.

This has a terrorising effect far beyond the nation's television studios, and with far more serious consequences. When these gang-rape cases came to court they did so in spite of local police, councillors and care-workers, many of whom were discovered to have failed to report such crimes involving immigrant gangs for fear of accusations of 'racism'. The media followed suit, filling their reports with euphemisms as though trying to avoid helping the public to draw any conclusions. So in cases like those in Oxfordshire the gangs were described as 'Asian' when they almost solely involved Muslim men of Pakistani origin. The fact that their victims were chosen precisely because they were not Muslims was only occasionally mentioned in the courts and rarely dwelt upon by the press. Instead of carrying out their jobs without fear or favour, police, prosecutors and journalists behaved as though their job was to mediate between the public and the facts.

Naturally none of this ever comes up in any 'acceptable' discussion on immigration. Introducing gang rape to a BBC discussion on immigration would be like introducing bestiality to a documentary on sickly pets. Only the good and happy can be dwelt upon, while the bad is ignored. And it is not only the harder edges of the discussion that get lost, but the softer, everyday concerns that people have: not savage denunciations, but simple regret that the society they grew up in has been changed without any care for the views of the majority of the people.

The other thing lost in the cosy, consensual Newsnight style of discussion is any reference to what we used to call 'our culture'. As ever, amid the endless celebrations of diversity, the greatest irony of all remains that the one thing people cannot bring themselves to celebrate is the culture that encouraged such diversity in the first place. In the whole political and press reaction to the 2011 census one saw once again the various staging-posts of a direction of travel that is profoundly self-annihilating.

One such claim is that even after a period of such extraordinary change as Britain has been through in recent decades, 'It's nothing new.' This argument can be heard across Europe, but in Britain it now most often goes as follows: 'Britain has always been a melting pot of people of different races and backgrounds. Indeed we are a nation of immigrants.' This was the claim, for instance, of a well-received book on immigration by Robert Winder that came out during the Blair years and was often used to defend the government's policies. Among other things the book argued that 'we are all immigrants: it simply depends how far back you go.' The book also claimed that Britain has always been 'a mongrel nation'.7 Here is Barbara Roche making the same claim in a talk in the East End of London in 2011: 'When we think of immigration or migration it's very tempting to think that it's something that happened in the nineteenth century. I'm Jewish. Some of my family came in the late nineteenth century. I'm Sephardi on my mother's side so some of my family came way before that. But there is a tendency to think that it's somehow quite recent – if it isn't nineteenth century then it's very much something that is a post-war phenomenon. Nothing could be further from the truth. I've always believed that Britain is a country of migrants.'8 Of course Ms Roche is welcome to believe this. But that does not make it true.

Until the latter half of the last century, Britain had almost negligible levels of immigration. Unlike America, for instance, Britain had never been a 'nation of immigrants'. And although there was often a trickle of people moving in, the mass movement of people was almost unknown. In fact immigration was so unknown that when it did happen people talked about it for centuries. When discussing migration into the United Kingdom today one can expect someone to mention the Huguenots – those Protestants forced to flee persecution in France to whom Charles II offered sanctuary in 1681. The Huguenot example is more resonant than people realise. Firstly, because despite the proximity of culture and religion enjoyed by French and English Protestants of the time, it took centuries for the Huguenots to integrate into Britain, with many people still describing themselves as coming from Huguenot stock. But the other salient point about the Huguenots – and the reason people cite them so frequently – is the matter of scale. It is believed that up to 50,000 Huguenots arrived in Britain after 1681, which was undoubtedly a huge movement for the time. But this scale was in a wholly different league to the mass immigration Britain has seen in recent years. From the period of the Blair government onwards Britain has seen an equal number of immigrants to that one-off number of Huguenots arriving not once in the nation's history, but every couple of months. And this immigration was by no means composed of French Protestants. Another example often given to defend the 'nation of immigrants' story is that of the 30,000 Ugandan Asians who were brought into Britain in the early 1970s after Idi Amin expelled them from Uganda. In the UK memories of this one-off influx are generally coloured with pride and good feeling, not just because it was a demonstrable and limited relief of a desperate people, but because those Ugandan Asians who arrived in Britain often made a palpable and grateful contribution to public life. In the post-1997 years of immigration the same number of people as that one-off 30,000-strong influx arrived into the country every six weeks.

The movement of people in recent years – even before the European migration crisis – was of an entirely different quantity, quality and consistency from anything that had gone before. Yet despite this fact, it remains one of the most popular ways to cover over the vast changes of recent years to pretend that history was similar to what is happening now. Not the least advantages of this suggestion is that any current problems arising from migration are nothing we haven't dealt with – and triumphed over – before. It falsely presents any current challenges as normal. But revising the past is just one attempt at a staging-post argument. After this come a whole range of implicit and explicit claims which respond to mass immigration by pretending either that the country of arrival does not have a culture, or that its culture and identity are so especially weak, worn out or bad that if it did disappear then it could hardly be mourned.

Here is Bonnie Greer again on Newsnight: 'There's always this failsafe, spoken or unspoken, that there is a British identity. That's always interesting to me. I think one of the geniuses of the British — of being British — is that there isn't this sort of rock-solid definition of identity that an American has.' It is hard to think of another part of the world where such a claim would be acceptable, let alone from the mouth of an immigrant: your culture has always been like this — it never really existed. If one even said anything similar in Greer's native Chicago – let alone on the main television network – it would be unlikely to receive such a polite reception as it was accorded on Newsnight.

Harsher examples of this argument have abounded during the era of mass migration. In 2006 Channel 4 screened a documentary called '100% English'. This programme took a group of white British people whom it clearly believed were racists — including Margaret Thatcher's loyal cabinet colleague Norman Tebbit — and performed DNA tests on them. The test results were then used to prove that all of the people in question were in fact 'foreigners'. The results were produced triumphantly to each of the subjects in order to point to the same conclusion: 'You see – we're all foreigners really. So there's no need to feel any concern about immigration or national identity.' Again, of course nobody would conceivably be so rude as to do this to any other group of people. But with British and other European peoples, different rules of engagement had begun to apply. All appeared to be methods of coping with a change that if it cannot be stopped must be solved by alterations in the minds of the host countries.

Down the line there is another, starker, rebuttal. That says that this form of destruction is exactly what our societies deserve. 'Do you know what white people did?' they ask. 'And you Europeans in particular? You travelled around the world and lived in countries and pillaged them, and tried to erase their local cultures. This is payback. Or karma.' The novelist Will Self (currently Professor of Contemporary Thought at Brunel University) played precisely this line of attack on the BBC in the same week that the 2011 census was published. On the network's main discussion show, Question Time, he declared, 'Up to the Suez crisis ... most people's conception of what being British involved was basically going overseas and subjugating black and brown people and taking their stuff and the fruits of their labours. That was a core part of British identity, was the British Empire. Now various members of the political class have tried to revive that idea quite recently without much success.'[9]

Leaving aside the claim that any member of the political class has tried to revive the British Empire in recent years, in these comments one can hear the authentic and undisguised voice of revenge. Demonstrating that such an instinct transcends racial or religious boundaries, and can as easily be self-induced as aimed at others, it suggests that on this occasion Britain must be uniquely punished for the deeds of history. The repercussions of the argument are striking to consider. For if this is even partially a spur for the recent transformation of our country, then what we are going through is not an accident, or a mere laxness at the borders, but a cool and deliberate act of national sabotage. Motivations aside, this also throws up the ultimate questions that our politicians remain so unwilling to address: How much longer must all this go on? Are we approaching the end of this transformation? Or is this only the beginning?

The 2011 census could have provided a wonderful opportunity to address this, and it was, like every other opportunity since the Second World War in the discussion around immigration, wretchedly missed. It was not just the fact that no answers were given, but that so few pertinent questions were asked. For example, amid all the complacency surrounding these developments, nobody asked this question: If the fact that 'white Britons' now comprised a minority in their capital city was indeed a demonstration of 'diversity' (as the spokesman from the ONS had said), when might it cease to be so? The census had shown that some London boroughs were already lacking in 'diversity'. Not because there weren't enough people of immigrant origin but because there weren't enough white British people still around to make those boroughs diverse.

In the years since the 2011 census the number of migrants into Britain has continued to soar. And the gap between the official figures and actual figures continues to vary hugely. One indication of the fact is that although the net migration figures for each year since the 2011 census has been far in excess of 300,000, the number of new National Insurance numbers issued each year (because they are required for work) has been more than double that. The rising population of the United Kingdom is now almost entirely due to immigration and to higher birth rates among immigrants. In 2014 women who were born overseas accounted for 27 per cent of all live births in England and Wales, and 33 per cent of newborn babies had at least one immigrant parent, a figure that had doubled since the 1990s.

On current population trends, and without any further rise in the number of immigrants, the most modest estimate by the ONS of the future British population is that it will rise from its current level of 65 million to 70 million within a decade, 77 million by 2050 and to more than 80 million by 2060.[10] But this estimate assumes immigration to be beneath current levels. Whereas if the post-2011 levels were to continue, the UK population would go above 80 million as early as 2040 and as high as 90 million (that is an increase of 50 per cent on 2011) by 2060.

Demographic predictions are a notoriously tricky area, with enough variables to make fools of many. But among serious academic demographers there is a consensus that even without migration at the rate it has occurred in recent years the demographic make-up of the country will change even more significantly within the lifespan of most people reading this book. For instance, David Coleman, a professor of demography at Oxford University, has shown that on current trends the people who identified themselves as 'white British' in the 2011 census will cease to be a majority in the United Kingdom in the 2060s. However, he stresses, if current levels of immigration to Britain continue, let alone rise, that number 'will move closer to the present'. It would be a time when, as Professor Coleman says, Britain would become 'unrecognisable to its present inhabitants'.[11]

Perhaps instead of simply celebrating such levels of immigration it would make matters easier if the proponents of mass immigration revealed what levels of 'diversity' they would like to get to and what they see as their optimal target figure? Is a ceiling of 25 per cent white Britons in London — or the country at large — a target? Or should it be 10 per cent? Or none at all? A final, and perhaps harder, question to ask would be when, if at all, given the range of claims against them, these 'white Britons' might ever be able to acceptably argue, let alone complain, about their odds?

Barring any drastic plan by a British government intent on averting such a trend, it is hard to see how this process could fail to continue. Not only because consecutive governments have shown themselves so incapable of predicting or anticipating anything in the arena of migration for the last 70 years, but because the objection to any such plan would continue to be so considerable. Consider Will Self again, speaking to wild studio applause on the BBC after the 2011 census findings were released: 'The people who line up on the opposition to the immigration line of the argument are usually racists [audience applause] ... [with an] antipathy to people, particularly with black and brown skins.' Having long ago reached the point where the only thing white Britons could do was to remain silent about the change in their country, at some point in recent years it began to appear as though they were expected simply to get on, silently but contentedly, with abolishing themselves, accepting the knocks and accepting the loss of their country: 'Get over it. It's nothing new. You were terrible. Now you are nothing.'

In all this it is impossible not to notice the striking level of vindictiveness around the manner in which the concerns of British people – and the white working and middle classes in particular – have been met by politicians and pundits alike. Perhaps at some point the 'just lying-down and taking it' period will stop, with repercussions quite as unforeseeable as all those to date. But in the meantime, if any politician wanted to try to pre-empt that eventuality and felt like indulging in an act of humility, he or she could do worse than go back to the point at which we started. Compare the statements derided as clichés that have come from so many working- and middle-class white voters in recent years and set them alongside the statements of the leaders of each of the mainstream political parties. All these years on, despite the name-calling and the insults and the ignoring of their concerns, were your derided average white voters not correct when they said that they were losing their country? Irrespective of whether you think that they should have thought this, let alone whether they should have said this, said it differently or accepted the change more readily, it should at some stage cause people to pause and reflect that the voices almost everybody wanted to demonise and dismiss were in the final analysis the voices whose predictions were nearest to being right.

3

The excuses we told ourselves

Throughout the late twentieth and early twenty-first century, European governments pursued policies of mass immigration without public approval. Yet such vast societal change cannot be forced upon a society against its will without a series of arguments being brought along to help ease the case. The arguments that Europeans have been given during this period range across the moral and the technocratic. They also shift according to need and the political winds. So, for instance, it has often been claimed that immigration on this scale is an economic benefit for our countries; that in an 'ageing society' increased immigration is necessary; that in any case immigration makes our societies more cultured and interesting; and that even if none of these were the case, globalisation makes mass immigration unstoppable.

Such justifications have a tendency to become intertwined and mutually replaceable, so that if one fails the others are always there to fall back on. They often start with economic arguments, but they can just as well start with moral arguments. If mass immigration doesn't make you a richer person, then it will make you a better person. And if it doesn't make your country a better country, then it will at least make it a richer country. Over time each of these arguments has produced sub-industries of people devoted to proving their truth. In each case the rationale comes after the events, so as to give the final impression of justifications being sought for events that would have happened anyway.

ECONOMICS

Over recent years there has been, for instance, a niche search to prove that the societal change Europe has been going through makes the continent significantly richer. In fact the opposite is true, as anybody who lives in a twenty-first-century welfare state can work out for themselves. Having paid into the system for all of their working lives, working Europeans know that the basis of the modern welfare state broadly consists of being able to take services out from the state (when you fall ill, become unemployed or reach retirement age), because you have paid into the system throughout your working life. There will be some people who have rarely paid in, but they will be covered by some who have rarely taken out.

Anybody can see that a family of people who arrive for the first time in their adopted country and who have never paid into the system are at the very least going to take some time before they have paid in as much in taxes as they will have taken out in housing, schooling, welfare, benefits and all the other advantages of the European welfare state. In the same way it is obvious to anybody involved in the labour market – especially at the lower end – that one which is comparatively closed off will operate differently from one in which the workforce can come from almost anywhere in the world. Although from an employer's viewpoint there is an obvious advantage to the mass import of cheap labour, it is equally obvious that a very open labour market will see people at the lower end of that market edged out of jobs by people from countries where wages and living standards are far lower and who are therefore willing to work for lower pay.

Other parts of the case are equally obvious. For instance, the United Kingdom has had a housing shortage for many years. Significant portions of green-belt land have to be built upon to make up a shortage of housing, which by 2016 meant that 240,000 new homes had to be built each year – or roughly one every few minutes. Even taking into account an increase in people living alone, this 240,000 figure is presented as just an unavoidable fact of life. But it is not just an unavoidable fact of life. This number of new homes have to be built in order to house all the new people who come into Britain each year. Indeed, with immigration at the rate it has been in recent years the UK needs to build a city the size of Liverpool every year. But of course construction has not kept up with demand. It is the same with school places. The shortage of school places in Britain is not an urban myth, nor a product of any increase in the birth rate among people already in the UK. It is the product of new arrivals into the country needing to send their children to school. By 2018 it is estimated that 60 per cent of local authorities will be suffering a shortage of primary-school places. Similar stretches are occurring in the National Health Service (which spends more than £20 million a year on translation services alone) and in every other area of state provision.

Because such things are so obvious, it requires a concerted effort to pretend they are untrue. One example of just such an effort is the report that was a foundation document for the wave of mass migration during the Blair government. 'Migration: An Economic and Social Analysis' was completed in 2000, a joint production of the Home Office Economics and Resource Analysis Unit and the Cabinet Office Performance and Innovation Unit (even their names seeming designed to bore any opponents to inattention). Both entities were staffed with people already known to be in favour of mass immigration and therefore clearly intended to provide 'intellectual ballast' to support the existing views of ministers.[1]

Among the claims of this seminal report was that 'overall, migrants have little aggregate effect on native wages or employment'. One of the ways it argued this was by painting exceptional migrants as being the norm and simply insisting that 'There is little evidence that native workers are harmed by migration.' It went on: 'Levels of entrepreneurship and self-employment also appear to be high among migrants (and higher among migrants in the UK than those elsewhere in Europe). For example, it has been estimated by *Le Figaro* that 150,000 French entrepreneurs have moved to the UK since 1995 (attracted in part by better transport links through the

Channel Tunnel). These have included internet and other high-tech ventures, one example cited was a computer design firm that had relocated to Ashford, Kent.'

After decades of immigration from the third world, to paint a French high-tech entrepreneur as a typical migrant requires a considerable level of dishonesty. Most people who came to Britain in the period after the Second World War were not highly educated but poorly educated and from poor societies: that was why they wanted to better their lot by coming here. And among those who had qualifications many were, in any case, entering a society where these qualifications were not recognised as having parity and so they had to start down the chain in their profession. But the only way to present migrants as contributing not just equally but actually more than those already working and paying taxes in Britain is if we talk almost exclusively about highly educated, high net-worth individuals from first-world countries. The cliché of the 'average immigrant' being an economic boon for the country only works when such exceptions are made to appear as though they are the rule.

All efforts to make an economic case for mass immigration rely on this trick. Among those to have used it are EU Commissioner Cecilia Malmström and UN Representative Peter Sutherland. In a 2012 piece they suggested that unless Europe opens its borders to mass migration, 'Entrepreneurs, migrants with Ph.Ds' and others will all be 'flocking to places like Brazil, South Africa, Indonesia, Mexico, China, and India', thus leaving Europe to be a more impoverished place.[2]

One of the few studies in this area is from the Centre for Research and Analysis of Migration at University College London. It is a study that is widely cited. In 2013 the centre published a working paper titled 'The Fiscal Effects of Immigration to the UK'. This working paper (rather than finished report) was exceptionally widely covered in the media. The BBC ran the story as a lead item with the headline: 'Recent immigrants to UK "make net contribution"'. The story claimed that far from being a 'drain' on the system, the financial contribution of 'recent immigrants' to the country had instead been 'remarkably strong'.[3] Following the lead of UCL's own positively spun press release, the national media focused on the claim that 'the recent waves of immigrants – i.e., those who arrived to the UK since 2000 and who have thus driven the stark increase in the UK's foreign born population', had 'contributed far more in taxes than they received in benefits'.[4]

Elsewhere the study made the claim that far from being a cost to the taxpayer, immigrants were in fact 'less likely' to be a financial burden on the state than the people of the country they were moving into. It also claimed that recent migrants were less likely to need social housing than British people and were even 45 per cent less likely to be receiving state benefits or tax credits than 'UK natives'. Doubtless some members of the public hearing this claim wondered when all the Somalis, Pakistanis and Bangladeshis had managed to put so much money into the exchequer. But the study had performed the usual sleight of hand. It had presented the best-off and least culturally strange immigrants as in fact being typical immigrants. So the UCL study focused attention on 'highly-educated immigrants' and in particular on recent immigrants from the European Economic Area (the EU, plus Norway, Iceland and Lichtenstein). The working paper highlighted the fact that these people paid 34 per cent more in taxes than they received in benefits while native British people paid 11 per cent less in taxes than they received in benefits. Anybody doubting the financial benefits of mass immigration was suddenly opposed to wealthy residents of Lichtenstein transferring to the United Kingdom for work.

Yet anyone who wanted to delve into this working paper would discover that the reality was wholly different from the spin that the media, and even the university from which it hailed, had given to the findings. For although UCL's own estimate suggested that 'recent migrants from the EEA between 2001 and 2011 had contributed around £22 billion into the UK economy', the fiscal impact of all migrants, regardless of origin, told an entirely different story. Indeed 'recent' arrivals from the EEA were the sole migrants for whom such a positive claim could be made. Away from the spin, what UCL's own research quietly showed was that non-EEA migrants had actually taken out around £95 billion more in services than they had paid in in taxes, meaning that if you took the period 1995–2011 and included all immigrants (not just a convenient high net-worth selection), then by UCL's own measurements, immigrants to the United Kingdom had taken out significantly more than they had put in. Mass migration, in other words, had made the country very significantly poorer over the period in question.

After some criticism for its methodology, manner of spinning and burial of crucial data, the following year UCL published its completed findings. By that point, and taking into account only UCL's own figures, the results were even starker. For the full report showed that the earlier figure of £95 billion far understated the cost of immigration to Britain. In fact, immigrants over that 1995–2011 period had cost the United Kingdom a figure more like £114 billion, with the final figure potentially rising to as high as £159 billion. Needless to say, the discovery that immigration had actually cost the UK more than a hundred billion pounds did not make the news and nobody was made aware on their news bulletins of a headline that should have read, 'Recent immigrants to the UK cost British taxpayers more than £100 billion'. How could they have done when the crucial findings didn't even make it into the conclusions of the publication that had discovered them?[5]

When it comes to immigration the same standards of proof apply everywhere, as do the same processes of reverse-engineering. For its 2000 report into migration the British government went to two of the academics most noted for their views in favour of mass immigration – Sarah Spencer and Jonathan Portes – to find justifications for the policies that politicians like Barbara Roche wanted to pursue. For such work the usual standards of academic rigour did not apply. Wherever a claim was desirable, 'evidence' was found to support it. Wherever a situation existed that was deemed undesirable, there was said to be either 'no evidence' or merely 'anecdotal evidence'. There was, for instance, only 'anecdotal evidence' that 'high concentrations of migrant children lacking English as a first language can lead to pressure on schools' and to 'some concern among other parents'.

Not only 'anecdotal', but an anecdote heard only from 'some'. It also explained that it was only 'in theory' that mass immigration 'may increase pressure on housing markets, transport and other infrastructure and exacerbate over-crowding and congestion'. The reality, it aimed to suggest, was wholly different. How could anyone imagine that an influx of more people would require more houses?

These were hardly surprising findings from authors with a track record of being in favour of mass migration as a good in itself. But while their work presented itself as an economic analysis of the benefits of migration, it was in fact not just a blueprint for societal change but a cheerleader for it. In arguing the case for mass immigration the authors insisted that migrant children would bring 'greater diversity into UK schools'. All potential concerns for British workers were similarly swept aside. There was, for instance, 'little evidence that native workers are harmed' by large-scale immigration. In fact, 'Migrants will have no effect on the job prospects of natives.'

The insertion of figures such as Spencer and Portes from the fringes of academia into Whitehall gave their opinions not only the veneer of respectability but the stamp of government. After publication of their report, ministers like Roche had something to point to when they insisted that mass migration brought unadulterated economic benefits. And if anybody wonders how the Labour government let immigration run away so wildly under its watch, it is in part because of the oiling effect of work like this.

The reality is that whatever its other benefits, the economic benefits of immigration accrue almost solely to the migrant. It is migrants who are able to access public facilities they have not previously paid for. It is migrants who benefit from a wage higher than they could earn in their home country. And very often the money that they earn – or much of it – is sent to family outside the United Kingdom rather than even being put back into the local economy. Those elements of the media which push the argument that mass migration makes everyone richer, and that we all rise on a tide of wealth created by immigrants, continually forget this one crucial thing. Even when the GDP of a country does grow – as it must with an ever-increasing number of people in the workforce – that does not mean individuals benefit from it. On the contrary only GDP per head does that. And there is no evidence that mass migration improves GDP per head. Which is why, having lost this argument, advocates of mass migration tend to move onto others.

AN AGEING POPULATION

If the economic argument for mass migration rests on the attraction of a bribe, then the outline of a threat hangs over another of the central justifications for migration on such a scale. This argument insists that Europeans are ageing, that Europe is a 'greying' society, and that in such a situation we need to bring in more people because otherwise our society will not have enough young people around to keep older Europeans in the lifestyle to which they have become accustomed.

This is, once again, one of the arguments of EU Commissioner Cecilia Malmström and UN Representative Peter Sutherland – both prominent international authorities on, and advocates of, mass migration. In 2012 they argued that 'The aging of Europe's population is historically unprecedented. The number of workers will decline precipitously, and could shrink by almost one-third by mid-century, with immense consequences for Europe's social model, the vitality of its cities, its ability to innovate and compete, and for relations among generations as the old become heavily reliant on the young. And, while history suggests that countries that welcome newcomers' energy and vibrancy compete best internationally, Europe is taking the opposite tack by tightening its borders.'[6] The best answer to this challenge, both conclude, is to bring in the next generation from abroad. Before noting why this is such a poor argument it is worth acknowledging the small kernel of truth within it.

In order for a population to remain at a stable level it is necessary for that society to have a fertility rate of around 2.1. That is, in order to maintain native population growth in the long term every two people would need to have 2.1 children. Across Europe in recent years this fertility rate has fallen below these levels. Portugal's fertility rate in

2014, for instance, was a mere 1.23, a factor that if left unaddressed would see the population almost halve in the next generation. At the turn of the millennium there was not one European country whose birth rate was at the crucial 2.1 level. Some, most notably Germany (at 1.38), were far below it.[7]

Interestingly, there was a time when parties of the far left and in particular 'Green' parties in the West used to campaign for precisely such an outcome in order to reduce population explosion. They argued for instance – and despite the unsavoury connotations after China's enforcement of a similar policy – that in order to attain an 'optimum population' for the world, every couple should restrict themselves to having one child. It was expected that developed countries might lead the way. It is a point of minor interest that as third-world migration to Europe has swelled, the Green movements have ceased to argue for population caps or to campaign for restrictions on reproduction. While happy to tell white Europeans to stop breeding, they became somewhat more reticent about making the same request of darker-skinned migrants. Nevertheless, the idea that Europeans have simply stopped having enough children and must as a result ensure that the next generation is comprised of immigrants is a disastrous fallacy for several reasons.

The first is because of the mistaken assumption that a country's population should always remain the same or indeed continue rising. The nation states of Europe include some of the most densely populated countries on the planet. It is not at all obvious that the quality of life in these countries will improve if the population continues growing. What is more, when migrants arrive in these countries they move to the big cities, not to the remaining sparsely populated areas. So although among European states Britain, along with Belgium and the Netherlands, is one of the most densely populated countries, England taken on its own would be the second most densely populated country in Europe.[8] Migrants tend not to head to the Highlands of Scotland or the wilds of Dartmoor. And so a constantly increasing population causes population problems in areas that are already suffering housing supply problems and where infrastructure like public transport struggles to keep up with swiftly expanding populations. Anybody concerned about quality of life for Europeans would wonder about how to lessen their populations, not substantially increase them.

But let us say that immigration is needed simply in order to keep the population levels static, if that were the case. If it is agreed that a particular country wishes to maintain a stable or slowly growing population, then before importing people from other states it would surely be more sensible to determine whether there are reasons why people in your own country are not at present having enough children. Is it because they do not want them, or because they do want them but cannot have them? If it is the latter then the question should be whether there is anything that government can do to create a situation in which people can have the children they want.

The evidence from most countries, including the United Kingdom, is that although the native population is below replacement levels, this is not because people do not want to have children. Indeed the figures show the opposite. For instance in 2002, at a central point of the Labour government's immigration explosion, a population study from the ONS showed that only 8 per cent of British women did not want to have babies. And only 4 per cent wanted one baby. The most popular desire of British women – the aim of a clear 55 per cent – was to have two children. A further 14 per cent wanted three children, another 14 per cent wanted four, and 5 per cent wanted five or more children, which if you were seeking a stable or slowly growing population would more than cover for the 8 per cent of women who wanted no children at all.[9]

Why are Europeans having too few children? This question has been approached from a biological as well as a sociological angle in recent years, but there is one missing observation that many Europeans will recognise. A middle- or average-income couple in most European countries worries about having even just one child and how they will afford that child, including suffering the loss of one household salary for at least a period of time. Having two children entails even more concern and even more worries.

Almost every European will know at least some couples who are both in good jobs and who would never feel able to afford to have a third child. In fact, only three types of people now have three children or more – the very rich, the poor and recent immigrants. Among immigrants – especially those who have come from third-world countries – any provision for their children paid for by the European welfare state will be better than anything they could have expected in their country of origin. Whereas native Europeans are concerned about competition for school places, housing shortages pushing average house prices up to between five and ten times average salary in their area, and how to afford one child, let alone three or four. It is also possible that, contra Spencer and Portes, some parents may not appreciate an endless amount of 'diversity' in their local schools and may want their children to be educated around people from a similar cultural background. This means, especially if those parents are in an inner-city area or suburb, that they are likely to worry about being able to afford a house in the kind of middle-class neighbourhood from which their child would be in the catchment area of a less 'diverse' school. If they cannot afford to bring up their children in the way in which they would like, many people will fail to have the number of children they would like.

The question of what your country is going to look like in the future also poses a huge question about the issue of producing, as well as raising, the next generation. When people are optimistic about the future they tend to be optimistic about bringing children into the world. However, if they contemplate a future filled with ethnic or religious fragmentation, they may well think again about whether this is a world they want to bring their children into. If European governments are really so worried about population decline that they would contemplate bringing in higher-reproducing populations from other parts of the world, it would be sensible for them first to work out whether there are policies that could encourage more procreation among their existing populations. In Poland, for instance, the Justice and Law Party has in recent years raised child benefit in order to try to raise the native birth rate and diminish any reliance on immigration. At the very least, governments should examine whether there are things they are currently doing that are making things worse.

Then there is the issue of a greying population. It is true that people in Europe live longer today than at any previous period in their history. Barring any major war or pestilence, medical advances should allow the next generation to live even longer still. And of course, although living longer is often painted as a terrible burden, indeed a scourge on a society, it should perhaps be remembered that for most individuals it is rather a good thing. It can also present a whole set of benefits for the rest of society, not least by balancing a cultural obsession with youth against the experience of age. The 'scourge' of a 'greying population' is only a scourge when it is depicted as such. In any case, even if you agreed that longevity is a curse for a society, there are many things you might do before deciding to import the next generation from another continent.

In the period following the Second World War people were expected to live for a few years after they retired. Today they are expected to live an extra couple of decades. The obvious solution to this economic challenge is to raise the retirement age in order to ensure that in retirement people are not taking out more in pensions and healthcare provisions than they put in during their years of work. In some countries this is happening naturally. For instance, between 2004 and 2010 the average retirement age in Britain rose by a year (63–64 for men, 61–62 for women).[10] Admittedly, this is neither always such an easy nor a voluntary process. After the financial crash of 2008 and the successive Eurozone crises, Greek citizens saw their retirement ages raised. Until then those covering a large, and somewhat eccentric, collection of professions (hairdressers, radio announcers, trombonists) were allowed to retire in their fifties. When economic realities hit, those retirement ages were hauled up. But it is always possible that governments in search of a cheap popular hit will refuse to bend to economic reality. In 2010 President Nicolas Sarkozy managed against stiff opposition to raise the retirement age in France from 60 to 62. Two years later his successor, François Hollande, lowered it back down to 60.

There will always be those who protest about the idea of working into their sixties. But perhaps some people will see working longer in a society they know as being preferable to dying in one in which they feel a stranger. And although there are those who argue that there would not be work for the greying workforce, this requires a serious consideration of how to shift the economy in order to improve productivity among the 'greying' community. In a 2012 interview Chancellor Merkel of Germany succinctly laid out the continent's challenge: 'If Europe today accounts for just over 7 per cent of the world's population, produces around 25 per cent of global GDP and has to finance 50 per cent of global social spending, then it's obvious that it will have to work very hard to maintain its prosperity and way of life. All of us have to stop spending more than we earn every year.'[11]

There are a huge range of possible answers to this problem and none of them are simple. But the most needlessly complex answer of all is to import huge migrant populations into a society to make up the workforce base of the next generation. Firstly, because the unpredictable factors in the area are legion. The history of post-war immigration into Europe has been a story of people not doing what they were expected to do. Although European governments may think that they know how the next generation of migrants is likely to contribute to the national economy, there is no evidence that they ever correctly predicted any of the previous ones. There are also predictable factors that are wholly ignored – such as the fact that immigrants get old as well. Surprising though it appears to be to many policy-makers, importing large numbers of young immigrants does not solve the 'greying' population issue, because immigrants become 'grey' as well, and when they do so they will expect – and deserve – the same rights as everybody else. The logical conclusion is that the short-term solution becomes an even greater long-term headache, because there will be a constant need to import larger and larger numbers of immigrants, as in a pyramid scheme, in order to keep more and more people in the style to which they have become accustomed.

At the same time in every European country we hear the argument that there are jobs young Europeans in particular 'won't do'. Where it is true, it is a consequence of welfare provisions that in some situations have made it better to avoid work than to take low-paid work. But it is also a result of young people being educated to a level at which they look down on apparently mundane or unglamorous labour. It is a societal viewpoint that is remarkably widespread. The suggestion goes, for instance, that we need to bring in people to stack shelves in supermarkets (a job that has become emblematic) because of its undesirability to native-born Europeans. During Britain's EU debate one millionaire pro-EU entrepreneur insisted that migration into Britain was necessary because he didn't want his daughter to become a 'potato picker'.[12] Aside from the racial insinuation that we are above such roles whereas others are eminently suited to them, we should ask ourselves why our young people are (if they are) 'above' such tasks. It is also necessary to ask ourselves whether we are entirely happy with this pay-off. There are many young people across Europe who are unemployed. Many do not have the skills necessary for high-end employment. So why import people to do low-skilled work when so many low-skilled workers already exist in Europe?

Sometimes mass immigration is advocated because of the advantage it gives in supporting pensioners, sometimes because of the advantage it allegedly gives in stopping young people from doing jobs they don't want. But in both cases it is an argument that if allowed to run will only encourage a greater and greater problem with every year that passes, as more ageing people need support and as fewer young people have any chance of getting into work. It is a habit Europe has got into, and one which becomes harder to kick with each passing year.

DIVERSITY

One of the most striking things about the arguments for ongoing mass migration into European countries is that they are so readily able to shift. Whenever the economic cases for mass immigration are briefly dislodged, along come moral or cultural arguments. Without making any concession they state a position along these lines: 'Let us pretend that mass migration does not make us financially richer. It does not matter, because mass migration makes us rich in other ways. In fact even if it makes us financially poorer, what you lose in economic benefits you will pick up in cultural benefits.'

This argument takes it as read that European societies are slightly boring or staid places, a presumption that would not go down as well in many other societies. The suggestion goes that whereas the rest of the world does not need the mass migration from other cultures in order to be improved, the countries of Europe do, and would especially benefit from such movements. It is as though it is agreed that there is a hole at the heart of Europe which needs filling and without which we would otherwise be poorer. New people bring different culture, different attitudes, different languages – and of course the endlessly cited example of new and exciting cuisine.

As with most of the arguments in favour of mass migration there is some truth in this. Despite Europe's already existing proliferation of languages, cultures and cuisine, who would not want to increase their knowledge of the world and its cultures? And if any other culture does not want to gain from a knowledge of the rest of the world, then it surely is the one that will be the poorer for it? Nevertheless the argument rests on a number of fallacies. The first is that the best way to learn about the world and its cultures is not to travel around the world but to encourage the world to come to you – and then stay. The second is that the value of migrants continues to increase as their numbers increase, so that if one person from a wholly different culture arrives in town then the town benefits from that culture, and that if another person follows then that town doubly benefits and thereafter continues to benefit with each new person. But the knowledge or benefit of a culture does not increase incrementally with the number of people from that culture. Food is one of the benefits that is rather embarrassingly seized upon in this argument. But to take that example, the amount of enjoyment to be got from Turkish food does not increase year on year the more Turks there are in the country. Every 100,000 extra Somalis, Eritreans or Pakistanis who enter Europe do not magnify the resulting cultural enrichment 100,000 times. It may be that Europe has already learned what it needs to learn from cuisine, and accordingly gained all that it needs to gain, and that in order to continue to enjoy Indian food it will not be necessary to keep on importing more Indians into our societies. If it is the case that 'diversity' is a good in itself, it does not explain why in each country immigrants overwhelmingly come from a small number of countries. If you actively sought to bring 'diversity' to Europe after the first decades of mass migration, it would have been sensible to search for people not just from former colonies but from countries that had never been colonies and countries about which there was a genuine lack of knowledge.

However, behind the insistence on 'diversity' as a good in itself lies another idea, albeit one that is perhaps less presentable to the general public. Although New Labour's 2000 document was meant to be an economic analysis, it was the social aspect of migration that most interested one of its authors. In a book she had edited in 1994 called *Strangers and Citizens: A Positive Approach to Migrants and Refugees*, Sarah Spencer, of the Centre on Migration Policy and Society at Oxford argued that 'The days when holding British nationality rested on a notion of allegiance are over.'[13] Elsewhere she and her co-authors had argued that the nation state had changed and that the modern state had become 'an open and formal association capable of accommo-dating diverse ways of life' and that in that state 'immigration policy must be seen ... also as a means of enriching the cultural diversity of the country'.[14] A year later Sarah Spencer was quoting approvingly in another publication the idea that 'the traditional concept of national-ity may be downgraded to the level of pure symbolism' and arguing herself that 'We are a diverse society of overlapping identities and are not bound, nor can we be bound, by universal values or single loyal-ties. If we are to be bound together it must be through the mutual enjoyment of rights and responsibilities.'[15]

This was a radically different understanding of what constituted a people or a country, and one with profound and – for most of the public – unpalatable connotations. Sarah Spencer outlined these in 2003 when she wrote about the idea of 'integration', that it is not something the migrant does to adapt to the host society but rather 'a two-way process of adaptation by migrant and host society'.[16] If you tell people they will gain from migration, that is a positive thing. If you tell them that they will have to change because of migration, that is likely to go down less well. And so the positive part is the only part that is stressed.

But the argument for mass migration on the grounds of 'diversity' as being a good in itself ignores one huge and until recently unspeakable issue. Just as most cultures have good and interesting things to say for themselves, all have some bad and disagreeable things about them too. And while the positives can be stressed and exaggerated from the outset, any negatives take years to admit, if they are admitted at all.

One need only consider the decades it has taken to admit that some immigrant groups hold less liberal views than the majority of people in the countries they have come into. A Gallup survey conducted in 2009 in Britain found that precisely zero per cent of British Muslims interviewed (out of a pool of 500) thought that homosexuality was morally acceptable.[17] Another survey carried out in 2016 found that 52 per cent of British Muslims thought homosexuality should be made illegal.[18] The common response to such findings is that these were the attitudes of many British people a generation or two ago. The unspoken follow-on is that homosexuals in Britain should be patient and wait another generation or two for the newcomers to catch up. All the while what is ignored is the possibility that this might not happen and that the views of the incomers may in time, through population growth or other means, change the national picture as a whole. So in 2015 when YouGov carried out a survey of British attitudes towards homosexuality, one of the questions asked was whether in general respondents thought homosexuality to be 'morally acceptable' or 'morally wrong'. Some people might have assumed that such a survey would smoke out latent homophobia in certain rural areas whereas the hip, diverse urban areas would show that they were relaxed about the whole matter.

In fact, the findings showed precisely the opposite. Whereas in the whole of the rest of the country around 16 per cent of people said that they thought homosexuality was 'morally wrong', in London the figure was almost double that (29 per cent).[19] Why should people in London have been almost twice as homophobic as the rest of the country? Solely for the reason that the ethnic diversity of the capital meant that it had imported a disproportionate number of people with attitudes which the rest of the country would now regard as being morally backwards. But if the views of some migrant communities on homosexuality were only a couple of generations out of date, the views of portions of those communities on the subject of women were shown to be out of date by many centuries, at least.

It was in the early 2000s in England that stories that the Sikh and white working-class communities had been telling for years were finally investigated by the media. These revealed that the organised grooming of often underage young girls by gangs of Muslim men of North African or Pakistani background was a theme in towns throughout the north of England and further afield. In each case the local police had been too scared to look into the issue, and when the media finally looked into it they too shied away. A 2004 documentary on social services in Bradford had its screening postponed after self-proclaimed 'anti-fascists' and local police chiefs appealed to Channel 4 to drop the documentary. The sections that dealt with the sexual exploitation of white girls by 'Asian' gangs were accused of being potentially inflammatory. In particular, these authorities insisted, the screening ahead of local elections could assist the British National Party at the polls. The documentary was finally screened months after the elections. But everything about this case and the details that followed provided a microcosm of a problem and a reaction which were going to spread across Europe.

Campaigning on, or even mentioning, the issue of grooming during those years brought with it terrible problems. When the northern Labour MP Ann Cryer took up the issue of the rape of underage girls in her own constituency, she was swiftly and widely denounced as an 'Islamophobe' and a 'racist', and at one stage had to receive police protection. It took years for central government, the police, local authorities or the Crown Prosecution Service to face up to the issue. When they finally began to do so, an official inquiry into abuse in the town of Rotherham alone revealed the exploitation of at least 1,400 children over the period 1997–2014. The victims were all non-Muslim white girls from the local community, with the youngest victim aged 11. All had been brutally raped, some had also been doused in petrol and threatened with being set on fire. Others were threatened with guns and forced to watch the violent rape of other girls as a warning should they tell anyone about the abuse. The inquiry into the abuse found that although the perpetrators were almost all men of Pakistani origin, operating in gangs, staff of the local council described their 'nervousness about identifying the ethnic origins of perpetrators for fear of being thought as racist; others remembered clear direction from their managers not to do so.' The local police were also found to have failed to act for fear of accusations of 'racism' and of what this might do to community relations.[20]

The story of Rotherham, like that of a whole series of similar cases in towns across Britain, partly emerged because a couple of journalists were determined to bring the story out. But all the time the communities from which the men came showed no willingness to confront the problem and every desire to cover it up. Even at the courts after sentencing, families of those accused claimed that the whole thing was a government stitch-up of some kind.[21] When one Muslim in the north of England spoke out against the gang rape of white girls by members of his own community, he said that he received death threats from fellow Muslims in Britain for saying so.[22]

Everywhere the story was the same. Girls were chosen, in the words of the judges who eventually presided over the trials, because they were from a different community, were non-Muslim and were regarded as 'easy meat'. Many of the men had brought ideas about women and especially about unaccompanied or 'unprotected' women with them from Pakistan and other male-dominated Muslim cultures. In the face of such attitudes towards women being expressed in the United Kingdom, every part of the British state failed to stand up for what had been British norms, including the rule of law. The kindest explanation would be that the influx of huge numbers of people from such cultures made the authorities nervous as to where to draw their own lines. But it was more than that. Every time grooming scandals occurred it transpired that the local authorities turned a blind eye for fear of causing community problems or being accused of racism. The British police remained scarred from the Macpherson Report of 1999, which had charged them with 'institutional racism', and feared any repeat of that accusation.

Everywhere in Western Europe the same truth came out at least equally slowly, often at almost precisely the same moment as the taboo shattered in Britain. In each country the period of silence was assisted by the refusal of the authorities to keep or break down any crime statistics based on ethnicity or religion. In 2009 police in Norway revealed that immigrants from non-Western backgrounds were responsible for 'all reported grab-rapes' – those in which the assailant grabbed the woman off a street or public place – in Oslo.[23] In 2011 the Norwegian state's statistical bureau was willing to note that 'immigrants are overrepresented in the crime statistics'. They did, however, also suggest that this was not due to any cultural differences, but rather perhaps to the predominance of young men among the immigrant populations. One former head of the violent crime section of the Oslo Police Department, Hanne Kristin Rohde, testified to the extraordinary unwillingness of the Norwegian authorities to admit to what was happening. In relation to the 'clear statistical connection' between rapes and migrants who came from cultures where 'women have no value of their own', she said that 'This was a big problem but it was difficult to talk about it.' As for the rapists' attitudes towards women, 'It is a cultural problem,' said Rohde.[24]

Obviously these and similar cases of rape gangs are an unusual and unrepresentative example of the behaviour of immigrants as a whole. They ought, however, to be the easiest misbehaviours imaginable to discover, investigate and punish. That it has taken years, and in some cases decades, even for police and prosecutors to face up to the problem, throws open a deeply troubling possibility. These cases – like female genital mutilation (FGM) – ought to be easier to deal with. But Western European societies have struggled for years even remotely to get to grips with the problem. Other less prominent or violent attitudes that some migrant groups bring with them are unlikely ever to achieve a similar degree of inspection if cases such as these are hard to grapple with. If the large-scale gang rape of children takes more than a decade to come to light, how long will less violent and horrific examples of untoward attitudes take to come to light, if they ever do?

One thing this demonstrates is that whereas the benefits of mass immigration undoubtedly exist and everybody is made very aware of them, the disadvantages of importing huge numbers of people from another culture take a great deal of time to admit to. In the meantime, the agreement seems to have been reached with the general public that it is not such a bad deal: if there is a bit more beheading and sexual assault than there used to be in Europe, then at least we also benefit from a much wider range of cuisines.

THE IDEA THAT IMMIGRATION IS UNSTOPPABLE BECAUSE OF GLOBALISATION

The final justification or excuse for mass immigration goes beyond reason and beyond excuses. Even if every other argument for the policy were debunked, this one would remain. It is the argument that none of this matters because nothing can be done anyway. It is all out of everybody's hands. It is our fate.

Towards the start of the current crisis I was involved in a debate in Athens about what Europe's policies towards the immigration situation should be. While presenting my argument I made the observation that the others present (including the Greek economist Antigone Lyberaki and the French politician and activist Bernard Kouchner) were likely to tell the audience that 'nothing could be done'. Only afterwards when Bernard put down his pre-prepared speech did I see that he had crossed out the first line before his delivery. The speech was indeed due to open with the insistence that Europe could not stop the flow coming into Greece and that 'nothing could be done'.

It is a familiar cry, though when alerted to it the wiser politicians often realise that it is a potentially disastrous one. Meanwhile leading politicians including, in 2015, Britain's then Home Secretary, Theresa May, have claimed that European countries must try to improve living standards in third-world countries in order to prevent people coming here. Yet the truth is — as many studies have shown — that it is only when living standards rise (though hardly to luxurious levels) that the mass migration truly begins. Truly poor people do not have the money to bribe the smugglers.

There are also attempts to give this view a veneer of academic respectability. In recent years a line has grown in academic discourse around the subject of migration, which insists that migration flows are actually caused by any and all migration controls. The work of, among others, Hein de Haas of the universities of Oxford and Maastricht, insists that migration controls not only do not work but actually boost migration by discouraging the normal circulation of migrants between Europe and their home countries. A favourite line in academia, this is also of course an argument that is only ever made by people who oppose any and all controls on migration.

Before pointing out the unexploded democratic explosive behind this, it is worth considering what is true in the claim. Certainly the prevalence of mobile phones, mass media – especially television – in the third world and the lowered cost of travel over recent decades means that the desire and opportunity of people all over the world to travel has never been greater. But if globalisation really has made it impossible to prevent people travelling to Europe from across the world, it is worth noting that this global issue does not affect other countries. If the cause is economic pull, then there is no reason why Japan should not currently be experiencing unparalleled waves of immigration from the West. In 2016 the country was the world's third largest economy if measured by nominal GDP, putting it ahead of Germany and Great Britain. But of course, despite being a larger economy than any in Europe, Japan has avoided a policy of mass immigration by implementing policies that stop it, dissuade people from staying there, and make it hard to become a citizen if you are not Japanese. Irrespective of whether one agrees with Japan's policy or not, the country shows that even in this hyper-connected age it is possible for a modern economy to avoid the experience of mass immigration and show that such a process is not 'inevitable'. In the same way, although China is the world's second largest economy, it is not a destination for asylum seekers or economic migrants on the scale of Europe. Ignoring whether this is desirable or not, it is obviously possible for even the richest countries not to inevitably become points of attraction for migrants from all over the world.

The reason people wish to come to Europe is not only because of the perception of wealth and work. It is also because Europe has made itself a desirable destination for additional reasons. Not least among them is the knowledge that Europe is likely to allow arrivals to remain in the continent once there. High among the reasons why people flock to Europe are the knowledge that its welfare states will look after migrants who arrive, and the knowledge that however long it takes or however poorly migrants may be looked after they will still enjoy a better standard of living and a better roster of rights than anywhere else, let alone in their home countries. There is also the belief – flattering to Europeans as well as true – that Europe is a more tolerant, peaceful and welcoming place than most parts of the world. If there were many such continents in the world then Europeans might be able to enjoy their status as one generous society among many. If the perception grows that Europe is in fact the only place where it is both easy to get in, easy to remain and safe to stay, then the continent may find the resulting attention less flattering in the long term than it does in the short term. In any case it is not inevitable that the world's migrants should come to Europe. They come because Europe has made itself – for good reasons and some bad – attractive to the world's migrants.

Something clearly can be done. Whether desirable or not, if Europe had to limit the flow it could take measures to make itself look and actually be – in a whole range of ways – less appealing to a world on the move. It could adopt a sterner face to the world, return people who should not be here, stop providing the welfare provisions to new arrivals and adopt more of a 'first-come first-served' basis for welfare policy in the future. If migration is caused by allure, then a way needs to be found to lose the allure. These are unpleasant things to consider, not least because they affect one of the views of ourselves that Europeans like to hold, and it might even in the long run alter that self-perception. But the road may not be as perilous as some people fear. Few would argue that Japan is a barbarous country for implementing its strict migration rules. In any case, the idea that what Europe is going through is unstoppable is a dangerous one, not just because it is untrue but because of the trouble it stores up.

For many years across Western Europe the issue of migration has been at the top of the list of public concerns. Opinion polls in each country consistently show the issue to be of almost overriding concern to the general public. If a concern is felt by a majority of the public for many years and nothing is done to address it, then trouble and resentment are certainly stored up. If the response is not just to ignore the concern but to argue that it is actually impossible to do anything about it, then radical alternatives begin to brew. At best such concerns will be expressed at the ballot box. At worst they will surface on the streets. It is hard to think of any other issue, let alone one so high up the list of public concerns, that would be responded to with a 'nothing can be done' response.

Even this final, fatalistic response to the problem is a result of a policy that was never thought through and now appears to have become – in the eyes of politicians and academics – essentially insuperable. After all, one after another the expectations about what would happen turned out to be false. And the realities of what did happen turned out either not to have been thought about or thought about erroneously. Consider the verdict of one of those who enabled the post-1997 Labour government to escalate their policy when they did. After her work for the British government Sarah Spencer was rewarded with the honour of a CBE. But by then, when some of the repercussions of her evangelism and that of others had begun to be felt, she made a more lachrymose assessment, admitting that during those years in government, when she and her colleagues had opened the floodgates, 'There was no policy for integration. We just believed migrants would integrate.'[25] All this was years before the biggest crisis that confronts us today, but all returned as foundational arguments to excuse the huge and continent-wide movement that was coming.

4

'Welcome to Europe'

The island of Lampedusa is the most southerly outpost of Italy. Closer to the coastline of North Africa than it is to that of Sicily, the main ferry from Lampedusa to Sicily takes nine hours. When you are on Lampedusa you can feel this isolation. These eight dry square miles of rock have a landscape far more like that of Tunisia or Libya than that of Italy. Over the centuries it has had the kind of history you might expect of an unprepossessing but useful post in the Mediterranean. It has changed hands repeatedly and its recorded history is one of constant depopulation and repopulation. Pirate raids were a problem throughout, notably in the sixteenth century when pirates from Turkey seized a thousand of the island's inhabitants and took them off into slavery. An English visitor in the eighteenth century found only one inhabitant.

The Princes of Lampedusa – who even after the gift of their title were sensible enough to stay in their palaces on Sicily – encouraged the island's repopulation. Today, if the island's name rings any bells apart from for its recent miseries it is for one holder of this title in particular. The author of *The Leopard* was the last of the line of Princes of that name. But there is nothing of him or his world on the island that shares his name. The decaying grandeur of his Sicilian Baroque feels as many miles away as it is from this dusty outcrop of plain, low-built houses. These days the island is inhabited by about five thousand people, mainly centred around the sole port. There is one main street of shops – the Via Roma – which leads to the harbour, and the island's youth hang around here in packs or speed about the town's few streets, two to a scooter. Old women group together on benches around the town square in front of the church, the men constantly greeting each other as though they haven't met for years. It is the sort of place from which any ambitious young Italian would do practically anything to escape. Yet every day thousands of people risk their lives trying to get here.

Of course, people have fled North Africa for years. And as the island's graveyard attests, it is not only in the last few years that the journey has proved deadly. Buried alongside the locals in the cemetery are some of those who set out for Lampedusa and whose journey ended in the sea. 'Migrante non identificato. Qui riposa', says one of the grave-markers put down by the local government: '29 Settembre 2000'. During the 2000s boatloads of migrants regularly arrived on Lampedusa, bringing people not only from North and sub-Saharan Africa, but from the Middle and Far East. People-smugglers charged high rates for the journey by boat, but desperate individuals paid their prices for the short crossing. With a journey time of less than a day, however badly propelled the boat, it became known as one of the best routes to a new life. Once onto Lampedusa you are into Italy, and once into Italy you are into Europe.

It is a strange first glimpse to get of the continent. Those whose boats come up on the shoreline see little to distinguish their point of arrival from the place they have just left. Those who sail into the south-facing harbour find a small port, lined with a few quiet shops and cafes meant to cater for the Italian tourists who used to come here for their holidays. Fishing remains the island's main business, and on a tall column over the harbour stands a statue of the Madonna and Child, watching over the ships as they go in and out of the port.

During the 2000s the local authorities began to get concerned by the number of arrivals coming from North Africa and were forced to build a holding centre for them. The original centre was designed to hold up to 350 people, the idea being that the migrants would be processed quickly and then moved on up by boat into Sicily or mainland Italy where their claims for asylum could be assessed. But the new centre swiftly proved inadequate for the task because of the numbers that started arriving. At 500 the centre is overcrowded. At points in the 2000s there were as many as two thousand people at a time and the migrant centre spilled out all around into a tent-city. At such moments local resentment risked becoming a problem.

Throughout this time, and cash-strapped though the country was, Italy carried the financial and human burden of this process almost unaided. Unsurprisingly, the government also improvised. During what would be the last decade of Colonel Gaddafi's rule in Libya the Italians entered into a covert agreement with his regime to return those Africans who had no right to remain and had to be deported from Italy. When the details of this arrangement emerged, Italy was roundly criticised by other European countries. But the country was only experiencing the sort of concerns and compromises that every-body else in Europe would encounter next. Soon, in a pattern that would also become familiar to everyone else, if it hadn't been before, almost everybody who arrived on Lampedusa stayed in Italy. Even when their asylum claims were processed and turned down, appeals lodged and also turned down and deportation orders issued, they still stayed. The numbers coming in were too great and the whole process was already far too costly for the additional costs of often forcible repatriation to be added in. At some point, whether as an official nod or as part of an unofficial acceptance of the inevitable, it was deemed not just too economically costly but too diplomatically costly to return people to where they came from. It was easier to let them dissolve into the country, perhaps to try to move around into the rest of Europe if they could, or if not to stay in Italy and find a way to live. Some would find a path to citizenship. Most would enter the country's or the continent's black economy, often working at rates not much above those they would get back home – and often for gangs from their own country that constituted their sole network in Europe.

While the rest of Italy hoped that the problem would melt into the length of the country, the holding centre on Lampedusa – just behind the harbour's centre – was regularly overflowing and had to come up with answers. At times the situation became dangerous. There were fights and riots among the residents, often sparked by inter-ethnic rivalries. The migrant centre was meant to be a holding centre, but migrants began to wander around the town. When the authorities tried to keep people from going out through the main entrance, some of the migrants made a hole in the fence at the back and walked out that way. The centre is not a prison and the migrants were not prisoners. The question of precisely what they were and what their precise status was took on an improvised air. Increasingly, the migrants knew what their rights were and what the Italian authorities could and could not do with them.

It was natural that the locals, who had in the main been extraordinarily understanding and sympathetic to the new arrivals, occasionally became unnerved by the numbers. At a high flow the number of people arriving in a few days could easily outnumber the natives. And though the local shopkeepers sold their limited wares to the latest arrivals and sometimes gave them gifts, the authorities knew that they had to become better at processing people. In particular they had to move them off the island faster and get them onto boats up to Sicily and the mainland faster than they were managing. This was Lampedusa during the relative 'trickle' of the 2000s.

From 2011, after the events that became known as the 'Arab Spring', this trickle became a flood. In part this was because of the number of people fleeing changes of government and civil unrest. In part it was because of the crumbling of the shady agreements with the old dictators that had limited some of the activities of the people-traffickers. From 2011 onwards hundreds and sometimes thousands of people were arriving in Lampedusa day and night. They came on rickety wooden boats, old fishing vessels from North Africa purchased (or stolen) by the smugglers who would make their clients pay the 'fare', however unseaworthy the vessel. Soon the question of what to do with all these boats became an issue on Lampedusa. Unable to find any further use for these wrecks, the local authorities piled them up behind the harbour front and at other places on the island – great graveyards of wretched vessels. At intervals, when the numbers got too great, the boats were heaped up together and burned.

That first year of the 'Arab Spring' was an especially bad time for the island. As five hundred people were lined up to be ferried off Lampedusa a thousand more would arrive. From 2011 onwards the migrant centre was often bursting with between one and two thousand people. And of course not all of those who set out managed to arrive in the increasingly inadequate vessels that the smugglers dispatched. On the island itself the authorities created more burial spots for the dead bodies that came in, identifying those they could and burying those they could not, with a cross and an identity number that was given to the body on arrival. 'Where are the other bodies?' I once asked a local. 'The sea has most' came the reply.

At the outset of the Syrian civil war many of the arrivals were Syrians, including the richer, middle-class Syrians. One day a yacht of well-dressed Syrians arrived into Lampedusa harbour and walked ashore to be processed in the normal way. But after 2011 the Syrians who came were the poorer ones and their numbers also declined. Those who came that way told of a route through Egypt that involved extensive tunnel systems where the children needed oxygen masks. Different ethnic groups came through different routes, but they also had different expectations and different wishes. Most expressed a desire to stay in Italy. Only the Eritreans did not, perhaps because of memories of their former colonial masters. They alone always expressed a desire to head on north into the rest of Europe.

As some observers noted from the outset, the demographics of the migration were suggestive in themselves. Perhaps 80 per cent of the people coming were young men. There were also children, including unaccompanied minors who caused the most concern for the waiting authorities. Nigerian children who were alone were often being sent into Europe to be trafficked. There were occasional women, generally promised work once in Europe. Met by their smuggler's contacts in Italy or further north, who would lend them money and to whom they would then be indebted, only at this stage did they find out that the 'job' they had been promised was prostitution. Most people know how dangerous the journey is for any unaccompanied woman. It is rare for Muslim women or girls to come alone.

Once they arrive on Lampedusa the behaviour of migrants also varies wildly. Those with money go shopping on the Via Roma. The Syrians are known for buying clothes when they arrive. Some migrants buy alcohol. Many immediately buy phone cards and use them to call home and tell their family that they have arrived in Europe and to make arrangements with whatever contacts they have for the next phase of their journey.

One day I met three young Eritreans in the street, no older than 16. They had just bought – and were proudly wearing – souvenir hats from the island bearing the legend 'I love Lampedusa'. Elsewhere, in the church square, eight young sub-Saharan boys seemed to be following instructions from an older migrant. They did not blend in. Among the small packs of immigrants who roam through the town some make an effort to wave or nod at locals. Others slope along the streets, glaring and already seemingly resentful. The overwhelming predominance of young men is noticeable at all times. They have come here on behalf of their families. In time they hope to send money back to them. Most of all they hope that they will be able to bring their families to join them.

By 2013 the flow was so great that the government took the unusual step of flying recent arrivals off the island and onto Sicily or the mainland. That July, Pope Francis visited Lampedusa to an ecstatic local reaction. He threw a wreath into the sea and presided over an open-air Mass during which he used a small painted boat as an altar. The Pope used the visit to condemn the 'global indifference' to what was going on and urged the world to a 'reawakening of consciences'. For the inhabitants it finally seemed some appropriate recognition of what was happening on their island.

Then on 3 October 2013 a boat that had set out from Misrata, Libya, filled mainly with sub-Saharan Africans, sank off the coast of Lampedusa. The Italian coastguard saved more than a hundred people, but over three hundred migrants drowned. There was a huge outcry. A day of public mourning was announced in Italy, with flags flown at half mast and a minute's silence observed in all Italian schools. On Lampedusa a silent candlelit procession and evening Mass were attended by most of the residents of the island. So many bodies were brought in that a hangar at Lampedusa's tiny airport had to be turned into a temporary mortuary.

A political outcry also ensued, not just in Italy but across the world. The Secretary-General of the United Nations, Ban Ki-moon, said that the tragedy proved the need for 'more channels for safe and orderly migration'. Further sinkings the same month, with the loss of dozens of lives, drew increasingly strong reactions. Whilst calling for more European aid, the Prime Minister of nearby Malta complained that the Mediterranean was becoming a 'cemetery'. Finally, international attention began to be paid to what was happening on the seas around Lampedusa. As a direct response the Italian government, with some wider support, launched 'Mare Nostrum' ('Our Sea'). The policy allowed the Italian navy to patrol the almost 70,000 square kilometres of water off Lampedusa and operate search-and-rescue missions for migrant ships. Navy frigates and helicopters were backed up with coastal radar networks at a cost to the Italian government of around nine million Euros a month. NGOs cooperated with the policy and arranged to be on board the government vessels to assist when migrant ships were intercepted. The policy undoubtedly saved many lives, but it also created new problems.

Among these was the fact that the people-smugglers operating from the lawless zones of the Libyan coastline now no longer had to try to use vessels even as able as those they had been putting out to date. Mare Nostrum had brought the border of Europe even closer to Libya. All that the smugglers now had to do was launch any boat into the water. If it happened to stay afloat the Italian navy would meet it half-way to Lampedusa or sometimes even closer to Libya. If the migrant vessel was seaworthy, the Italian navy would tow it into port at Lampedusa. Normally, the migrants would first be brought aboard the Italian vessels. This operation – which lasted under a year – was applauded by the International Organisation for Migration (IOM), among other international bodies, which later estimated that during this period Italian vessels brought around 150,000 people into Europe. The IOM repeated the official line that the operation did not encourage more people to come.[1]

Nevertheless with the numbers so substantial, and no end in sight, the cost of Mare Nostrum soon proved too much for an Italian state still staggering through the various Eurozone crises. And so after a year during which officials had sought help but been given hardly any, the job of Mare Nostrum was turned over to the EU's Frontex border agency under the title 'Operation Triton'. This too sought out boats crossing from North Africa and either assisted the migrants onto the Frontex vessels or guided their boats into harbour at Lampedusa or Sicilian ports such as Augusta towards which many boats were also heading. Throughout this period, Frontex and other officials also continued to deny that the operation was causing any pull factor.

Yet how could it not? On one side of the Mediterranean were people from across Africa, the Middle East and the Far East, some of whom had been travelling for months to get to the shores of Libya and to embark on this final journey. Word of Italian government policy and European attitudes to what was happening undoubtedly filtered back. The advantages this gave the smugglers were considerable. Not least because the greater the demand the higher the prices they could charge and the more people they could pack onto their boats. The stories of the behaviour of the smugglers obviously also came with the migrants, some of whom had paid up to 4,000 Euros for the crossing alone. But the bargain was rarely straightforward. Rape was commonplace, especially of women – whether accompanied or not. Many migrants made it to Libya only for more money to be demanded from them than they had already paid. Possessions were seized. Some migrants told of the smugglers using a migrant's mobile phone to video their abuse and torture. The video was then sent to the migrant's family with a threat of further torture unless they sent more money. The officials who process the migrants once they arrive in Italy get to know where the traffickers' safe-houses are, but next to nothing can be done inside Libya to punish the gangs.

Although the world sees all these people as 'migrants', or 'refugees', between and among themselves they are very different people, with different backgrounds and different reasons for finding themselves on this same journey. One demonstration of this is the hierarchy that exists among the migrants even once they are on the boats. Racism between and among the migrant groups is routine. For instance, Tunisians and Syrians look down disapprovingly on sub-Saharan Africans, and not only metaphorically. When the boats set out the best places in the vessel – at the front and on the deck – are occupied by these better-off groups from the Middle East and North Africa. The Eritreans, Somalis and others sit or stand in the hold of the boat. If the boat goes down it is these people who are most likely to drown.

During the summer of 2015 on Lampedusa I got speaking to two Eritreans in their late teens or early twenties, sitting in silence on the edge of the harbour, picking at their feet and looking back over the sea they had crossed. While huge naval vessels scoured the horizon beyond, these two showed me the boat, sitting between the Italian government vessels in the harbour, that they had arrived on the previous week. It was, among the battered old boats that set out from Libya, comparatively seaworthy. It had been spotted by the coastguards and escorted into harbour by a helicopter with accompanying rescue boats. The two Eritreans had travelled at the lowest point, in the dark hold of the boat, but it had stayed afloat and so they had stayed alive.

The NGO workers who are tasked with getting the people off these rickety boats in the middle of the sea have terrible stories to tell. When a boat is spotted at any time of the day or night and the workers are not on an official vessel, they have an hour or two at most to get down to the harbour. One worker says that when the migrants board the naval vessel at sea, or the harbour on land, they are told 'You're in Italy!' Then the workers reassure them that they are safe. Again, apart from the Eritreans most are very happy and smile. In the countries they come from, people are suspicious of officials and especially of police, so for third parties to reassure the migrants that here in Europe the police and officials will actually work for them is a very important reassurance. One NGO worker relates that the first thing she says to the migrants when they get onto the naval vessel in the middle of the sea or into the dock at Lampedusa is simply, 'Welcome to Europe.'

After what the migrants have been through even before the treacherous crossing from North Africa, it is hardly surprising that many of them arrive at Lampedusa exhausted and traumatised. Some will have lost a family member on the journey. In 2015 a big Nigerian man sat on the harbour ground weeping like a child and hitting it with his hand. The boat he had come in on had gone down and though he had saved one of his children, his wife and another of his sons had drowned in front of him.

Yet still they come, knowing the risks, because for all the stories of sinking boats and deaths on board, most of those who set out will stay afloat, reach Italian waters and once there become European citizens. Whether they are fleeing political, religious or sectarian persecution, or whether they are after a better life in the developed world, all will claim asylum. Many will have legitimate claims and Italy has a duty to give these people asylum: under the Geneva Conventions and the EU Dublin Treaty the first country into which a migrant enters and claims asylum is the country that must assess the claim and offer protection. But the bitter truth is that there is almost no way to find out who is who, or what is true. If the flow of applicants was not at the levels it has been for years then the finger-printing, interviews and everything else that follows could be carefully assessed. Backstories could be cross-checked and followed up on. But with the arrivals coming at this speed and in these numbers there was never any chance of this.

Two other elements make all of this far worse. Many – and sometimes most – of the people arriving deliberately bring no paperwork with them because being unidentified is an advantage. Amid the demands on the time of the agencies people can pretend to be other ages, other people or even from another country. When it became known that a particular group were being put to the front of the asylum queue – Syrians, for instance – then a large number of people would claim to be Syrians, even though some of those working with the refugees noticed they were neither speaking any Syrian dialect nor knew anything about the country they claimed to be from.

This phenomenon is at least partly caused by NGOs that advocate for any and all migration into Europe as part of the 'borderless world' movement. As the flow of migrants grew in the 2010s, some NGO groups decided to help migrants before they even got to Europe. They provided easily accessible information on the web and on phone apps to guide would-be Europeans through the process. This included advice on where to go and what to say once there. Front-line workers notice that as time goes on the awareness of the migrants about what will happen to them and what they should expect becomes ever clearer. In part this is the result of word filtering back to their countries of origin from people who have successfully made the journey. But it is also because a movement exists that seeks to teach migrants how to stay in Europe whatever the justice of their application. All these groups are correct in their assumption that in the twenty-first century Italy has neither the money, time nor will to painstakingly go through every application. Of course, there are people who are refused asylum, at which point they can appeal the decision. But even if their appeal is turned down it is rare for anything further to happen. It is hard to find any cases of someone arriving in Italy, being refused the right to remain and then being sent back to their home country. Very occasionally someone who has been convicted of a crime in Italy is repatriated. But even then the bar is set exceptionally high. It is easier to let everyone dissolve into Italy and then into Europe than it is to hold the line of the law. The truth is that once you survive Lampedusa's waters you are in Europe for good.

Of course, even those who may be lying about asylum are looking for an infinitely better life than the one they have left behind. From Lampedusa it seems easy to imagine schemes to distribute this vast and continual wave of people equitably and harmoniously across the continent. But anybody who knows even just Italy should know better than this. Aside from the tiny number of earlier and better-off migrants, most people who arrive will eventually find themselves sleeping outside the train station in Milan or in a car park in Ravenna. The lucky ones will end up working for gangs or trying to sell imitation luxury goods on the bridges of Venice or down the side streets of Naples. Whenever they see a policeman or the flash of a police car's lights they will hurriedly gather up their counterfeit bags or wheel away their tray of imitation-brand sunglasses and hurry from the scene. They may be more protected, free and safe than they were at home, but their future can hardly be said to be bright.

And Lampedusa is only one small island. During recent years boats full of migrants have also come ashore on the islands nearest to Lampedusa, including Malta and Sicily. In 2014 alone – the year before the migrant crisis 'began' – 170,000 people arrived this way. Officials talk of solving the problem by filling Libya's recent government vacuum. But they forget that the flow of migrants continued even during the period when European governments (including the French) were paying bribes to Gaddafi. And they forget that the boats do not only head out from Libya, but also launch from Egypt, Tunisia and Algeria. What is more, this is in any case only one route. Over to the west of the Mediterranean is another route entirely, going up from Morocco and into Spain. Migrants have flowed across this narrowest gap between Africa and Europe, the Straits of Gibraltar, for decades. And despite Morocco having the best relations of any North African government with any European country – and therefore the best chance of doing deals to stop the smugglers – the migration to Spain has not been stopped. Indeed, during the early 1990s the movement of migrants through this route proved to be a harbinger of what was to come. In those days the going rate for the people-smugglers to traverse 10 miles of sea was $600. Then as now boats set off on a daily basis and the bodies of those who didn't make it (often because the smugglers make migrants swim the last portion of the journey) washed up on the beaches of Spain.

Then, as now, the movement was not only continuous but diverse. One report from 1992 documented that of 1,547 illegal migrants detained by the Spanish authorities in Tarifa alone over a ten-month period, there were 258 Ethiopians, 193 Liberians and 64 Somalis.

As the report observed, 'word of the new route had spread far beyond Morocco, with not only Algerians and growing numbers of sub-Saharan Africans, but also Filipinos, Chinese and even the occasional Eastern Europeans among those detained'. Among those who were fleeing, some were escaping oppression while others were simply looking for work or a better quality of life. As Santiago Varela, Spain's then Deputy Interior Minister, said, 'In North Africa, there is a structural problem. We don't know how its political and economic situation will develop. And the demographic pressure is enormous.' He was referring to a situation in which even then 70 per cent of the Moroccan population was under the age of 30 and official unemployment figures sat at 17.5 per cent. 'You can't yet compare our problem with that of other European countries,' Varela said. 'But it's a warning of what can happen here in the future. Spain has passed very quickly from being a land of emigration to one of immigration.'[2]

Varela was speaking after a period in which North Africans who had previously headed towards France and Belgium were instead looking to find jobs in Italy and Spain at a time when neither country required visas. The migrants could enter either country as tourists and then travel on to the rest of Europe. And part of the pull factor even then was Europe's commitment to lower the internal borders between countries, making free movement easy once anyone was in Europe. In the 1990s efforts to clamp down on illegal entries were hampered by Morocco's refusal to take back any non-Moroccans who had left the country. Thus, as one Spanish official noted, even if the government did manage to deter boats in his region, 'They'll find other ways of getting in. They'll use bigger boats and land away from here. They'll try Italy or Portugal. While there's so much misery over there, they'll keep coming.'[3]

Although efforts to stem the flow of migrants has been more successful in Spain than in Italy or Greece, the flow still continues today. In the 2010s it is concentrated on the Spanish North African enclaves of Melilla and Ceuta, which remain tantalising positions for anyone seeking to make their way into Europe. Regular efforts by migrants to break down the fences and walls surrounding the enclaves mean clashes with police and frequent unrest. At the same time – and powerful though the pressures of those enclaves remain, the migrant boats still continue to head for the Spanish mainland or tiny pieces of territory like the islet of Alboran. In December 2014 in bad seas one boat of more than fifty sub-Saharan Africans headed off from near Nador in northern Morocco to the southern coast of Spain. The Cameroonian Muslim captain blamed the bad weather on a Nigerian Christian pastor who was praying on board. The captain and crew beat the pastor and threw him overboard before searching the other passengers, identifying the Christians, then beating and throwing them overboard in the same manner.[4]

This is only one more major route – one that has existed for years and where once again nothing is new but the scale. It was to this other side of the Mediterranean that the world's attention turned in the crucial year of the crisis.

5

'We have seen everything'

As in the Italian islands, the boats have been coming into the islands of Greece for years. And like the Italians, for years the Greek authorities had to try to deal with this problem on their own. Once again there could hardly have been a more unfortunate country to have to deal with such a challenge. By 2015 the Greek economy had been in a debt-repayment crisis for six years. While struggling with economic astringency enforced by the other Eurozone countries, with Germany at the helm, Greece was also struggling with a humanitarian crisis along its ragged borders.

As with the Italian islands, the migration went on for years before the rest of the continent even began to pay attention. And as with Lampedusa, the Greek islands are a prisoner not only of their geographical proximity to another continent but their own history. The dozens of Greek islands within short sailing distance of the Turkish coastline makes the northern Aegean and Dodecanese islands an even softer underbelly of the continent than those nearest North Africa. Like Italy, the Greek islands were already so consumed with financial and social problems when the flow of arrivals increased that they too pushed the migrants on up into the mainland in the hope that they would find their way north from Greece and through into the rest of Europe.

Throughout history the vulnerability of this piece of coastline has been unusual even by the standards of the region. It is the reason why the Byzantines, Ottomans and others all battled for these islands and held them at different times. From the northernmost parts of the island of Lesbos you can see Turkey clearer than most Greek islands are visible one to another. Five miles of water is all that divides this portion of Europe from Turkey. You can see why the people-smugglers get away with telling their charges that the final stretch of their journey into Europe consists of crossing a river. With a shorter journey time than the one from North Africa to Lampedusa, the going rate for the final part of this journey into Europe is $1,500. In the winter when the waters can get rough some of those lured to the shore see the rickety vessel they are being offered and refuse to get in. They are told that if they do not get in then they will still have to pay their $1,500, followed by another $1,500 for the boat they do get in.

Once they are pushed off from the shore, the boats take between 90 minutes and two hours to reach Greece. Unlike the smugglers from Libya into Italy, the people-smugglers of Turkey do not bother to use wooden vessels for such a short crossing. Their preferred boats are plastic ones, and unlike the great funeral pyres of wooden boats intermittently burned on Lampedusa, these plastic vessels cannot be burnt. Nor can they be recycled on the island, so cheap is the type of plastic they are made from. And so intermittently great piles of these plastic boats are collected and sent by a bigger boat to the Greek mainland for recycling. But of course the boats can still go down, in good weather and bad.

As with the inhabitants of Lampedusa, throughout all the years that the world took no interest in the locals on these Greek islands, they responded with a similar sense of charity and history, aware not just of what was happening now, but also of their own history. Many of the families on these islands have their own memories of migration. When the Greco-Turkish war ended in 1922 these islands were flooded with Greek citizens fleeing Asia Minor. More than three million Greeks fled what is now Turkey, via islands like Lesbos where today one in three residents is descended from those refugees. On the days when the 'river' between Turkey and Lesbos is dotted with boats like a low-key Armada, one of the first sites many of the migrants see is the tiny village of Skala Skamnias on the northern coast of Lesbos. Its tiny port, with a couple of bar-restaurants hugging the water and its tiny chapel on the harbour's promontory, was founded by some refugees from 1922.

Yet although movement and migration has been the story of these islands for centuries, what has happened in recent years is new. Not just in the regularity with which the numbers of arrivals have kept rising, but in the places from which they come. Although few islanders insist on the distinction, these newcomers are not Greeks fleeing conflict abroad and returning home. They are people fleeing conflicts far away, often having passed through many safe countries in the process. They also include a growing number of people fleeing poverty, joblessness or a lack of prospects, and who see Europe as the answer to their problems and Greece as their way into Europe.

As with the Italian points of entry the flow into the Greek islands sped up in the wake of the 'Arab Spring' and in particular with the civil war in Syria. But, again as in Italy, the arrivals also came from further afield. From countries with insurgencies and unstable governments – not least Afghanistan – but also from countries that were allied to the European powers and with ostensibly stable governments, such as Pakistan. This flow of people who had made their way through four or five countries before getting to the launch sites on the shores of Turkey also came the long way around from Africa.

But even in Greece, where this tide of people had been coming for years, it was 2015 that changed everything. Not because of anything new that had happened in the Far East or Middle East or Africa, but because of something that happened far to the north, in Germany.

The broadcast news that told Africa and the Middle East about the life to be lived in Europe had also of course told Europeans about the lives of people in Africa and the Middle East. And few things made a greater impression on the evening television news than the stories of boats capsizing and sinking in the Mediterranean: the turning of the southern portion of Europe into a watery graveyard. After 2011 such stories of human misery that had already touched the hearts of those living in Italy and Greece slowly at first began to be noticed in the rest of Europe.

Nowhere were they more commented upon and worried over than in Germany. But what was to happen developed against a backdrop that was far from propitious. An upsurge of migrants coming into Germany meant that already by 2014 immigration into the country had reached a twenty-year high. That year an estimated 200,000 people claimed asylum in the country. As a response some Germans began to feel security concerns and also identity concerns. How could Germany cope if it had to take in refugees and asylum seekers at this rate, on top of the decades in which the country had – like everyone else – already opened its borders to people who were honestly or otherwise admitted as guest-workers? What would be the likely impact on the country given that most of these new arrivals were also of the Muslim faith? During 2014 these often-uttered private concerns began to be voiced more loudly on the streets. A movement calling itself Pegida (People against the Islamisation of the Occident/West) began in Dresden and other German cities that objected to this upsurge in immigration.

In her New Year message on 31 December 2014 Chancellor Merkel singled out these movements for criticism. The German people, she insisted, must not have 'prejudice, coldness or hatred' in their hearts, as these groups did. Instead she urged the German people to a new surge of openness to refugees. She explained that wars and crises worldwide were creating 'more refugees than we have seen since the Second World War. Many literally escaped death. It goes without saying that we help them and take in people who seek refuge with us.' She also talked about Germany's demographics and explained that with an 'ageing population' this immigration that many people were worried about would in fact prove to be 'a gain for all of us'.[1] The following May the Federal Interior Minister Thomas de Maizière announced in Berlin that the German government was expecting 450,000 refugees to arrive in the country that year.

Then in July 2015 the human side of the migration story burst into the German news in the form of a 14-year-old Palestinian girl whose family had left Lebanon. On a live television programme involving a question-and-answer session between children and the

Chancellor in Rostock, this girl told Merkel she was worried that her family might be deported. The Chancellor's response epitomised the difficulty of meeting natural human sympathy with a wider political problem. She told the girl sitting in front of her that she seemed 'a very likeable person'. But then she added, 'Politics is hard.' Thousands and thousands of other people were also in Lebanon, the Chancellor told her, and if Germany said 'you can all come' and everyone from Africa alone came, then she should realise that Germany 'cannot cope with that'. Merkel promised that cases would be dealt with faster but was clear that some people 'will have to go back'. Then in the type of gruesomely gripping moment that the producers and presenter clearly realised was about to make all the nightly news programmes, as the Chancellor prepared for another question there was a noise from the young girl. She had begun to cry. Merkel walked over to comfort her. There was a dispute with the presenter, who seemed to be hoping for an on-air amnesty. The huge recent upsurge of migrants from Greece and Italy was clearly on the Chancellor's mind. But seized by the personal stories, much of the German media criticised Merkel for the 'coldness' of her response. This coldness, if that is what it was, soon left her.

With both Greece and Italy allowing recent arrivals to push on up into Europe, the next month the German Interior Ministry had already revised Germany's expected arrivals for 2015 up to 800,000 – more than four times the total number of arrivals in 2014. A week later the Ministry along with the Federal Office for Migration and Refugees pondered the question of what they would do with people coming up through Greece and Hungary and into Germany. Would they be sent back to Hungary as they ought to have been under the proper protocols? An agreement was reached that they would not be. On 25 August this fact was announced on Twitter by the Office for Migration, which said, 'we are at present largely no longer enforcing Dublin procedures for Syrian citizens'. The message swiftly went around the world. Then on the last day of August the Chancellor made her most important statement. Before an audience of foreign journalists in Berlin she announced, 'German thoroughness is super, but now German flexibility is needed.' Europe as a whole 'must move and its states must share the responsibility for refugees seeking asylum. Universal civil rights were so far tied together with Europe and its history. If Europe fails on the question of refugees, its close connection with universal civil rights will be destroyed. It won't be the Europe we imagine.'[2] The German Chancellor was opening the doors of Europe, and the words of encouragement she gave to her countrymen were motivational: 'Wir schaffen das' ('We can do this'). Germany, she insisted, was politically and economically strong enough to succeed in this task, just as it had succeeded with tasks in the past. Much of the media backed her up. 'Merkel the bold' was the headline in *The Economist*, with the accompanying article claiming: 'On refugees Germany's Chancellor is brave, decisive and right.'[3]

Though it was not only Merkel's decision to make, nevertheless the German Chancellor's powerful statement dragged the whole continent along with her, whether they wanted it or not. In a Europe whose borders had come down and in which free movement had become a doctrinal principle, the mass movement through Europe by people from outside began to cause continent-wide problems. Germany's neighbours saw hundreds of thousands of people walking through their territory on their way north into Germany. During 2015 around 400,000 migrants moved through Hungary's territory alone. Fewer than twenty of them stopped to claim asylum in Hungary. And this great surge of people broke out all over the rest of Europe as well. Tens of thousands of people from the Balkans, who had otherwise been unable to find a legal way to go north into Germany, joined the great movement of people moving across their countries from the south. At the same time the movement even further north swelled. The Swedish government announced an upsurge in its desire to take the flow and soon every day thousands of people were heading into Denmark, sometimes to stay rather than moving on to Sweden. During 2015 more than 21,000 people applied for asylum in Denmark (three times the figure of two years before), but far more surged on up into Sweden. Of course there were quibbles, and of course there were those who protested against this policy outright. But at this crucial moment a movement that risked becoming depersonalised by the sheer numbers suddenly took on a human face.

Already, at the end of August as some domestic opposition to Merkel's policy had begun to be voiced, an abandoned truck with 71 dead migrants inside was found on an Austrian road just as the German Chancellor was arriving in Vienna for a meeting. The debate was already noisy with echoes. And then, two days after Merkel's key announcement, a family of Syrian Kurds set out in a plastic boat from Bodrum in Turkey, hoping to reach the Greek island of Kos. Their boat sank and among those who drowned was a three-year-old boy called Aylan Kurdi. His body soon washed up, face down, on a beach in Turkey where a photographer captured the image. This image went around the world. An issue that was already a contest between head and heart, practicality and emotion, saw the heart override the rest of the system at the crucial juncture. The photograph dampened respectable opposition to Merkel's open-door policy in Europe. Opponents had to explain how they could be immune to the image of dead Aylan. Newspapers that ordinarily called for tight immigration suddenly changed their tune to fit with their cover image. Some papers and politicians questioned whether this wasn't the time to start bombing Syria, in order to alleviate such suffering. Meanwhile actors and other celebrities took to Twitter with the hashtag 'Refugees Welcome' and insisted that Europe must open its doors. To be opposed to this was suddenly to be indifferent to dead children. Unsurprisingly, even the British Prime Minister – who had struggled to resist any EU-enforced migrant quotas to date – buckled and agreed to start by allowing in a further 20,000 Syrian refugees (albeit over the course of five years). Dams broke elsewhere in Europe too, with media cameramen running alongside migrants as they poured through fields, down roads and across borders. For her part, Angela Merkel announced that there was 'no limit' on the number of migrants Germany would accept, announcing, 'As a strong, economically healthy country we have the strength to do what is necessary.' Over the next 48 hours *The New York Times* reported a surge of migrant movement from Nigeria, among other countries, as people saw that a window of opportunity had opened for citizenship in Europe.

It is easier to scorn such decisions than it is to make them, and easier to make them than perhaps it should be. In each country the continent's politicians were stuck in a moment akin to that of any person standing on a shoreline seeing a boat coming in. If the people in front of you are struggling to get ashore, the instinct of most observers – certainly most modern Europeans – would be to help those in difficulty to safety. Very few would push them back into the sea. Only months after saying that 'politics was hard' and trying to hold the line before the 14-year-old Lebanese girl, Angela Merkel had decided to show softness. Although her decision was taken on behalf of the continent rather than merely herself, the impulse she demonstrated was not an untypical one. The wish to welcome all comers ashore may not have been a natural compulsion throughout history, but it had become a natural one to Europeans now, and its opposite seemed unimaginable.

The inhabitants of Lesbos, like those of other islands, are a perfect example of this. Their main port – Mytilene – is one of the nearest ports to Turkey. At Mytilene too the migrant boats can see Europe in front of them when they set out. Illuminated and towering over the central point of the harbour is the dome of Saint Therapon, named after the bishop of Cyprus, massacred by the Arab Muslims as he said Mass. Inside is the sarcophagus of Bishop Ignatios, a leading opponent of the Ottoman occupation in the nineteenth century. Along the port front are shops, bars and hotels including the Sappho Hotel, a name replicated everywhere on the island from which the ancient poetess came. With a population of 87,000, this is in size and population one of the bigger Greek islands. In the heat of the day, the smell of oil, fish and brackish water makes the vast harbour less appetising than it at first looks. But by evening, with a breeze, the port-front bars and cafes come alive and buzz as the sound systems pump out pop songs.

As in Lampedusa, the contrasts can be jarring. On the Italian island an aid-worker had described the occasional moments in the summer months when a boatload of migrants would be brought in from the sea, corpses among the living, while the music of the better-off Italians who still come to the island in the summer to party could be heard along the cliff edges and beaches. In Mytilene migrants who have often escaped from or walked through their own version of hell, take their first footsteps into their new life in a scene that shows the best of Greece's good life.

In 2015 there was a period during which people were arriving in Mytilene (a town of 30,000) at the rate of 8,000 a day. Boats pulled up on the side of the long coastal road between the airport and the town. Some migrants walked into town. Others hailed a taxi when they got out of the boat and asked the driver to take them to Moria, the main reception centre behind the town. Local drivers remarked on the fact that the people from the boats all knew in advance that the taxi fare to Moria was 10 Euros.

As in the Italian islands, so in the Greek islands, the local authorities felt left alone. The mayor of Lesbos instigated his island's reaction. The mayor of nearby Samos did the same. Did they cooperate? No, the mayor's office says: everyone went their own way. But even on each individual island the organisation is complicated. When the flow became a flood the former army camp of Moria was converted into a temporary centre, that is, under the control of the relevant ministry in Athens. Whereas the other camp on Lesbos – Kara Tepe – is under the control of the local municipality. Whenever you ask why, people sigh. In any case, for a time the effort to get everybody processed and quickly given papers for their onward journey worked well. Around two days after arrival the migrants would be back down at the port and off on another boat, this time a ferry, to Athens or Kavala (just along the coast from Thessaloniki). From there the Greek authorities did not mind losing them. Most – as they knew – would not want to stay in a country where unemployment was bad enough for locals. They would keep travelling, through south-eastern Europe and up towards the countries they thought would receive them: particularly Germany and Sweden. When the process took longer because the numbers overwhelmed the authorities, unrest began. In September

2015, as the inflow resulting from the German Chancellor's invitation grew to its height, there were serious disturbances between some of the migrants on Lesbos and local riot police. After processing delays meant some migrants had been on the island for two weeks, crowds of them down in the port chanted 'Asylum' and also 'We want go Athens'. Some Syrian migrants threw stones and bottles at police. Others tried to stop them.

Although there were temporary solutions, during the winter of 2015 and into 2016 the process began to stall. The numbers kept coming as before, but the initial enthusiasm of the rest of Europe was already beginning to flag. At one point there were 20,000 refugees in Mytilene. Neither Moria nor Kara Tepe is designed to keep even a quarter of that number. But the people of Mytilene did not turn on the arrivals, though they were close to being outnumbered by them. With both migrant centres in overflow, tents sprang up across the centre of the city, on any available green or rubbly place, on roundabouts and sidewalks. When the winter was at its worst, locals opened their homes or cleared out their garages to house migrants trying to escape the worst of the weather.

In the summer of 2016, when deals with foreign powers and warnings from within Europe were meant to have stopped the flow of people to these islands, the boats kept coming. But an emergency deal in March between the EU and Turkey had somewhat eased the pressure and slowed the flow. In return for a payment from the EU to the Turkish government of six billion Euros as well as visa-free travel across Europe for many Turks, the number of migrants coming into Europe had lessened considerably. During August the arrivals to Lesbos were down to a couple of hundred, sometimes a couple of dozen, a day. One night that month when the sea was glassily calm, three boats managed to come across, two to the north of the island and one up to the harbour in Mytilene. A fourth was stopped by the Turkish naval forces, who are said by migrants and aid-workers alike to take a laissez-faire approach to the boats which the EU-Turkey deal should force them to turn back. In reality, when they see them coming they stop some but let others through.

The island's second facility, Kara Tepe, set up by the municipality in 2015, is aimed at housing families, women and children – though not unaccompanied minors, who are placed in houses. Although Kara Tepe has the capacity for 1,500 migrants, during parts of August 2016 it was only half full. Even though the recent coup in Turkey had put the agencies on alert for the possibility of a restart of the previous summer's flows, at this point the island was comparatively calm. At the camp's entrance there are opportunities for providing a service and for making money. Stall-holders had set up food vans and drinks stalls. The only other person trying to get into the camp was a young man from the Congo, who was based up the road at the camp at Moria but had come to visit his sister and her children at Kara Tepe. Outside he drank beer and smoked while we waited in the midday sun. He said that it was not possible for him to remain in the Congo. He had relations with the country's political opposition and so it was no longer safe for him to be there. He said he was university educated, worked in a psychiatric hospital in the Congo, and could not get his phone to work to get through to his sister in Kara Tepe. People are not locked in, but nor can anybody simply wander in.

Inside the camp is all that a poor, makeshift shelter designed for more than a thousand people can be. There are tin huts for families to live in as well as medical huts and other necessities. A children's football pitch has been set up and there is a small tin-covered amphitheatre for occasional musical performances to lift the inmates' spirits. The elderly and disabled – like the ancient Syrian man in a traditional keffiyah, staring out from his tin hut – have special facilities, including toilets, away from the large complex set up for everyone else. The people in this camp are mostly Syrians – perhaps 70 per cent today. The next largest groups are Afghans and Iraqis. The woman from Athens who runs the camp on behalf of the municipality is very proud of it and the innovative attitude she says they foster here. Here the people are not called 'refugees' or 'immigrants', she insists: they are 'visitors'. The camp is progressive in other ways, which is why they are happy to allow journalists with the required permits to enter. The visitors are served three meals a day and unlike in other camps, including Moria, they are not made to queue. Meals are delivered to the doors of their huts. Clothes are provided for them to change into when they need them. A family from Syria sit by their hut, while a young man almost not yet ready to shave, his face still pimply, uses an electric shaver to remove his little stubble, a mirror in the other hand. A little girl of two or three has lost one of her shoes and struggles in the dust to put it on. We help her, she gets back up, runs on and falls straight over again.

For all the advantages of being in the camp at Kara Tepe, the problem for the 'visitors' here in the summer of 2016 is that they are stuck. Since the migrant flow of 2015, the other countries of Europe have shut their borders, meaning there is no opportunity for the flow across Europe of last year to recommence. These visitors cannot even flow up to Athens because the authorities realise that if a bottleneck is created on the mainland they risk creating entirely new problems. And so where once they would have spent no more than 48 hours in this place, and where a fortnight has caused troubles, some of these families have been here for months. Outside the camp, buying chips in sauce, are a girl of 17 and her seven-year-old younger sister. They are from Aleppo and have been here for between four and five months. They now have lessons here and there is an attempt to teach other skills, including music – even violin lessons – at the camp. But they do not know when they will go or where they or the other visitors will go to.

Understandably, the authorities and NGOs who help run and fund the camps are wary about letting 'visitors' speak with journalists. Many are traumatised and as in Lampedusa nobody knows exactly what to do with the migrants or what restrictions – if any – are legal or possible. But along the road and down on the beach is an impromptu collection of tents. On the highway wall opposite someone has graffitied in huge capital letters 'Refugees! Condemn the deal! No person is illegal! Welcome refugees!' Similar messages are scrawled in Spanish. If you were to come off a boat at this point, as some of the migrants do, these are the first words you will see in Europe.

The collection of tents opposite is run by a 'No Borders Group'. A young German called Justus comes over smoking a roll-up cigarette. He is from Dresden, he mentions apologetically. A fortnight ago he and a group of like-minded Germans, French and Swiss people opened a social centre in a decrepit ruin of a building on the other side of the road. It was not intended to be an asylum centre, but a day centre to give the migrants somewhere to come and escape the tedium of the camps. But after only a few days the bank that owned the building, fearing that they were setting up an illegal camp, threw them out. So here they are on the beach opposite, with a few large makeshift tents, trying to keep their movement going. Oda, a German woman in her forties, from Hanover, who is coping badly in the midday sun, explains, 'It is not enough to simply keep going to demonstrations and chanting "No borders". It is also necessary to do something.'

Here is where this group, mainly comprised of Germans, are trying to do their bit to help. It is ramshackle, underfunded and slightly shambolic. A family who walk blithely past all the refugee signs and come each day to this encampment to help themselves to tea turn out to be a local Roma family who already live on Lesbos. Oda shows the photographs of the building they have just had to vacate. On the wall in the main rooms of what had been their social centre they had whitewashed the walls and hung brightly coloured baubles. The centre's rules were painted in blue and red on the walls. These were (bullet-pointed), 'No racism. No violence. No sexism. No homophobia.'

Oda and her colleagues say that what the fifty or so people a day who currently come to the group's tents really want is not the tea, the water, or some of the three to six hundred portions of food a day they hand out to supplement the food people get at the main camps. What the Afghans, Pakistanis, Moroccans, Eritreans – evenly mixed – who come here want, they say, 'is people to respect them'. They had recently met a Christian from Pakistan whose family had all been killed by the Taliban. Asked what he wanted most now, he said 'a smile'.

But the German 'No Borders Group' are not universally welcomed. Aside from their problems with their former landlord and the island authorities, some locals are suspicious of their presence. And not only because they think the presence of the group suggests that the Greeks cannot cope. One local says the group are 'bad people. They are political activists.' But other local people are helpful. Some even give extra aid. A local vegetable dealer gives them free supplies. And at least here, unlike up the road at Moria, people do not have to stand in 200-metre-long queues for food. Complaints of food shortages, food poisoning and other squalid conditions at the Moria camp make it clear why this facility is one that the authorities refuse to allow anyone to visit. Three 16-year-old Afghans explain that they are not even allowed to take photos in the Moria facility where there are currently 3,000 people. The nearest a non-migrant can get to is the gate, but even from the outside it is clear that this is a different proposition to Kara Tepe.

The former army camp of Moria now has three or four different sections of barbed wire on each side. Its present occupants are from all over the Middle East, Africa and Asia. Whereas most are from Syria, Iraq, Africa and Afghanistan, there are also migrants from Bangladesh, Myanmar and Nepal. A young Eritrean explains his route to Sudan from where he took a plane to Iraq, travelled to Turkey, and from there to the beach on Lesbos on which we end up sitting. The Afghans, by contrast, came through Iran and sometimes via Pakistan before getting to Turkey. All say that these days they do not meet the smugglers they pay to traffic them here. Everything is done by phone, with instructions given to them at steps along the way. A nine-year-old Afghan boy with his father explains his route. He has now been in Europe for two months. The father signals that he would like to speak in private.

We find a ruined building on the seafront in which he tells their story. They came in on a boat that went down twice during what should have been the hour's journey from Turkey. On the second sinking they were picked up by the Greek coastguard. He is thirty-one years old. He has come with his wife, his two sons and two daughters.

The girls are five and one and a half. Handsome, strongly built and with a single quiff of white in the centre of his head of black hair, he is wearing sports clothes he has clearly been given since his arrival. In Afghanistan he had a job in the Ministry of Education with responsibility for schools in the Herat region. As the Taliban regained their strength he received a phone call from them telling him to leave his job. He didn't and so they kidnapped him and jailed him for three days. While he was there they broke both his hands. Each has large protruding lumps where bone sticks out at the wrists. He says he managed to escape from the jail but, stumbling in the Afghan mountains he injured himself further, breaking his head open on the rocks when he fell.

In two months at home he was unable to work. But after that he did go back to work. At which point the Taliban kidnapped him again. This time they kept him for twenty-one days. They tortured him again (the scars are on his side as well as his arms). They also raped him, or as the Afghan from the camp who acts as our translator puts it, 'attacked him from the backside'. 'You know what he means?' he asks helpfully, making miming signals as the man looks away. Each night the Taliban raped him. While they did so they told him 'That I no longer had a god. That they were my god and that this meant I must do anything they asked of me.' At this point he says that he agreed to help them. They told him that they wanted him to use his position to put one of their own men into the education authority. They had a plan to put something into the water system at the schools with 600 to 700 children between the villages of Adraskan and Gozareh. If the children could all be poisoned at school then parents would stop sending their children to school, reasoned the Taliban. Because he agreed to help them this second time they allowed him to go home.

But once home he fled, taking his family with him, and without allowing the Taliban to get their man into the position he wanted. When he arrived in Turkey, he says he phoned back home to an official to tell him of the Taliban plan, to try to stop it from happening. 'I lost my everything,' he says. 'But I am happy to have saved the children's lives.' He cannot go back home he says, and 'If the Greek government deport me I will kill myself.' What does it mean to be in Europe, I ask him? 'I am happy to be here because I can be alive here. Because I am safe now,' he says. Then he turns away. He tries to hide the tears that fall down his face. We sit in silence. Later he shows me some more scars from the Taliban's torture, on his legs. We shake hands and out on the road we bump into his family. He introduces me to his wife and daughters, the older of whom is wearing a bright pink children's cap that one of the agencies has obviously given her, and they walk back up to the camp together as a family.

Among the other migrants at the camp in Moria are a pair of brothers from the Ghazni region of south-eastern Afghanistan. They say they are 20 and 18, and are from the Hazara peoples, a minority Shia group who are a particular target of Isis in Afghanistan, the group having carried out mass beheadings of this 'heretical' sect. Isis is only the latest worst thing to have happened to their homeland. Before them the Taliban burned down their school and then attempted to recruit the brothers. They say that Isis also tried to recruit them when they moved into the area. Offered the chance by Isis to either 'join our group or we'll kill all your family members', the boys left their village and fled to Kabul. Both their father and mother are ill so they, as the biggest boys, had become responsible for supporting their household.

While we're sitting on the stony ground of Greece, all the Afghan boys and men who have come to join us play in the dust with their hands. An older man of 62, from the same province as the brothers, has heart trouble but is hoping to join a daughter in Austria. He has come through Iran where there are more Hazara people. If Afghanistan was not safe, could he not have stayed in Iran? 'I know no one in Iran,' he says, his eyes filling with tears. 'What would I do in Iran'? As we speak he gathers up little mounds of dust and fills in holes in the ground. But I notice that the younger of the two brothers, with a dark fringe almost covering his deep dark eyes, picks up small pebbles and repeatedly strikes the ground with them while we talk.

The Hazara people, they explain, are persecuted wherever they go. Even life in Pakistan – where many other Hazara live – is made hard. Their money gets taken and they are kidnapped with demands of up to one million US dollars ransom for their return. The brothers entered Pakistan illegally, then went illegally to Iran, then illegally to Turkey. The older brother explains that his younger brother suffers particularly from psychological problems. It is not a surprise. When the younger one speaks it tends to come out in bursts of exasperation. 'Every country has good or bad people,' he says at one point. 'Why are Europeans seeing us all as dogs and criminals? They are not good with us. Why?' They complain that while they accept the country of Greece they are not accepted by it. People look at them and are unfriendly on buses. In Moria, he complains, the camp police make noises to them with the food as though they were coaxing animals. Many people have complaints about the camp in Moria, but he says there are snakes that have made holes in the tent walls and have already killed two inmates – a fact he says the authorities are covering up.

At one stage, in passing, the older brother mentions that his younger brother was raped by the Taliban back in Afghanistan. The younger one speaks for himself when asked what he has seen along the way. 'We are Afghans,' he says. 'We have seen everything. The cutting of heads. The dead bodies. Everything.' He wants to commit suicide, and like all the others he says he will do so if sent back. Asked what they would like to do if they could stay, the older brother says he had started a pharmacy course at university before they fled Afghanistan. He would like to continue that. The younger says that all he wants 'is to find a life in these bad situations'.

All the Afghans are angry with the Syrians. It comes down to a general feeling that the Syrians are being favoured. It is true that Chancellor Merkel's 2015 invitation specifically suspended any need to prove asylum if the migrants were Syrian. 'Why?' the Afghans want to know. 'In Syria there has been war for five years. In Afghanistan we have had war for fifteen years.' What about the allegation that people are coming here because they want a better life? One of the Afghans, a young man who speaks good English, responds, 'Every day there is a bomb blast in Afghanistan. Yet they think we are coming here for happiness, for enjoyment. We do not have economic problems in Afghanistan,' he insists. 'In Afghanistan we can find money. It is about our security problem.'

Hearing such things, at such times, from people who have been in such places, the instinct that Chancellor Merkel and her ministers displayed in 2015 can seem eminently justified. She and her colleagues landed on a portion of the answer by recognising that our continent is probably doing the only thing that a civilised people can do in rescuing such people, welcoming them and trying to give them safety. But this generous instinct may well prove – both for the people who have crossed the water and for the continent trying to welcome them in – to be the easiest part of the journey.

6

Multiculturalism

It was in Berlin, on 31 August 2015, that the German Chancellor indicated her new intentions and provided her motivational statement: 'Wir schaffen das' ('We can do this'). Yet even these few words raised questions. What was the 'this' that she wanted to be done? What were its aims and intentions? Was there an endpoint or a point of completion to the process? What would success in this endeavour look like? These would be large enough questions on their own. But her three short words begged another equally considerable question. Who was this 'we'? What was the entity being urged to accomplish this hard-to-define thing? In making her statement Angela Merkel had taken for granted the existence of a 'we'. But in the years preceding her speech Europe had been scrutinising itself deeply and constantly to find an answer to this question. And this constant reversion to the psychiatrist's couch was not an abstract question, but one with an urgent aspect, all the time fuelled by an awareness – as the Dutch author Paul Scheffer had put it eight years previously – that 'without a "we" it's not going to work'.[1]

Chancellor Merkel herself was more than aware of this. Five years before her grand gesture she had given another speech in which she had addressed one of the fastest-growing concerns of her nation. In the process she led a stampede of European leaders into saying what had gone wrong with the reigning European policy regarding immigration and integration. In October 2010 Merkel gave a major 'state of the nation' speech in Potsdam. She did so in the middle of a significant public debate already going on in her country. Weeks earlier Thilo Sarrazin, a former Senator and member of the executive board of the Bundesbank, had published a book titled *Deutschland schafft sich ab* (*Germany Is Abolishing Itself*), which was like an explosion in such a consensus-driven society. In his book Sarrazin had explained how low birth rates among Germans and an overly high level of immigration – Muslim immigration in particular – was fundamentally transforming the nature of German society. What perhaps caused most controversy was his argument that a higher birth rate among less well-educated people and a lower birth rate among more highly educated people was putting at risk Germany's post-war success and prosperity.

The evidence that migrants in Germany were failing to integrate, just as Sarrazin had argued, was all around them, but the political and media class fell on Sarrazin for his heresy in making these arguments. In the resulting fallout Sarrazin himself was forced to resign from his position at the Bundesbank. And despite himself coming from the political left in Germany, his own party (the Social Democratic Party) as well as Angela Merkel's CDU distanced themselves from him. Various Muslim organisations in Germany attempted to take him to court and most damagingly (if also baselessly) he was accused of anti-Semitism. Nevertheless the book hit a public mood. A poll taken around the same time found that 47 per cent of Germans agreed with the statement that Islam doesn't belong in Germany. Although German politicians had put a firm *cordon sanitaire* around the debate on immigration, integration and Islam, the two million copies sold of Sarrazin's book, among other things, suggested that this was not restraining wider society from thinking things that their political representatives did not want them to.

With typical political skill Merkel chose to speak to this issue, trying to keep people with concerns within the camp of her party and also to correct where she believed Sarrazin and those who supported his views had gone wrong. In her speech in Potsdam she started by referring to the country's *Gastarbeiter* programme and the mass movement of Turks and others to live and work in Germany from the early 1960s onwards. She conceded that the country had – like the post-war labour-market immigration in Britain and other European countries – 'kidded ourselves for a while'. She continued, 'We said "They won't stay, sometime they will be gone", but this isn't reality.' It failed to anticipate any of the consequences flowing from the policy. She went on to criticise more current mistakes in the German immigration and integration debate.

The speech was reported around the world. What made it so newsworthy was that it included the most damning summary by any mainstream politician to date of a European country's integration failures. Some of it had previously been said on the political margins, but had never been so decidedly voiced in the mainstream. Discussing what had gone wrong between Germany and its immigrants, the Chancellor said, 'Of course, the approach to build a multicultural society and to live side-by-side and to enjoy each other has failed, utterly failed.' That was why, she insisted, 'integration is so important'. Those who wanted to participate in German society must follow the laws and constitution of Germany, she said, and must also learn to speak the German language.[2]

Press reports inside Germany speculated that the Chancellor was positioning herself ahead of elections scheduled for the following spring. An opinion poll published the same month had shown a sharp increase in the percentage of the German public who were becoming concerned about levels of immigration, revealing that 30 per cent feared their country was being 'overrun by foreigners' who had come to Germany because of the social-security benefits the country provided them with.[3] The political ingenuity of Merkel's speech is that these people would, like almost everyone else, hear what they wanted from a speech that was also careful to give credit to immigrants and insist on how welcome they still were in Germany. Nevertheless, the uttering of the idea – and the use of that particular word twice, that multiculturalism had 'failed, utterly failed' – struck a chord. From the moment that her audience in Potsdam gave her a standing ovation, Merkel found herself praised for having the courage to speak out on such a difficult issue. Across Europe she was compared favourably with other political leaders, with the newspapers of other nations suggesting that only the German Chancellor had the strength and courage to tell such a difficult truth.

So it was not surprising that other political leaders soon wanted a bit of this, and dived into waters that Merkel had shown to be surprisingly warm. The following February Britain's Prime Minister, David Cameron, used a speech at the Munich Security Conference to declare that, 'Under the doctrine of state multiculturalism, we have encouraged different cultures to live separate lives, apart from each other and apart from the mainstream. We've failed to provide a vision of society to which they feel they want to belong. We've even tolerated these segregated communities behaving in ways that run completely counter to our values.'⁴ A few days later, in a televised debate, the French President, Nicolas Sarkozy, also pronounced multiculturalism to be a 'failure' and said, 'The truth is that in all our democracies we have been too preoccupied with the identity of those who arrived and not enough with the identity of the country that welcomed them.'⁵ These leaders were soon joined by others, including the former Australian Prime Minister John Howard and the former Spanish Prime Minister José María Aznar.

Within the space of a few months the apparently unsayable had been said by almost everybody. In each country, on each occasion, a great debate began. Was David Cameron right to twin the issue of national security and national cohesion? Was Merkel simply trying to respond to pressures and cleverly keeping a bloc of the centre-right within her political fold? Whatever the reasons, in each country the 'multiculturalism has failed' debate seemed to mark some kind of watershed moment.

Yet despite the prolific nature of these debates, it was unclear even at the time what these statements meant. The word 'multiculturalism' (let alone *multikulti* in German) already sounded notoriously different to different people. For many years, and still today for many people, the term seemed to mean 'pluralism' or simply the reality of living in an ethnically diverse society. To say you were in favour of multiculturalism might mean that you didn't mind people of different backgrounds in your country. Or it might mean that you believed that the future for all societies was to become a great melting pot in which every possible culture contributed: a sort of miniature United Nations in each country. On the other hand, saying that 'multiculturalism had failed' may have sounded to some voters as a concession that post-war immigration as a whole had been a bad idea and that immigrants should not have come. It may even have sounded like a call to stop mass immigration and even reverse such policies. In each country these different understandings of the same phrase were undoubtedly politically beneficial, giving politicians the opportunity to embrace voters they might otherwise have had to avoid courting. It was no coincidence that each of the political leaders who took this plunge was from the political right and trying to keep together a fractious political movement that risked going on the move.

But the confusion over what these speeches meant also had an old cause, because 'multiculturalism' had always been a hard-to-define term. To the extent that it was possible to draw any clear inferences from their speeches it would seem that Merkel, Cameron and Sarkozy were addressing a specific variety of state-sponsored multiculturalism. Theirs was certainly not a criticism of a racially diverse society or a society that welcomed immigration. On the contrary, outside the headline-grabbing parts of their speeches, all professed their support for large-scale immigration. What they were claiming to criticise was 'multiculturalism' as a state-sponsored policy: the idea of the state encouraging people to live parallel lives in the same country and particularly in living under customs and laws that stood in opposition to those of the country they were living in. These European leaders appeared to be calling for a post-multicultural society in which the same rule of law and certain societal norms applied to everybody.[6] Late in the day to argue such things, but a significant step perhaps.

Many critics on the political left objected to the whole discussion, claiming that these were straw-man arguments and insisting either that such problems did not exist or that they did exist but were not problems. But by 2010 growing public concern about precisely such parallel societies was growing across Europe. The sharpest cause of this growth was the increasing tally of terrorist attacks and thwarted terrorist attacks involving people born and brought up in Europe. But while these attacks gave the concerns their edge, concern over the less violent or non-violent expressions of difference were also growing – and not always because they were being expressed by minorities.

In 2006 the Dutch Justice Minister, Piet Hein Donner, caused significant anger in the Netherlands when he suggested in an interview that if Muslims wished to change the law of the land to Sharia by democratic means (that is when Muslims were large enough in number), then they could do so. In 2004 Donner had briefly proposed the resurrection of the country's blasphemy laws to address the concerns of some Muslims. Then in 2008 there was at least equal public outrage in Britain when the Archbishop of Canterbury, Rowan Williams, gave a lecture at the Royal Courts of Justice that addressed parallel legal jurisdictions growing inside the country. During his lecture the archbishop had suggested that the adoption of elements of Sharia law in the UK 'seems unavoidable'. In the wake of the initial public anger the archbishop had insisted he had been misunderstood. But in a BBC radio interview the following day, intended to clarify his remarks, he went even further, stating that the idea 'there's one law for everybody and that's all there is to be said' was 'a bit of a danger'.[7]

Coming on top of years of growing concern about immigration and security it suddenly seemed as though some of the absolute bases of Western civilisation were being offered up for negotiation. It also sometimes seemed as though the past was up for grabs as well. Only a fortnight before Merkel's Potsdam speech the President of Germany, Christian Wulff, gave his speech on the 'Day of German Unity'. Among his comments, also aimed at answering the Sarrazin question over the place of Islam in Germany, Wulff implied that Islam was as much a part of the country's history as Christianity and Judaism had been. There was an outcry in Germany, including from within his own party. But the President was not alone in appearing willing to alter the past in order to adapt to present realities.

In each case the backlash against comments such as these came because of a wider sentiment that in the multicultural era Europe was being expected to give up too much of itself – including its history – while those who had arrived were being expected to give up next to nothing of their traditions. If that was indeed one direction in which Europe might have been heading, Cameron, Merkel, Sarkozy and other politicians of the right were attempting to outline another route. None of them was denying that the process of adaptation might be a two-way street, but they were being careful to stress what was expected of the immigrants, in particular to be able to speak the language of the country they were in and to live by its laws.

The virulence with which such basic demands were debated was a reminder that absolutely none of this had been planned for in the post-war years. It was just the latest part of a 'make it up as we go along' process. And it meant that even the terms being used were constantly changing. As the historian and critic of multiculturalism, Rumy Hasan, said in a book published at this time, the distinct phases of Britain's post-war immigration was one demonstration of this fact. During the first phase (from the 1940s to the 1970s) non-white settlers from the Commonwealth were known as 'coloured immigrants' and recognised as different from the rest of society. Then during the 1970s and 1980s, partly in an effort to tackle discrimination, these people became 'Black British' and began to be viewed as normal and equal citizens. Soon afterwards the country became characterised as a 'multicultural' society in the sense that it contained people from different cultures. As Hasan says, a 'multiracial' or 'multi-ethnic' society would have been a better description, but the discrediting of the idea of 'race' by that time meant that 'multiculturalism' seemed to be the best term on offer. However, if its intentions were to unite people under one national umbrella, the new definition ended up having the opposite effect. Indeed, rather than leading to a unified identity it led to a fracturing of identities, where instead of making society colour- or identity-blind, it suddenly made identity into everything.

A version of 'pork barrel' politics entered society. Organisations and interest groups were thrown up that claimed to represent and speak for all manner of identity groups. The ambitious, generally self-appointed figures who claimed these roles became the middlemen between the authorities and a particular community. They were not the only ones to benefit from this approach. Local and national politicians were also able to gain from a process that made their lives so much easier, giving as it did the impression that it was possible to pick up a phone and get a particular community. Of course, to be on the side of a particular community created the potential for getting that allegedly monolithic community's votes, and in some cases the communities delivered.

Inevitably, local councils and others funnelled money to particular ethnic and religious groups. And although some of this was done to win votes, some of it was also done for nobler reasons, not least a genuine desire to tackle any existing discrimination. Yet even 'anti-racist' groups tended to be political beyond the realms they had at first set out to address. Those groups that aspired to tackle actual discrimination in time sought increasing influence, access and funding. And they were aware that they could only get this if the problem was not solved. In time this had the effect of making discrimination appear worse – and needing to be fought harder – at the very points at which things were getting better. Complaints against society presented an opportunity to grow. Satisfaction became a dying business.

At the same time the only culture that couldn't be celebrated was the culture that had allowed all these other cultures to be celebrated in the first place. In order to become multicultural, countries found that they had to do themselves down, particularly focusing on their negatives. Thus the states that had been so open and liberal that they had allowed and encouraged large-scale migration were portrayed as countries which were uniquely racist. And while any and all other cultures in the world could be celebrated within Europe, to celebrate even the good things about Europe within Europe became suspect.

The multicultural era was one of European self-abnegation where the host society appeared to stand back from itself and hoped that it would not be noticed other than as some form of benign convener. It was for this reason, among others, that the celebrated American political philosopher, Samuel Huntington, wrote in his last book, 'Multiculturalism is in its essence anti-European civilisation. It is basically an anti-Western ideology'.[8]

In every European country the period in which nothing could be said about this broke down at different speeds over a similar period. In the United Kingdom the work of 'Race Relations' quangos helped hold a lid on it until the summer of 2001. At that point, partly as a result of riots in the north of England involving young Muslim men, and partly because of events in New York and Washington, the existence of parallel communities began to be discussed more widely and the concept of 'multiculturalism' began to come in for criticism. In Holland the dams broke a little earlier. In France they stayed tight until the *banlieue* riots of 2005. Germany and Sweden took a while longer. But in the 2000s dissidents from the multicultural consensus began to break out everywhere.

Some of those who broke that consensus were politicians of the left. Their apostasy had a particular impact, because while politicians and commentators of the right were almost expected to have a problem with multiculturalism and could always be suspected of harbouring nativist tendencies, those from the left were generally seen to have less easily assailable motives and could even be believed. Nevertheless, the breakages that were most liberating (not least because they gave cover for other people to speak) came from European citizens from ethnic backgrounds. In Britain the slow apostasy from the race-relations industry of one of its former leaders, Trevor Phillips, opened up territory that others had not dared to walk in. His realisation that the race-relations industry was part of the problem, and that partly as a result of talking up difference the country was 'sleepwalking to segregation', was an insight others soon began to share across the continent. Among other dissidents from multiculturalism to emerge during the same decade, some entered politics whereas others remained outside as opinion formers. But the emergence during the 2000s of, among others, Ahmed Aboutaleb and Ayaan Hirsi Ali in Holland, Nyamko Sabuni in Sweden, Naser Khader in Denmark and Magdi Allam in Italy, had a palpably liberating effect. All spoke from within their communities to countries that needed people of such backgrounds to break the ice. They managed to do so with varying degrees of success.

In every country the early criticisms alighted around the same issues. The most extreme and unacceptable practices of some communities became the first way in to split open the prevailing orthodoxies. In each country the issues of 'honour' killings and female genital mutilation received massive attention. This was partly because many people were genuinely shocked that such things were going on and had feared saying so if they had known about it before. Partly it was due to the fact that these issues were the 'softest' or easiest concerns to express about the multicultural era. If not entirely unopposed, these issues were at least capable of uniting opinion from the widest possible political spectrum: from a left-wing feminist to a right-wing nationalist. Almost everybody could agree that murdering young women was wrong. And most people could unite in expressing their horror at the thought of a young girl's genitals being mutilated in twenty-first-century Europe.

Over the course of the 2000s the criticisms of such extreme examples of multiculturalism in European society grew. Everywhere the questions Europeans were pondering coalesced around the limits of tolerance. Should liberal societies tolerate the intolerant? Or was there a moment when even the most tolerant society should say 'enough'? Had our societies been too liberal and in the process allowed illiberalism or anti-liberalism to thrive? Around this time, as Rumy Hasan pointed out, the era of multiculturalism quietly transformed into the era of 'multifaithism'. Ethnic identity, which had previously been the focus of the multiculturalism debate, began to recede and faith identity, which to many people seemed to have come from nowhere, instead became the crucial issue. What had been a question of blacks, Caribbeans or North Africans now became a question of Muslims and Islam.

As with each of the previous periods of post-war change, the process of seeing through this period did not occur overnight. It had taken European governments decades to recognise that the *Gastarbeiter* era had not gone as planned. In the same way it took time for European governments to realise that if migrants were staying in their adopted country then they needed laws to protect them from discrimination. The period of multiculturalism also took a couple of decades to burn itself out. But like those previous episodes, even as its death was recognised and in this case announced, it was unclear what all this meant and what might replace it.

A CORE CULTURE?

One of the few people who had already done the thinking on this was Bassam Tibi. The academic who had himself migrated to Germany from Syria in 1962 spent years urging the integration of minority communities into Germany. In an initially discouraging atmosphere he also evolved a specific concept of how to go about this. European countries, he suggested, should move from a policy of multiculturalism towards one that advocated for a *leitkultur* or 'core culture'. This notion – first put forward by him in the 1990s – argued for a form of multi-ethnic society that embraced people of different backgrounds but united them around a set of common themes.[9] Like jazz it could work if everyone knew the theme that they were riffing around. But it could not possibly work if the theme was unknown, forgotten or lost. In such a situation a society would not only fail to hang together but would represent a cacophony. It was one of the first attempts to present a solution to the European multicultural problem, in particular the question of how to unite people of such disparate backgrounds as now existed in Europe. The most straightforward answer was that they should be united not necessarily by a dedication to precisely the same heritage but at least a unified belief in the core concepts of the modern liberal state such as the rule of law, the separation of Church and State and human rights. Yet even as a few figures like Tibi were thinking through this era, most of the rest of society was having to just live its way through it. If there was a painful slowness about finding any way through this, it was at least in part because of a set of ongoing and painful cognitive dissonances.

Once Europe had realised that the immigrants were going to stay, it held two wholly contradictory ideas that were nevertheless able to cohabit for several decades. The first was the idea that Europeans began to tell themselves from the 1970s and 1980s onwards. This was the notion that European countries could be a new type of multi-racial, multicultural society into which anyone from anywhere in the world could come and settle if they so wished. This never received public support, but it had some elite support and most importantly was propelled by the inability of any government to turn around the process of mass migration once it had started. During the first waves of migration (and certainly when it was expected that many immigrants at least would still go back home at some point) few people minded if the newcomers failed to assimilate. In fact, they rarely wanted them to.

To varying degrees in each country, the new arrivals were put into towns and suburbs on their own, generally in places where they would work. Even when the work dried up, people coming in from the same communities still tended to move to the areas where other people of their background lived. If they were not always encouraged to do so, certainly there was little effort to discourage them from doing so. Governments were subsequently blamed for the segregation, but many of the immigrants self-segregated through a perfectly understandable wish to retain their culture and customs in a society that had no connection to them.

When people realised that the newcomers were not going anywhere, there was also some native resistance to their presence, and any suggestion that the migrants should change their ways was inevitably tainted by association. If the immigrants were going to stay then they should be made to feel at home. To do so it was necessary to do a whole range of things. But it was easier to do the abstract things than the practical ones. Among the abstract things was a clear effort to adapt or change the story of the host nation. Sometimes this was simply a process of rewriting history or changing its emphases. On other occasions it seemed to involve an active denigration of it.

One such effort, as practised by President Wulff, involved talking up any and every aspect of non-European culture in order to raise it to a level at least of parity with Europe. So, for instance, the more Islamic terrorist attacks occurred the more the influence of the Islamic neo-Platonists was raised and the more the significance of Islamic science was stressed. In the decade after those attacks the rule of the Muslim Caliphate of Cordoba in Andalusia, southern Spain, between the eighth and eleventh centuries moved from historical obscurity to being the great exemplar of tolerance and multicultural coexistence. This itself required a careful new version of history, but the past was being conjured up to provide some hope in the present.

Such aspects of Islamic culture soon had to sustain an almost unbearable burden. An exhibition called '1001 Islamic Inventions' toured London's Science Museum among others, insisting that almost everything in Western civilisation had in fact originated in the Islamic world. Ahistorical though such claims were, they developed the aura of faith. People needed them to be true and ceased challenging all such claims. It became a matter not merely of politeness, but of necessity to stress and indeed over-stress how much was owed by European culture to the cultures of the most troubled communities. When in 2008 a French medievalist academic, Sylvain Gouguenheim, published an essay arguing that the texts from Ancient Greece often said to have been saved by Arab Muslims with no knowledge of Greek had in fact been preserved by Syriac Christians, the debate became a heated political issue. Public petitions and letters denounced Gouguenheim for his 'Islamophobia' in coming to this finding. Few other academics even spoke out in support of his right to say what the evidence he provided showed. Cowardice aside, this was just one demonstration of an urgent need – as with the argument 'we've always been a nation of immigrants' that took hold at the same time – to change Europe's fairly monocultural past to fit in with its very multicultural present.

At the same time there were people who took these methods to their extremes. For a further way of trying to arrange a point of equal standing between the incoming cultures and the host culture was to talk down the host culture. One notorious as well as high-profile example of this came from the Swedish Minister of Integration, Mona Sahlin, while speaking at a Kurdish mosque in 2004. The Social Democratic minister (who wore a veil for the occasion) told her audience that many Swedes were jealous of them, because the Kurds had a rich and unifying culture and history, whereas the Swedes only had silly things like the festival of Midsummer's Night.[10] Another way of achieving the same effect was to insist that there was in essence no such thing as European culture. In 2005 a journalist asked the Swedish government's Parliamentary Secretary and lead integration official, Lise Bergh, whether or not Swedish culture was worth preserving. The reply she gave was, 'Well, what is Swedish culture? And with that I guess I've answered the question.'[11]

It is hardly possible to blame immigrants alone for the resulting confusions of this era. It was the European societies who let them in who had no idea what attitude to take towards them once they were here. That it took six decades of immigration for the political leaders of France, Germany and Britain (among others) to state that immigrants should speak the language of the country they were in demonstrated the problem. Only a few years earlier such a demand would have been – and was – attacked as 'racist'. That it took until 2010 for a German Chancellor to insist that the law of the land and the Constitution of Germany must be followed by migrants pointed to a failure of Germany at least as much as the failure of any immigrants. Again, only a few years earlier, anyone who made such a call would have been subjected to accusations of the basest motives. But in the years before the multicultural era was announced as having ended, and before the political ground began to move, there were so many confusions.

The question of whether immigrants were expected to assimilate or be encouraged to retain their own culture was just one confusion. If, as by 2011 most mainstream politicians agreed, something between the two was expected then what were the bits of the incomer's culture that should be dropped and what were the bits of the native culture that should be adapted? Presumably one reason for the lack of public discussion on this was an awareness of how painful it would be to most Europeans. Which parts of their own culture would they volunteer to give up? What reward would they get in return, and when would they experience the effects of that reward? Of course, such an idea was never passed by the public because the European publics almost certainly would never have given their approval. Yet even worse presumptions lay beneath.

If the host country was not going to give something up then surely the incomers must? But what were those things, and who ever spelt them out? And what were the punishments for failing to abide by them. For example, what would happen to migrants who once they were in Europe refused to learn the native language? If there were no punishment or disincentive then any such suggestion was no more than words. All the time it was also unclear how many immigrants simply wanted to enjoy their rights in Europe and how many wanted to become Europeans. What was the difference between the two and what were the incentives to be one rather than the other? Did Europeans ever really want the incomers to become like them?

All the while the official line remained that once a passport or visa was issued, then the country or continent's latest arrival became as European as anyone else. And all the while that governments discussed the possible measures needed to encourage millions of people already in Europe to become Europeans, the minds of the European publics mulled over another idea – one ordinarily pushed to the very recesses of the public debate, but always capable of breaking out.

This was the fear that all of this was bogus and that if not all, then at least much of the existing plan was going to fail. It was a concern based on the thought that if integration were to happen then it would take a very long time – perhaps centuries – and that in any case it had certainly not happened yet in Europe. Here the everyday experience of Europeans is more important than any survey and the experience of their eyes is more important than official statistics from any government.

'THE GREAT REPLACEMENT'

Any trip to thousands of locations across Europe can spark the fear of what the French writer and philosopher Renaud Camus has characterised as 'Le Grand Remplacement'. Take the suburb of Saint-Denis on the northern outskirts of Paris. This is one of the central locations of French history and culture, named after the great Basilica Cathedral at its centre in which lie the relics of the third-century Bishop of Paris who is now the city's patron saint. The present building, dating from the twelfth century, is also famous for another reason. From the sixth century onwards it was the necropolis of the French royal family. Their memorials, featuring elaborate likenesses in stone, include those of the Capetian dynasty, the Bourbons, the Medicis and the Merovingians. At the time of the French Revolution these tombs were desecrated, but today in the crypt lie the stark, marble tombs of the King and Queen that revolution overthrew: Louis XVI and Marie-Antoinette.

Not least among the earlier tombs in Saint-Denis is that of Charles Martel, the Frankish leader who a century after the death of Mohammed, when the Umayyad Caliphate was pushing relentlessly into Europe, forced the Muslim armies back. Martel's victory at the Battle of Tours in 732 is recognised for having prevented the spread of Islam throughout Europe. Had his Frankish armies not succeeded no other power in Europe could have stopped the Muslim armies from conquering the continent. When those armies had crossed into Europe in 711 one of their leaders, Tariq bin Zayad, famously ordered their boats to be burnt, saying 'We have not come here to return. Either we conquer and establish ourselves, or we perish.' Martel ensured that they perished and that other than having gained a foothold in southern Spain, Islam would never progress further into Europe. As Edward Gibbon famously wrote a millennium later, were it not for the victory of the man who became known as 'The Hammer': 'Perhaps the interpretation of the Koran would now be taught in the schools of Oxford, and her pulpits might demonstrate to a circumcised people the sanctity and truth of the revelation of Mohammed.'

As Gibbon went on, 'From such calamities was Christendom delivered by the genius and fortune of one man.'[12]

Today a visitor to the basilica in which Martel's tomb sits may well wonder whether he did indeed succeed – or at least reflect that after he succeeded his descendants failed. To wander the district of Saint-Denis today is to see a district more resembling North Africa than France. The market square outside the basilica is a souk more than a market. Stalls sell different styles of hijab and radical groups hand out literature against the state. Inside, though all the clergy are elderly white men the residual congregation is black African, part of the non-Muslim wave of immigration into the area from Martinique and Guadeloupe.

This area has one of the highest Muslim populations in France. Around 30 per cent of the population of Seine Saint-Denis, also known as the 93rd district, are Muslim. No more than 15 per cent are Catholic. But with most of the immigrants in the area from the Maghreb and sub-Saharan Africa and a growing youth population, it is not surprising that even in the district's private Catholic schools around 70 per cent of the students are Muslim. Meanwhile the area's Jewish population has halved in recent years. According to the Interior Ministry the district has around 10 per cent (230) of the total number of known mosques in France. If you visit them you can see that there are nowhere near enough for the needs of the community. At Friday prayers worshipers spill out onto the streets and a number of the major mosques are struggling to create larger facilities to meet the demand.

Of course, if you mention Saint-Denis to anyone in the centre of Paris they grimace. They know it is there and try never to go to it. With the exception of the Stade de France stadium there is little reason to go anywhere near the area. Having been scarred by waves of de-industrialisation and re-industrialisation, in recent years the government has attempted to do some social engineering, building municipal offices in the area for state employees to work in. But these employees (around 50,000) who have jobs in the area almost never live there. They come in from elsewhere in the morning and leave again in the evening, when their office blocks are carefully locked and the security fences secured. It is France's immigration challenge summed up in one district.

The same phenomena can be witnessed in the suburbs of Marseilles and many other areas of France. But it can also be noticed by any visitor or resident, however unwilling to go to Saint-Denis, on a simple trip on the RER and Métro in the centre of Paris. Travelling on the deep underground RER, stopping infrequently and with long distances between stops, often feels like taking an underground train in an African city. Most of the people are black and they are making their way far out to the suburbs. Those places where the RER stops in Paris's chic centres – Châtelet for example – are known as areas where there can be trouble, especially in the evening when bored youths from the banlieues hang around in town. Always there lingers the memory of 2005 when riots and car-burnings from the banlieues were repeated as far into the centre as the Marais district.

However, if you travel in the Métro train above the RER lines, which serves the shorter stops around the centre of the city, you enter a different world. The travellers on the Métro are mostly white people going to work whereas the RER is mostly full of individuals either going only to low-paid service jobs or appearing to be heading nowhere. Nobody can experience this light airy feeling in the centre of Paris and the deep swell of other people underneath and not sense that there is something amiss. The same feeling will strike anybody travelling through certain towns in the north of England, or neighbourhoods of Rotterdam and Amsterdam. Today it can also be experienced in the suburbs of Stockholm and Malmö. These are places where the immigrants live but they bear no resemblance to the areas inhabited by the locals. Politicians pretend that this problem could be solved by more elegant or innovative town-planning, or by an especially talented housing minister. From 2015 onwards they had to continue trying to pretend this in capital cities some of whose areas had started to resemble refugee camps. Although the police continually tried to move the migrants on to keep their city looking as it is meant to, in Paris in 2016 huge encampments of male North Africans moved around the suburbs. In places like the Stalingrad area of Paris's nineteenth *arrondissement*, hundreds of tents were put up on traffic islands running along the middle of the main roads or on the sides of the pavements. When the police moved them on, they simply sprang up somewhere else. But even before 2015, the theories of so-called experts and politicians as to what could happen or is meant to happen to alleviate this ongoing problem have simply been colliding with the experience of what is actually going on in front of their very eyes.

Everyday awareness of this problem as well as an awareness of it going largely unsaid means that many Europeans chew over another dark concern. Which is that seeing these very large numbers of people and seeing them going about their very different lives, it might be the case that in the future these people will come to dominate – that, for instance, a strong religious culture when placed into a weak and relativistic culture may keep itself to itself at first but finally make itself felt in more definite ways. Again, studies and polls are not much use in pinning down this sense of imminent change. Occasional polls are used to 'prove' that immigrant communities are integrated into existing society. But if the integration that politicians and some pollsters say has happened had in fact occurred, then we would be witnessing quite a different reality. For example, pubs very often close in those areas of the United Kingdom where Pakistani and other Muslim migrants have moved in in large numbers. If the newcomers were becoming 'as British as anybody else' – as government ministers and others insist that they are – then the pubs would remain open and the new arrivals drink lukewarm beer like everybody else who had lived on the street before them. It is the same with churches. If the incomers were indeed to become 'as British as anybody else', then they would fail to turn up to church most Sundays but would be there for weddings, occasionally christenings, and most likely just once a year for Christmas. But that is clearly not what has happened. The churches have closed like the pubs and these buildings have had to be put to other uses.

Although the pretence remains that the mosque-going, teetotal arrivals constitute a seamless transition of native traditions, from such visible aspects of identity it is obvious that the results will be very different. And the causes that lie behind such differences are the harder ones to deal with. The same story and the same silence can be applied to the Turkish and North African suburbs of Amsterdam, the suburbs of Brussels like Molenbeek, areas of Berlin such as Wedding and Neukölln, and any number of other cities across the continent. In each case the price that local people were made to pay, for taking anything but the most positive attitude towards the arrival into their towns and cities of hundreds of thousands of people from another culture, was just too high. Whole careers not only in politics, but in any walk of life, could be ruined by any recognition of the new facts, never mind any proposed alteration to them. And so the only thing left for people to do – whether locals, officials or politicians – was to ignore the problem and lie about it.

In time both politicians and the public began to favour the wilfully optimistic version of events. So a minor or unimportant cultural trait – such as queuing or complaining about the weather in Britain – would be picked up on and run with. The fact that a particular immigrant enjoyed queuing or talking about the weather would be used as a demonstration that this immigrant – and by extension all immigrants – had become as integrated as anybody else. After the suicide bombers of the July 2005 attacks on London Transport were identified as British-born Muslims, it was discovered that one of them had worked in a fish-and-chip shop and had played cricket. Much was made of this, as though the hijacking of this perfectly English individual by a terrible hatred remained the main mystery. The idea that an entire culture had been transmitted to him through the medium of fish and chips was a way to delay facing up to the unpleasant discussions that lay beneath.

As the multicultural era started to break down, a scramble began to identify any country where the experiment had been working. During the aftermath of the 2005 attacks on London the British debated whether the model of French *laicité* did not perhaps point the way towards dealing with problems of integration. Then, after the growing number of home-grown terrorist attacks in France, there was a discussion over whether perhaps the Anglo-Saxon model had some merit. Meanwhile, much of the time Scandinavia was held up as providing a particular solution, until the problems of those countries in turn became clearer. Overall, members of the public could see what the policy-makers could not, which was that despite the differences between these various European countries, each one had failed in turn to assimilate the new arrivals.

There were criticisms of the 'doughnut' planning technique in French towns that seemed to keep the migrants to the edges of the city. But the same problems arose in countries that had tried to avoid such policies. So when a French politician would criticise the 'parallel communities' that had arisen in Britain because of the British model, precisely the same accusation could be made back in his own country.[13] It would seem that although differences in planning laws between the various countries of Europe are a matter of interest, they are not in fact seismic. As for the educational systems of the various countries and their emphasis on one part or another of the curriculum, these are subjects of academic debate. But again, no one system seems to have worked especially well nor are any particularly more admirable than any other when it comes to the matter of actual results.

And so all the time the European brain has held onto two contradictory things. The first is the dominant established narrative of a generation: that anyone in the world can come to Europe and become a European, and that in order to become a European you merely need to be a person in Europe. The other part of the European brain has spent these years watching and waiting. This part could always recognise that the new arrivals were not only coming in unprecedented numbers but were bringing with them customs that, if not all unprecedented, had certainly not existed in Europe for a long time. The first part of the brain insists that the newcomers will assimilate and that, given time, even the most hard-to-swallow aspects of the culture of the new arrivals will become more recognisably European. Optimism favours the first part of the brain. Events favour the second, which increasingly begins to wonder whether anyone has the time for the changes that are meant to happen.

Nobody should be surprised that simmering under all this are darker, subterranean fears. Nowhere are these more pronounced than in France which, in the aftermath of the Second World War, suffered the same labour shortages as other Western European countries. The country responded in precisely the same way, opening its borders to workers from around the world. In the 1950s and 1960s, as the effects of French decolonisation in North Africa were felt, it became as impossible for France to stop the inflow of people from its former colonies as Britain and other countries had found in their turn. And the influx of largely poor and ill-educated manual workers gradually changed the culture and appearance of swathes of France, as it did elsewhere.

One subterranean response to this – a response that the French philosopher Bernard Henri-Lévy has posited as the country's 'dark specialism'[14] – was a concern about population replacement. With the largest Muslim population per capita anywhere in Western Europe and the perpetually looming electoral threat to the established parties from the Le Pen family's Front National, the boundaries of this discussion and the expression of any such concerns were policed as assiduously as anywhere else in Europe. Yet it was in France that one of the most discomfiting and prophetic treatments of this fear emerged.

THE 'DARK SPECIALISM'

In 1973 a strange novel appeared in France that swiftly became a best-seller. The author of *Le Camp des Saints* (*The Camp of the Saints*) was already known as a travel writer and novelist. Well-travelled, cultured and curious, his vision for this most notorious work came to him one morning in his home on the shores of the Mediterranean. In his own words, that morning in 1972 he saw a vision of 'A million poor wretches, armed only with their weakness and their numbers, overwhelmed by misery, encumbered with starving brown and black children, ready to disembark on our soil, the vanguard of the multitudes pressing hard against every part of the tired and overfed West. I literally saw them, saw the major problem they presented, a problem absolutely insoluble by our present moral standards. To let them in would destroy us. To reject them would destroy them.'[15]

The novel that Jean Raspail spent the next eighteen months writing was set at some point in the coming decades and depicted a France – and Europe – in the process of being swamped by mass migration from the third world. The general catalyst for the migration is the growing disparity between the numbers of poverty-stricken people in the third world and the diminishing percentage of the world's population living in the comparative paradise of Europe. With modern communications media, word of this disparity is no longer possible to hide and the third world turns to Europe. One million people set sail in a fleet of boats, but all the time untold millions are watching and waiting to get on boats themselves. Everything depends on the reaction of Europe to this first million. For strategic political reasons (as he later explained) Raspail chose to make the migration come not from North Africa but from Calcutta, and head from there towards the French Riviera.

The novel's memorable opening presents an elderly, cultured professor sitting in his house on the south coast of France, listening to Mozart as the armada is landing. He thinks he is alone, as the ensuing anarchy has already caused the local population to flee. However, a young hippy-ish man invades his study. He is glorying in the 'new' country that is going to emerge, a country that will be 'born all over'. And the young man instructs the professor that he is 'through. Dried up. You keep thinking and talking, but there's no more time for that. It's over. So beat it!' For his part the professor accepts that the young man may be right: 'My world won't live past morning, more than likely, and I fully intend to enjoy its final moments.' And so he shoots the young man.[16]

In Raspail's novel the specific catalyst for the mass migration is an announcement from the Belgian government that it will admit some young children from the third world who are in need. Soon mothers are thrusting their young through the consul general's gates in Calcutta. Belgium tries to reverse the policy but by then it is too late.

A crowd storms the consulate, trampling the consul general to death. From the crowd a hideously deformed leader emerges who calls for the people of the third world to advance on Europe: 'The nations are rising from the four corners of the earth and their number is like the sand of the sea,' he says. 'They will march up over the broad earth and surround the camp of the saints and the beloved city …'[17] The last is a quote from the Apocalypse of St John the Divine – a quotation that also finds its way into the novel's epigraph. It is an apt quotation, for the novel is indeed apocalyptic.

It is also deeply unpleasant. The messianic figure who leads the third world onto the great armada that takes them to Europe is a 'turd-eater', monstrously deformed and monstrously depicted. Elsewhere the great sea of humanity is almost uniformly equally grotesque, its poverty unforgivable and its uncleanliness endemic. It is not hard to see why Raspail's novel was swiftly and almost unanimously dismissed by the critics as a racist tract. But its uncomfortable precision, not least its depiction of the failure of European society once the migration begins, saves it from being only that.

In the wake of the threat to the French Republic every arm of the state – like its European neighbours – buckles. When it is clear that the armada is on the way and that France will be overwhelmed not by force but by people simply landing peaceably on their beaches, everybody fails in their own particular way. The politicians dither, incapable of working out what their attitude should be and flipping wildly between attempts to accept the armada and their ideas of how to scupper it. When some of the French military are ordered to torpedo the boats, they refuse to obey orders. Meantime the leaders of the Church, weighed down by the guilt of their own worldly wealth, urge that the doors of France be opened. And all the time celebrities and media stars polish and preen their reputations in front of the media by depicting this moment only as a wonderful opportunity. Perhaps aware that any other ending would have made his novel even more unacceptable, in the end Raspail allows the armada to land. France does not repel them.

Despite being a best-seller in France, a *cordon sanitaire* was imposed around the novel by French critics, and so *The Camp of the Saints* sank in plain sight. In the ensuing decades a number of translations of the novel appeared but these tended to be issued by small publishing wings of anti-immigration organisations. Yet in spite of its nearly unreadable luridness, something about the book stuck in the subterranean portion of the European conversation. Whatever its critical or publishing fate, Raspail's dystopian vision of the European future – described by two writers at *The Atlantic* in 1994 as 'one of the most disturbing novels of the late twentieth century'[18] – had an uncomfortable habit of bobbing back to the surface, and occasionally breaking above it.

In 1985 Raspail made a rare return to a theme of his novel in an article for *Le Figaro* Magazine. The front-page article, co-authored with the respected demographer Gérard François Dumont, asked 'Will France still be French in 2015?'[19] The cover image was of Marianne, France's national symbol, covered with a Muslim veil. The article itself argued, with reference to demographic projections, that ongoing immigration and the disproportionate population growth among the existing immigrant communities meant that France's non-European population would soon grow to endanger the survival of the country's culture and values.

The piece was leaped upon with relish. Government ministers queued up to publicly denounce the article. Georgina Dufoix, the Minister of Social Affairs, called the article 'reminiscent of the wildest Nazi theories'. The Culture Minister, Jack Lang, called *Le Figaro* Magazine 'an organ of racist propaganda' and said the article was 'grotesque and ridiculous', while Prime Minister Laurent Fabius told the French Parliament, 'Immigrants have contributed in large part to the richness of France. Those who have been manipulating immigration statistics are going counter to our country's genuine national interest.'[20] Dufoix's ministry released its own figures to try to counter those of the article. Among other things they claimed that Raspail and Dumont had exaggerated the possible future demographics because they had assumed that immigrant birth rates would continue to be high and that native birth rates would continue to be low. Raspail and

Dumont's projection interestingly assumed an ongoing annual net migration into France of 59,000 people. In fact, according to the official French figures,[21] by 1989 the number of asylum-seekers alone had reached 62,000 (a threefold increase from the start of that decade). By 2006 annual net migration into France had reached 193,000. By 2013 that figure had risen to 235,000 (assisting a population rise of 2.6 million in just eight years).[22] Perhaps most controversially the authors of the *Figaro* piece predicted that by 2015 Islam would be the most important religion in France.

In a 1985 reprint of his most famous book Raspail reiterated that he both understood and felt the central contradiction that would lead to his prophecy in *The Camp of the Saints* coming true. Faced with the choice of opening the door or slamming it in the face of the disadvantaged of the world: 'What's to be done, since no one would wish to renounce his own human dignity by acquiescing to racism? What's to be done since, simultaneously, all persons and all nations have the sacred right to preserve their differences and identities, in the name of their own future and their own past?'[23]

In 2001 a boat packed with Kurdish refugees from Iraq came aground on a beach in the south of France at 4 o'clock one morning. Among the 1,500 people on the boat some walked ashore and began to knock on the houses of locals. As chance would have it, the boat landed only 50 metres from the house on the Riviera from which Raspail had written his novel almost three decades earlier. Another ten years later and mainstream media were conceding a certain prophetic strain to *The Camp of the Saints*. On the occasion of yet another republication of the novel the then 86-year-old author appeared on the television programme *Ce Soir (ou jamais!)* on France 3 in a strikingly lenient interview in which the author suggested that perhaps some of the broad outlines of the book were no longer as controversial as they had once been. Reminded of the 2001 landing he referred to it as 'a sign'. The sole thing he conceded that he had got wrong in his vision of the boat people coming across was the numbers. It is true, he conceded, 'Currently there is no fleet with a million people.' This was in February 2011.

Long before 2015 the controversial and denounced vision of Jean Raspail was one that people across Europe had intuited. Even before the media started showing daily footage of the boats coming in and phalanxes of young men from the third world trudging up, through and across the continent by foot, he had tapped into a fear that already existed. And if this particular fear – this 'dark specialism' – seemed to have arisen most seriously in France, it was not confined there. Politicians and cultural figures at the time, and for decades afterwards, seemed certain about how to control this. Any and all such fears could be responded to by a simultaneous dismissal and pandering. So at the same time that French politicians derided the vision of Raspail as racist and without foundation, they competed with each other to be tougher in their rhetoric on how they would limit the flow of migrants and increase repatriations. For years even – perhaps especially – the country's socialist politicians participated in this game.

Whether they realised it or not they were responsible for bringing a crisis to bear on their country. Every year the facts changed. Every year the same political class, through successive governments of every stripe, continued to see an ever greater upsurge of the foreign-born population of France. Throughout this process the official statistics continued to cover over the change that politicians said was not happening but which the population could see with their own eyes. This was not all badly intentioned. Thanks to an old law intended to prevent any future Vichyite possibilities, throughout the 1970s, 1980s and 1990s the Republic collected neither ethnic, racial nor religious numbers for the make-up of the French population. During the mid-2000s the law in France relaxed. But analysis of the existing population, never mind projections about future demographics, remained a fraught political matter in France more than in almost any other country. Even as the Muslim population rocketed towards being the highest per capita in Europe, and only expected to grow in the years ahead, any demographer in France who did not understate all future population changes would be tarred with the brush of assisting the far right. For instance, one highly respected demographer, Michèle Tribalat, had her professional reputation badly tarnished when the 'well-connected' demographer Hervé Le Bras dismissed her as 'the National Front darling'.[24]

It is easy to assume that the facts don't lie. But in immigration statistics, let alone demographic projections, they often do – and nowhere more so than in France. It can hardly be a surprise that in a country where the facts have become so malleable, portions of the population might believe their eyes over the statistics, with consequences that have yet to be imagined. Raspail and Dumont were not correct in their 1985 prediction that in 2015 Islam would be the dominant religion in France. At least not numerically speaking. An Ipsos poll released by France's leading liberal publication, *L'Obs*, on 4 February 2016 revealed that among high-school students in France 33.2 per cent identified as Christian whereas 25.5 per cent identified as Muslim. But nobody could any longer deny that in France it was Islam that had the wind in its sails. The same poll revealed that less than half of the non-Muslims surveyed (and just 22 per cent of Catholics) described their religion as 'something important or very important' to them. Conversely, among young Muslims 83 per cent said their religion was 'important or very important' to them.[25]

And, of course, the one million people Raspail had prophesied would come was an underestimation. The numbers when they came, not on huge ships but in flotillas of countless small boats, carried numbers far in excess of his dystopian vision. And this was before the migration crisis. By the time the crisis began in earnest, France was already taking in that number of people every few years. The official figures said that legal immigration into France was at 200,000 a year, but around a similar number were believed to be entering the country each year illegally. In private some French officials will quietly admit that the only reason they have managed to avoid German levels of immigration over recent years is the widespread perception among migrants that France is a racist and unwelcoming country. It is a reputation that even the most left-wing officials do not find unhelpful to have at times such as these.

While in 2015 Marianne was not covered in the Muslim veil, the country had seen things Raspail had never predicted even in his worst nightmares. He would never have considered portraying Muslim captains on numerous migrant boats in the Mediterranean hurling Christian passengers overboard because of their faith. He would never have dared to record some incomers slitting a priest's throat at the height of the Mass. Nor would even he have predicted that on a Sunday morning in 2016 in Saint-Denis, while the priests were inside celebrating Mass for the remaining congregation, those priests and the tombs of the French kings had to be guarded from outside by multiple heavily armed soldiers. Not for the first time in Europe, the worst prophets of doom turned out to have understated their case.

7

They are here

At the time she gave her Potsdam speech in October 2010, Angela Merkel seemed to have made an important concession about the past and even signalled a change of direction for the future in the relationship between Europe and its immigrants. Yet within just a few years those much-applauded statements seemed almost entirely meaningless. In the speech the Chancellor admitted that Germany had failed to integrate the people who had arrived to date. In 2010 Germany had a total of 48,589 people apply for asylum.[1] Just five years later Merkel allowed (if leaked internal estimates from the government were correct) up to 1.5 million people into Germany in the space of one year alone.

If multiculturalism was not working with around 50,000 people claiming asylum in Germany each year, how was it expected to work with thirty times that number coming in each year? If not enough was being done in 2010, how was it the case that five years later the German government's integration network was so much – indeed thirty times – better? And if Germany had been fooling itself in the 1960s about the return of the guest-workers, how much more was it kidding itself that those applying for asylum in 2015 would return to their homes? If multiculturalism had not been working well in 2010 it was working even less well by 2015. The same goes for Britain. If multiculturalism in Britain had failed when Prime Minister David Cameron said it had, in 2011, why was it any less failed in 2015 when the British government oversaw a new record high of net migration into the country?[2] Was the relationship between France and its immigrant populations better by 2015 than it had been a few years before? Or Sweden's or Denmark's? All across Europe the migration surge of 2015 piled further numbers of people into a model that all the existing political leaders had already admitted to be a failure. Nothing noticeable had occurred in the years between to have made the model any more successful than it had been in the past.

At one stage in the crisis Chancellor Merkel telephoned the Israeli Prime Minister, Benjamin Netanyahu. It is said that she asked for advice. Israel is the only country in the world to have successfully integrated a comparable number of arrivals in an even slightly comparable timescale, namely Russian Jews entering Israel after 1990 – not to mention other large-scale influxes in the decades since the founding of the state. How had Israel managed to absorb so many people and yet held together a remarkably united country, indeed perhaps an increasingly united one? There are various reasons she could have been given – not least the bond formed in Israel through the common experience of compulsory service in the Israeli Army and government sponsored absorption programs. What diplomatic discretion may have prevented Prime Minister Netanyahu from pointing out, but which might have been apt, was that Israel had an advantage in that nearly all of the arrivals into the country for decades had a common link in their Jewish heritage – whereas in the months and years to come Angela Merkel and her nation would have to recognise that few of the people they let in during 2015 were German Lutherans.

Even as the migration into Europe increased exponentially the justifications that officials reiterated were the same ones that had been used for decades, and they permeated everywhere from the heads of supranational organisations down to the level of local government. In the middle of August 2015, as the Chancellor prepared to open the borders, the mayor of the town of Goslar in Lower Saxony insisted that his town would welcome migrants with 'open arms'. Mayor Oliver Junk – a member of Angela Merkel's own centre-right party – highlighted the fact that Goslar had been losing a small part of its population each year. Over the last decade the population of 50,000 had diminished by around 4,000 people – a factor caused by young people leaving the area to look for work as well as a diminishing birth rate among local people. In 2014 the town had taken in 48 migrants. Now the mayor announced that in his opinion there could not be enough migrants coming to Goslar. Migrants would, he said, 'give our town a future'.[3] Rather than find a way to create jobs that would attract the town's young people to stay in Goslar, the mayor thought it a sensible policy to largely replace the population of Goslar with a wholly different population.

During that same crucial month of August 2015 the EU head of the International Organisation for Migration (IOM) took to the pages of *The Wall Street Journal (Europe)* to outline another familiar argument. In the opinion of Eugenio Ambrosi it was 'troubling' that the continent was having 'difficulty' accepting the unprecedented wave of migrants that had already come that year. Ambrosi claimed that Europe could easily cope with the influx of migrants. The greatest scandal, he claimed, was that Europe was 'experiencing the most widespread and intense anti-immigrant sentiment seen in decades'. This should change, he insisted, and one way of doing so was to explain the basic argument that he and his colleagues chose to push – which was that this influx of migrants presented a great opportunity for Europe. Migrants, he said, bring 'new ideas and high motivation' and also 'pitch in and contribute to our economies and societies when given a fair chance. Sometimes they have a better work ethic than native Europeans.' And then there came the familiar claim: 'Europe is getting older and will soon be dealing with a serious shortage of working-age people ... Germany alone could experience a labour shortage of up to 2.4 million workers by 2020, according to the Boston Consulting Group. Our existing social-security systems are not threatened by migration. Quite to the contrary: The contribution of migrants will ensure that the support Europeans receive now will continue into the future.'[4] This was another argument for population replacement, this time dressed up in the language of palliative care.

Even if Europe's demographic fall-off was as severe as Mr Ambrosi claimed, the most obvious answer was not necessarily to import people from a wholly different culture to make up the next generation. If Ambrosi and other officials were so concerned to fill any existing or future labour shortages in Germany, surely it would have been sensible, before casting a net across the globe, to look closer to home to the 25–50 per cent of young people in Spain, Portugal, Italy and Greece who were suffering from unemployment at exactly the same time. People as dedicated as Ambrosi to the free-marketeer argument were not even making sense of events on their own terms. More worryingly, they seemed to assume that their free marketeer arguments were the only arguments that would matter and that the young populations of southern Europe, among others, would not mind being leap-frogged over by anyone and everyone from the non-European parts of the world.

And of course, as migration into Europe reached an unheard-of historical peak there remained those willing to argue that this was all perfectly normal. The only country to have taken in the same number of migrants per head of population as Germany in 2015 alone was Sweden (1–2 per cent). The country's 2015 arrivals alone numbered somewhere between 160,000 and 180,000 – an historically unprecedented number even for a country with a recent history of taking refugees. So whereas in 2004 Sweden had absorbed around 400 child refugees, in 2015 alone it had to absorb 35,000 child arrivals at the cost of tens of thousands of Euros per child per year. During the summer of 2015 migrants flowed into the country daily not only across the famous Øresund bridge from Denmark (between Denmark and Sweden there was no border) but also from the north. Most of those who arrived had no identity papers at all, and this was not always an accident. Residents of Malmö attested to seeing bins at the railway station filled with destroyed identity papers.

Yet even as Sweden was going through this abnormal year the authorities there continued in the pretence that this was nothing new. In October 2015 the government put on a conference in support of its migration policy entitled 'Sweden Together'. The King and Queen of Sweden were in attendance along with most of the rest of the political establishment. Among the speakers was Ingrid Lomfors, the head of Sweden's 'Living History Forum' (a Holocaust education body). In her much-praised speech Lomfors insisted upon three things: that immigration to Sweden is nothing new, that everyone is a migrant really, and that in any case there is no such thing as Swedish culture.[5]

In its way the 'Living History Forum' crystallised the problem piled upon problem that post-war immigration across Europe had presented. Even as events were occurring before the public's eyes the authorities refused to concede that what was happening was anything new. When they did concede it they could only dress it up as an opportunity for the country. Nowhere was there a willingness to concede that some public suspicion about the consequences of these movements might be justified. From the 1950s onwards the continent had been united in a tendency to underestimate the number of people expected to arrive and then to massively overestimate the country's ability to integrate those arrivals. There were few moments of humility from the people who were making these decisions, not even over one of the grandest and most evident failings, which was the unwillingness to notice that the immigrant groups who came to Europe might have different views not just from mainstream society, but from each other, and that these facts would bring consequences of their own.

Nothing demonstrates this failure in the multicultural and 'post-multicultural' eras better than the fact that the ideologies – political and religious – of the incomers were rarely a subject of consideration and were almost never a permissible subject for debate. So it was that in each country post-war immigration was discussed when it was discussed as an issue of race. The racial identities of the incomers were discussed and any and all concerns raised about this were returned along the terms of anti-racism. What very few people saw or mentioned was that the racial background of incomers was an insignificant matter alongside the far greater issue of creed. When Moroccans first came to Holland in large numbers they were discussed as Moroccans. When Pakistanis first came to Britain in large numbers they were discussed as Pakistanis. The same went for Turks in Germany. But around the turn of the millennium the period of multi-faithism crept up on Europe and the significance of the race of migrant groups declined, Europe began to wonder whether the issue was not in fact religion. It was a subject that took most politicians and commentators in Western Europe entirely by surprise.

In the 1980s or 1990s almost nobody predicted that the first decades of the twentieth century in Europe would be riven by discussions about religion. The increasingly secular continent had expected to be able to leave faith behind it, or at least recognised that after many centuries the place of religion in the modern state had been pretty much settled. If, more specifically, anybody in the late part of the twentieth century had said that the early years of the next century in Europe would be rife with discussions about blasphemy and that death for blasphemy would once again have to be expected in Europe, any audience would have scorned the prediction and doubted the sanity of the claimant. It was not that the early-warning sirens that went off were not heard. How could some of them not be? The problem was that they were consistently ignored.

Britain had one of the earliest warnings, from Valentine's Day 1989 when the Supreme Leader of the Revolutionary Islamic Republic of Iran, Ayatollah Khomeini, issued a document calling on 'all zealous Muslims of the world' to know that 'the author of the book entitled *The Satanic Verses* – which has been compiled, printed and published in opposition to Islam, the Prophet and the Qur'an – and all those involved in its publication who were aware of its contents, are sentenced to death'. The Ayatollah went on: 'I call on all zealous Muslims to execute them quickly, wherever they may be found, so that no one else will dare to insult the Muslim sanctities.'[6] The head of a Tehran 'charitable foundation' followed this up with a $3 million reward for the British novelist's murder (the bounty to be reduced by

$2 million if the murderer was a non-Muslim). Britain – and the rest of Europe – learned the word *fatwa* for the first time.

Within less than 24 hours Rushdie was in hiding, with protection provided by the British state. Soon thousands of British Muslims were on the streets supporting the imposition of Islamic blasphemy laws in Britain. In Bradford, in the north of England, the novel was nailed to a piece of wood and then burnt in front of crowds of thousands of Muslims. One man who thanks to the controversy was on the fast-track to Muslim leadership status, Iqbal (later Sir Iqbal) Sacranie, was asked whether he thought the author of *The Satanic Verses* deserved death. Sacranie replied, 'Death perhaps, is a bit too easy for him.'[7] Britain's most famous convert to Islam, Yusuf Islam (formerly known as the singer Cat Stevens), was asked on a television programme whether he would give Rushdie shelter if he were to turn up at his door. He replied, 'I'd try to phone the Ayatollah Khomeini and tell him exactly where this man is.' Asked whether he would go to a demonstration where an effigy of Rushdie was being burnt, he replied, 'I would have hoped that it would be the real thing.'[8]

Across the cultural and political worlds people debated this reawakened question of blasphemy. On both the political left and right there were those who believed that the novelist had transgressed the rules of courtesy. Among the high Tory right Lord Dacre (Hugh Trevor-Roper) told a newspaper, 'I would not shed a tear if some British Muslims, deploring his manners, should waylay him in a dark street and seek to improve them.'[9] The Foreign Secretary, Sir Geoffrey Howe, stressed on television that he himself had no love for *The Satanic Verses* and that it was rude about Britain. Others dug up earlier criticisms of Rushdie's about Britain and concluded that chickens were coming home to roost. The Prince of Wales allegedly said in private that Rushdie deserved everything he got.[10] Faith leaders, meanwhile, competed to mollify the Islamic Republic. The Archbishop of Canterbury, Robert Runcie, said that he 'understood the Muslims' feelings'.[11] The Chief Rabbi, Immanuel Jakobovits, said that 'Both Mr Rushdie and the Ayatollah have abused freedom of speech.'[12] There were similar pronouncements from the leadership of the Catholic Church and other denominations.

From the political left John le Carré declared that, 'there is no law in life or nature that says great religions may be insulted with impunity'.[13] And the Labour MP Bernie Grant – one of the first black MPs in the British House of Commons – told a meeting of fellow MPs that white people were trying to impose their values on the world and that although he didn't agree with the Ayatollahs, Muslims in Iran should have the right to live their own lives. Besides which 'burning books,' he claimed 'was not a big issue for blacks'.[14]

Still a small but determined group of people did realise what the fatwa meant and supported the novelist whom Ayatollah Khomeini referred to as 'that blasphemous bastard'.[15] The novelist Fay Weldon was sitting opposite Cat Stevens when he made his comments and remarked with amazement that a police chief superintendent who was also in the studio did not simply walk across and arrest the singer for incitement to murder. In a subsequent pamphlet Weldon claimed that Britain was paying the price for the fact that too few people had bothered to read the Koran and had instead been happy to murmur 'platitudes about "great world religions" '.[16] This broadside in turn was viewed by some British Muslims as hate-speech, with even a fairly moderate Muslim writer of the period, Ziauddin Sardar, writing that, 'It seemed Weldon could fabricate whatever she wished and produce a prejudiced diatribe simply because Muslims were fair game.'[17] In fact, it was only people associated with Rushdie who were 'fair game'. In 1991 Rushdie's Italian translator was stabbed and beaten up in his apartment in Milan. In 1993 the Norwegian publisher of *The Satanic Verses*, William Nygaard, was shot three times outside his house in Oslo. In Britain two bookshops were firebombed for stocking the book. Other shops, including a London department store that housed a Penguin bookshop, had bombs planted in them. And in 1989 a young man called Mustafa Mahmoud Mazeh blew himself up and destroyed several floors of a London hotel while priming a bomb intended for Rushdie.

There were some people who realised that this was a matter of free speech, in America as well as Europe. For instance, that year's president of the writer's group PEN, Susan Sontag, organised an event at which prominent authors would read from Rushdie's novel: 'A bit of civic fortitude is what is required here', as she put it.[18] But although there was some civic as well as governmental fortitude, there was barely any wider understanding of what was happening. Broadsides like Weldon's were highly unusual during the period in realising that Rushdie had not simply had the bad luck to poke a hornet's nest that happened to be inhabited. He had poked a hornet's nest that had been recently imported into the country and that was growing. When Hilaire Belloc published *The Great Heresies* in 1938 he had devoted a chapter to 'The great and enduring heresy of Mohammed', a passage that makes *The Satanic Verses* look tame. But Belloc had not had to escape into hiding or live under police protection for a decade because in the 1930s there were a negligible number of Muslims in Britain. At the time of the Rushdie affair there were just under a million Muslims in the United Kingdom, a number that would treble in the two decades after the affair. Britain was undergoing a crash course in the rules of Islam, just as everybody else was going to have to in the years ahead.

Thanks to the protection measures put around Rushdie by the British government, he survived the *Satanic Verses* affair. But as the author Kenan Malik put it much later, society as a whole – and the publishing industry in particular – internalised the fatwa.[19] Things that were published before 1989 would not be published again. The assassin's veto took over and soon it was not only novels that might be critical of Islam but even fawningly uncritical novels that became unpublishable. In 2008 security concerns persuaded the same British publishers that had published Rushdie's novel to withdraw from publishing a work of romance about the founder of Islam called *The Jewel of Medina*. A small independent publisher in London that picked up the novel to make a point against censorship was subsequently firebombed by three British Muslims.

Apart from making a society internalise the threat of violence the Rushdie affair had another important effect in Britain. It embedded the idea of 'community politics' along faith-based lines, because as soon as thousands of angry Muslims appeared on British streets the question arose of who spoke for these people. In Britain the Rushdie affair created the first organised Muslim 'representative' organisation. The UK Action Committee on Islamic Affairs (UKACIA) was put together as a direct effort to coordinate anger about, and preclude any repeat of, the *Satanic Verses* affair. In the years afterwards this led to the creation of the Muslim Council of Britain (MCB), the largest umbrella group claiming to represent British Muslims. The organisation was not only political but sectarian. Although the group was financially supported by Saudi Arabia, then vying with Iran to be the dominant Muslim power, it was dominated by people from the Pakistani Islamist group Jamaat-e-Islami. The creation of such an entity obviously benefited those who were almost overnight promoted from obscurity into positions as 'community spokesmen' (always men). It also benefited their own hardline branch of Islam, with each apparent or actual escalation of the crisis strengthening their hand and sidelining more liberal and independent elements within the community.[20]

In the short term the creation of such groups appeared useful for government. As Henry Kissinger reportedly asked, 'What number do I dial to get Europe?', so the British government in the wake of the Rushdie crisis asked, 'What number do I dial to get the Muslim community?' Those who claim this was a familiar brand of left-wing politics forget that in Britain it was a Conservative Home Secretary – Michael Howard – who encouraged the creation of the MCB and made it into the interlocutory group for the government. The alleged success of the model meant that it was exported across other Western countries, where even France – despite its traditions – chose to encourage representative bodies for French Muslims, notably the Conseil Français du Culte Musulman (CFCM). In France, as in Britain, this was the creation of a right-wing government and one right-wing politician in particular – Nicolas Sarkozy.

The downsides should have been obvious from the start, but were not. These included the fact that ordinary Muslims suddenly had a branch of religious representation inserted between them and their political representatives. The model also favoured those who were already politically active and engaged, while disadvantaging those too busy with their lives or careers to bother with community politics, let alone community politics already tied up by sectarian groups. The model favoured the loud, the extreme, the offended and those like Jamaat that were already organised – a fact that meant their brand of sectarian politics, which was often unpopular in their country of origin, became the mainstream voice for Muslim representation in Europe. Four years after 11 September 2001, Rushdie gave an interview in which he discussed Islamist efforts to dominate in the wake of the *Satanic Verses* affair, and in particular to exclude 'progressive' Muslim voices. 'People weren't interested in hearing about this at the time,' he pointed out. 'And then along comes 9/11, and now many people say that, in hindsight, the fatwa was the prologue and this is the main event.'[21]

But even before that 'main event' there were warning signs across Europe that the continent's twenty-first century was going to be consistently entangled with the demands of one religion in particular, because its adherents had been brought to Europe in such large numbers. One country that had a noticeable head start in these arguments was Holland.

8

Prophets without honour

When labour in the Netherlands was scarce, in the 1960s, immigration into the country had mainly come from Morocco and Turkey. The immigrants brought their wives and families and by the 1990s the continuing immigration and higher birth rates among these communities meant that they were growing at a faster rate than any other community in the country. The Dutch government's policy had been to emphasise 'integration without prejudice to everyone's own identity'. The few people in public life who objected to the government's immigration and integration policies during this period were not treated kindly. In the 1980s one maverick politician, Hans Janmaat, proclaimed that the Netherlands was full and expressed himself opposed to the multicultural model, insisting that immigrants should either assimilate into the Dutch way of life or leave. Not only was Janmaat politically shunned but in 1986 left-wing activists set fire to a hotel in Kedichem in the south of the country, where his small party was holding a meeting. Janmaat's wife was among those forced to jump from the building to save their lives. She lost a leg in the process.

Perhaps in part because of its reputation as the most liberal country in Europe (thanks to its legalisation of soft drugs and liberal attitudes towards sexual minorities) by the 1990s Holland was beginning to experience tensions with its fastest-growing minority group. During this period a number of politicians privately agreed that the increasing number of Muslims in the Netherlands presented problems too large for any one political party to address, that mass immigration and integration in Holland were not working, and that simply attacking those who raised concerns would no longer address the problem. Free expression was an early clash-point. On 5 October 1990 a Muslim religious leader said in a radio programme on a Dutch-subsidised radio station in Amsterdam, 'Those who resist Islam, the order of Islam or oppose Allah and his prophet, you have permission to kill, hang, slaughter or banish, as it says in the Sharia.'

In 1991 the head of the Dutch Liberal Party (VVD), Frits Bolkestein, gave a speech and wrote a follow-up article in which he voiced what some other leaders from across the political spectrum were also beginning to worry about. Bolkestein noted that Islam is 'not only a religion, it is a way of life. In this its vision runs counter to the liberal separation of church and state.' He also highlighted the differences between Islamic attitudes towards women and that of Dutch law and custom. While recognising that the new populations in Holland were clearly not going to go anywhere, Bolkestein concluded that real, full integration into Dutch life was the only answer to the questions he was raising. But there was a final problem: 'The problem is that we cannot afford to be wrong.'[1] Both speech and article were greeted with huge amounts of criticism. Prime Minister Ruud Lubbers called the article 'dangerous' while another minister accused its author of being 'insulting to the Muslim community'. One prominent opinion journalist claimed that it would 'fan racist sentiments'.[2]

In a culture where ideas still matter, the sociologist Paul Schnabel's 1998 book *The Multicultural Illusion: A Plea for Adaptation and Assimilation* brought many of these issues further into the acceptable mainstream; as in 2000 did the essay 'The Multicultural Drama' by the academic and Dutch Labour Party member Paul Scheffer.[3] But the public and the politicians were still at a wild divergence. A survey carried out in 1998 discovered that already about half of Dutch people thought that 'Western European and Muslim ways of life are irreconcilable.'[4] The leadership of Bolkestein and others gave their country the advantage of going relatively early through the issues that every other Western country would stumble through in the decade ahead.

Nevertheless among the political class there remained a serious reluctance to tackle the problem. In the end it took a popular pundit and professor from the political left to make this discussion normal.

Until he got onto the subject of Islam there was nothing remotely 'right wing' about Pim Fortuyn. A Marxist university professor and a gay man, Fortuyn was also a high-profile advocate of promiscuity and almost every other libertarian attitude. Only once he got onto the subject of Islam did he become 'right wing'. His 1997 book *Against the Islamisation of our Culture* focused on the range of challenges that he said Islam posed to Dutch society.[5] All were issues that had until then been campaigning points of the political left.

They included the fact that Islam had not achieved the separation of church and state which had been the achievement of Dutch Christianity – a separation that gave the Dutch not only freedom of speech, freedom of the press and other human rights but without which the public space had no guard against clerical intrusion based on 'holy' texts. Another of Fortuyn's principal objections to Islam was the difference in attitude towards the sexes. He argued that Muslim women in Holland should have the same right to emancipation as all other Dutch women. And he seized with fury upon Islamic attitudes towards sexual minorities. Dutch society had led the world in passing legislation and creating a culture in which equality between men and women and between heterosexuals and homosexuals had become the norm. The practices of Muslim-majority countries demonstrated, with varying degrees of austerity, that these principles were not compatible with Islam. Yet despite these obvious clashes, Dutch society was trying to pretend that its own tolerance could coexist with the intolerance of the fastest-growing portion of Dutch society. Fortuyn felt that it could not.

Through his newspaper columns and on popular television programmes, Fortuyn became a master not only at expressing his own views, but also at teasing out the views of other people. On a television discussion show he acted as flamboyantly as he could in front of a Dutch Imam until the Imam exploded in rage over Fortuyn's homosexuality. Mainstream Dutch politicians also told him what they thought of him. During a television debate in 1997 about his 'Islamisation' book the leading Labour Party politician and former cabinet minister Marcel van Dam told Fortuyn, 'You are an extremely inferior human being.'[6] It was only a taste of the vitriol to come.

By the time of the 9/11 attacks in America, Dutch society had been around the central parts of this discussion several times and Fortuyn had begun to devote his energy to politics. He was expelled from the party he had joined when he described Islam as an *achterlijk* ('backward') culture, but promptly started his own political party, Lijst Pim Fortuyn (LPF). Because of its voting system Dutch politics, more than perhaps any other country in Europe, is comparatively easy for new outsider parties to break into. In a matter of weeks in the lead-up to the 2002 national elections Fortuyn upturned the whole of Dutch politics.

Unrestrained by colleagues, he increasingly warned of the threat to Dutch identity, and in particular to the country's liberal identity. He warned that multiculturalism was not working and was instead seeing the growth of parallel societies, especially in the growth of Muslim ghettos. He warned that it was 'five minutes to midnight' and that Holland had only this brief window to turn itself around. Combined with an innate showmanship and a refusal to play the media's games on its own terms, in the run-up to the 2002 election it looked as though the population was willing to trust Fortuyn with their country. His political opponents threw everything they had at him. They said that he was a racist. They said that he was Hitler. The more moderate opponents compared him to Mussolini. In a television interview shortly before he died Fortuyn talked of the threats to his life that were coming in and said that if anything were to happen to him his political opponents, who had so demonised him, should take some of the responsibility for lining up the assassin.

They didn't, of course. Just over a week before the election, as Fortuyn was leaving a radio interview in Hilversum a man in his thirties shot him in the head repeatedly at close range. The nation took a deep breath for fear that the killer might turn out to be a Muslim.

But the culprit turned out to be a far-left vegan activist who at his subsequent trial explained that he had killed his victim because he felt Fortuyn was targeting Muslims. In the aftermath of the murder the Netherlands went into mourning, and in the ensuing election voters gave Fortuyn's party the largest number of seats, a gift it repaid by petty infighting and a total inability (perhaps inevitable given the swiftness of their rise) to deliver on its mandate.

The Dutch public's desire to deal with their challenges at the ballot box were thwarted. And although those who picked up his political mantle included Geert Wilders (who left the main VVD 'liberal' party also to form a party of his own), none of Fortuyn's successors were able to pick up the working-class and young entrepreneurial vote that Fortuyn had been able to appeal to. Although the murder of the man who would later be voted the greatest Dutchman of all time shuttered one part of electoral politics, it did, however, allow the debate to widen in the society as a whole. It was not sustainable to believe that Fortuyn was a fascist and that a large proportion of the Dutch public supported a fascist.

One of those who continued to speak out in the vacuum left by Fortuyn was the filmmaker Theo van Gogh. As well as being friends, the two had appeared on television together many times, not least on van Gogh's show 'A Pleasant Conversation', at the end of which the presenter would hand his guest a cactus. After Fortuyn's murder van Gogh worked on a film about the murder and also continued to write books and articles. His 2003 book *Allah weet het Beter* (*Allah Knows Best*) included a cover image of van Gogh wearing a Muslim head-robe and staring out as a mimic of the fundamentalists of Islam.

In television appearances and public debates van Gogh took on the most outspoken Islamists in the Netherlands, including on one occasion the Hezbollah-trained extremist Dyab Abou Jahjah, who he described as 'the pimp of the prophet'. After that event (which stopped when Jahjah refused to be on a stage with van Gogh) Jahjah's retinue were heard saying, 'We'll get that fat pig and cut him open.'[7] Around this time, at public events, including book-signings for *Allah Knows Best*, van Gogh started to become nervous for his own security. Then in 2004 he made a short film called *Submission* about the mistreatment of women within Islam. The script was written by a young Somali immigrant to the Netherlands, Ayaan Hirsi Ali, and around the time that the film was screened on Dutch television at the end of August the threat to the film's makers grew. Van Gogh refused to accept the security that was offered. It was his view, according to those closest to him, that any Islamist assassins would be unlikely to target 'the village idiot'.[8]

Village idiot or not, an assassin did catch up with him as he cycled to work in Amsterdam on the morning of 2 November 2004. Mohammed Bouyeri shot van Gogh, slit his throat and stabbed him in the chest. In his dying moments van Gogh said to Bouyeri, 'Can't we talk about this?' The knife stuck into van Gogh's body included a threat to the life of Ayaan Hirsi Ali. She was immediately spirited out of the country by the Dutch security service, while a number of other Dutch critics of Islam, including the Iranian-born academic Afshin Ellian, were also put under police protection. For a period even the most careful critics of elements of Islam – like the Dutch academic Paul Cliteur – silenced themselves. Politicians, academics, journalists and others had learnt the tough lesson that criticising Islam, in the manner in which Dutch society was able to criticise every other religion, was at the very least something that changed your life and was also – unless you had police protection – likely to be deadly. The country that in the past had fostered religious doubt and produced rationalist thinkers like Spinoza, was now very anxious on the subject of religion.

This fact put even more pressure on the few people who were not willing to play by the assassin's rules. Among those willing to continue to defy the extremists was the young Dutch woman of Somali origin who had fled to Holland ten years before to escape a forced marriage. Hirsi Ali was in every way a model migrant. Having arrived in the country she claimed and was given asylum, and while working basic factory jobs she learned the Dutch language and was soon able to apply to university. She studied at the University of Leiden whilst working with other immigrants as a translator. Just over a decade after arriving in the Netherlands she received her MA in Political Science, worked as a researcher and entered the country's Parliament as an MP for the Liberal Party. It was a meteoric immigrant success story. Her success was due to her intelligence, charisma, hard work and exceptional personal bravery. But the swiftness of her rise to prominence also occurred because Dutch society desperately needed immigrant success stories. Yet it seemed to come as a shock to some on the left in particular, that this immigrant refused to say the things they expected of her.

Hirsi Ali herself would later write that the 9/11 attacks caused her to 'investigate whether the roots of evil can be traced to the faith I grew up with: was the aggression, the hatred inherent in Islam itself?'[9] Six months later she read a book on atheism she had been given several years earlier and dared to admit that she was no longer a believer.[10] In her own time she announced her evolving thoughts in public. But the Dutch media-class in particular seemed intent on pushing her – trying to make her say things they would not say. One interviewer pressed her to use that same crucial word Fortuyn had used, *achterlijk*. Was Islam backward compared to Dutch society? There seemed to be two movements pushing at Hirsi Ali. One, broadly coming from the political left, wanted her to say things for which they could then attack her. Another – coming from left and right – wanted her to say things in order to free things up for everybody else. It was harder to accuse a black woman of racism than it was a white man. Nevertheless the supporters of the status quo found a way around this by claiming that Hirsi Ali did not know what she was saying because she was 'traumatised' by her experiences – experiences they insisted were wholly uncommon.

As a victim of female genital mutilation (a subject about which she would write graphically in her autobiography),[11] someone who had as a teenager believed death was a suitable punishment for Salman Rushdie, had fled a forced marriage and understood at first hand the challenges of integration, Hirsi Ali tackled the most brittle issues. A sign that the coming years were not going to go well was that this exemplary immigrant found herself assailed not just by a large proportion of the Dutch political class but with extraordinary vitriol by the country's Muslim community.

Early in her public career a friend had asked Hirsi Ali, 'Don't you realise how small this country is, and how explosive it is, what you're saying?' As she recounted her response in her autobiography, 'Explosive? In a country where prostitution and soft drugs are licit, where euthanasia and abortion are practised, where men cry on TV and naked people walk on the beach and the pope is joked about on national TV? Where the famous author Gerard Reve is renowned for having fantasized about making love with a donkey, an animal he used as a metaphor for God? Surely nothing I could say would be seen as anything close to "explosive" in such a context.'[12] But it was. Hirsi Ali had put her finger on the sorest point of Dutch society. A people who liked to think of themselves as tolerant and open and decent were wondering whether this tolerance and openness and decency had gone too far. How could they enforce any limits? Hirsi Ali was telling them that there were limits and she was living proof of some of them. And so in spite of the threats to her life both before and after the murder of her colleague van Gogh, she believed that 'some things must be said, and there are times when silence becomes an accomplice to injustice.'[13]

Everywhere in Europe these same concerns were growing. During the decades in which European governments allowed immigration to run at the levels they did, few if any expected that one consequence would be that they would spend the foreseeable future trying to balance Islamic laws and demands with European culture and traditions. Yet as the immigrant populations grew, everywhere the same problems erupted. Sometimes it occurred because of the discovery of what was going on within the communities. In France in 2004 a young Muslim woman called Ghofrane Haddaoui was stoned to death in Marseille for refusing the advances of a young Muslim man. In the United Kingdom the police admitted that they had failed to investigate scores of suspicious deaths of young Muslim women because they had thought these potential 'honour killings' were community matters. In 2006 the British Medical Association reported that at least 74,000 women in Britain had been subjected to genital mutilation.

At the same time individuals from the Muslim communities in Europe who had spoken out publicly about any negative aspects of their culture, or had appeared to go against their community in any way, were increasingly the subject of physical intimidation and violence. From the Norwegian pop singer Deepika Thathaal, who was attacked onstage in Oslo for her 'immodesty', to the columnist and activist Nosheen Ilyas in Italy, minorities within the minority turned out to be perhaps the most threatened people of all. And all the time there was a slowly growing awareness that the newest incomers to Europe might not all look favourably on some of the oldest. Throughout the multicultural era it had been assumed that minorities would have their minority status in common with other minorities. The idea that they would bring any of their ancient animosities with them seemed to occur to almost no one in power. But as the numbers grew, this presumption began to crumble.

In 2003 a report into anti-Semitism by the European Monitoring Centre was quietly shelved when it found that the upsurge in anti-Semitic activity in Europe was caused by a rise in attacks on Jews by young Muslims. Yet despite such attempts to cover over the facts, the facts kept on breaking out – often in the most brutal ways possible. In 2006 there was horror in France when a French Jew called Ilan Halimi was tortured to death over the course of three weeks by a gang of Muslims in Paris who called themselves 'the barbarians'. His torturers believed they could get money out of Halimi and his family because 'Jews have money'. In the years of mass migration attacks on Jews began to increase everywhere. According to the body that records attacks in France, the BNVCA (Bureau National de Vigilance Contre l'Antisémitisme), the number of recorded anti-Semitic attacks in France doubled between 2013 and 2014 alone, reaching 851 incidents in that year. Despite accounting for less than 1 per cent of the population, Jews were the victims in almost half of all recorded racist attacks in France: on Bastille Day 2014, worshipers at a synagogue in Paris were barricaded inside by immigrant protesters chanting, among other things, 'Death to the Jews'; a Muslim gunman shot dead three children and a teacher at a Jewish school in Toulouse in 2012; another Muslim gunman shot dead four people at the Jewish museum in Brussels in 2014; another Muslim gunman killed four Jews at a kosher Hypercache in Paris in 2015; and yet another Muslim gunman killed a Jewish man on security duty at the Great Synagogue in Copenhagen in 2015. These, killings, among other attacks, caused the issue of Islamic anti-Semitism finally to get discussed.

But in the case of resurgent anti-Semitism, as with a whole set of new or revived problems, the journey to acknowledging what was happening was slow and almost wilfully sluggish. In Germany in 2013 a new political party, Alternative für Deutschland (AfD), was formed. Once the party's anti-immigration stance became clear, the German media and political class were intent on proving that the party was anti-Semitic. Yet in 2014 it was not AfD supporters but mainly immigrant protesters who gathered on the streets of German cities including Frankfurt, Dortmund and Essen to chant 'Hamas, Hamas, all Jews to the gas' and 'Jewish shit'. It was not an AfD politician but a Muslim Imam in the Neukölln area of Berlin who stood in the mosque in 2014 and urged God to 'Destroy the Zionist Jews. Kill every last one of them.'[14]

In each country there had been people who had tried to issue warnings. Some like Hirsi Ali were people who had been brought up as Muslims but left the religion. Others had been born as Muslims and were intent on remaining in the religion and pushing a liberal reformist agenda from within. Other warnings were issued by non-Muslim Europeans who insisted on their right to speak about their continent.

Few did so with greater passion than the famous Italian journalist and author Oriana Fallaci. The only Western journalist ever to have got an interview with Rushdie's persecutor in Iran, Fallaci was in her seventies at the turn of the millennium. In younger days her celebrated interviews with Khomeini as well as Colonel Gaddafi, the Shah of Iran, Henry Kissinger and others had made her perhaps the world's most feared interviewer.[15] These encounters up close with power, as well as her travels around the world's war zones, had given her a deadly rage about many things – and a rage against Islam was among them.

The daughter of anti-fascists, she had grown up in Mussolini's Italy. Through her father Fallaci became involved in anti-fascist activities and at the end of her life she would recall the errands she would run as a girl – hiding hand grenades in lettuces to take them to the opposition headquarters, gun-running and posting partisan materials.[16] Her country and her home city – Florence – were occupied from 1943 to 1944 by the Nazis, and though she was only in her teens at the time, Fallaci, like her family, fought to get her city and country back. When she talked of fascism she talked with the benefit of experience.

After her many years of uncompromising and brutal interviews, Fallaci turned to fictionalised accounts of her life, including a novel (*Inshallah*) based on her experiences of the civil war in Lebanon. In the 1990s she retreated into an ever greater solitude, living above her publisher's shop in New York and working on a novel about her family and childhood. When 9/11 happened one of the things it did was to waken this dormant literary volcano in Manhattan. Within a fortnight she had completed a long essay that made up a special supplement of the Italian paper *Corriere della Sera*. It was a characteristically tumultuous, heartfelt, torrential and furious assault: on the people who had brought down the Twin Towers, on the people who had turned a blind eye to the threat, on the Muslims around the world who celebrated the act and on the religion of Islam itself. It was a distinct and passionate production.[17]

That edition of *Corriere* sold out and Fallaci swiftly turned the polemic into a short book published in 2002. *The Rage and the Pride* sold more than a million copies in Italy and hundreds of thousands more copies in translations across Europe. It was the subject of vicious counterattacks from the outset, and fierce defences in her homeland from the religious as well as those like Fallaci who were atheists. In the ebb and flow of intellectual and political fashions it is easy to forget or dismiss as 'overnight sensations' works like *The*

Rage and the Pride. But almost no work had such a wide and powerful impact on its readers or retained such a strong effect away from polite society.

Taking, by her own admission, the form of a 'J'accuse' or sermon to the West, Fallaci's work attacked those who carried out terror in the name of Islam, on the increasing number of Muslims in the West and on those in the West who 'have no balls' to stand up for themselves against these incomers.[18] 'I am very, very, very angry. Angry with a rage which is cold, lucid, rational,' she wrote at the beginning. 'A rage which eliminates any detachment, any indulgence, which orders me to answer them and to spit in their face.'[19] The pitch did not lower from there.

Writing of the fight that she and her family were engaged in when she was a child, she compared it with the recent reaction of public officials to the 'occupation' of the Duomo square in Florence when Somali Muslims in Florence erected tents around the cathedral. The camp lasted for three months and was a major controversy in Florence at the time. In her polemic Fallaci told of how she had contacted every public official in Florence and then in Italy demanding to know why they could not clear away this site in the centre of the city, only to be greeted on each occasion with professions of incapability. She relates that eventually she phoned a local policeman and told him that if he didn't clear the tents away she would burn them down herself and he would then have to arrest her and incarcerate her in her own city.

Such emasculated Italians, Europeans and Westerners in general were as much the target of Fallaci's rage as Muslims. As were all those who would draw comparisons or equality between the world of the West and the world of Islam. While acknowledging the failings and sins of the West, Fallaci insisted 'I want to defend my culture, not theirs, and I inform you that I like Dante Alighieri and Shakespeare and Goethe and Verlaine and Walt Whitman and Leopardi much more than Omar Khayyam.'[20] She had, she claimed, as much veneration for any work of art as any Muslim professed to have for Mecca.[21] The cultural pride and defiance of Fallaci perhaps stood out because it was so rare in that period.

Yet Fallaci's fiery style undoubtedly sometimes tipped over into something else. In relating the desecration by Somali Muslims in the Duomo square she obsessed about their bodily functions, about the excrement and especially the trails of urine from the camp: 'the yellow streaks of urine that profaned the millenary marbles of the Baptistery as well as its golden doors. (Good Heavens! They really take long shots, these sons of Allah!)'.[22] Though it was when discussing the reproductive habits of the new Muslims of Italy that Fallaci walked into trouble.

A fixation on the numbers of Muslims coming into Europe and the number of children they brought or had once they were here was not something that Fallaci plucked from nowhere. Nor was her suggestion that this migration or *hijra* was a declared intention of some Muslim leaders. In *The Rage and the Pride* she quotes Islamic leaders who boast that they intended to do exactly what she was describing. She quotes an Islamic scholar who allegedly told a synod at the Vatican in 1999, 'By means of your democracy we shall invade you, by means of our religion we shall dominate you.' It was, she said, 'a reverse crusade'.[23] All this leads Fallaci to conclude that Europe's Muslims are attempting 'not only a conquest of souls but also a conquest of territory.' And then, 'They breed too much. Italians don't produce babies anymore, the idiots. For decades they have had and still have the lowest birth-rate in the West.'[24] This is the slightly watered-down version that Fallaci's publishers released when the author translated her own work into her own idiosyncratic English. But in the original edition Fallaci had flavoured this with her observation that Muslims 'breed like rats'.[25]

Muslim groups in Italy pressed for Fallaci to be prosecuted on the grounds, among others, of 'vilification of religion'. Similar prosecutions against her were attempted in France. This happened in 2002 at the same time as a spate of similar prosecutions were attempted against public figures. In France the actress turned animal-rights campaigner Brigitte Bardot was prosecuted for statements including her attacks on the practice of Halal slaughter.[26] French Muslim groups also attempted the prosecution of the novelist Michel Houellebecq for saying in an interview that he thought Islam 'the most stupid religion' and the Koran 'badly written'.[27]

The prospect of prosecution in her home country for offending Islam was not the only threat to Fallaci after the publication of *The Rage and the Pride*. When she returned to Italy she had to be protected around the clock by the Carabinieri.[28] These and other outrages to her in her home country spurred Fallaci to a less disciplined work than *The Rage and the Pride*. Her follow-up sermon, *The Force of Reason*, sold almost as many copies in continental Europe and saw the same preoccupations taken up a notch. The argument was not devoid of historical or present-day evidence. In defence of her view that Muslims were trying to outbreed Europeans inside Europe, Fallaci quoted the former Algerian President Houari Boumedienne who in 1974 told the General Assembly of the United Nations, 'One day millions of men will leave the southern hemisphere of this planet to burst into the northern one. But not as friends. Because they will burst in to conquer, and they will conquer by populating it with their children. Victory will come to us from the wombs of our women.'[29] A third and final book by Fallaci in a similar vein followed.[30]

A noisy wing of the Italian left excoriated Fallaci for her final works. But millions of others listened to her and revered her. In 2005, shortly after becoming the new Pope, Cardinal Joseph Ratzinger invited Fallaci to come and speak with him at his summer residence on the understanding that what they discussed would never be made public. The following year Fallaci died of the cancer she had been battling for decades. Until the end the legal cases against her were still coming, and the debate around Italy's Cassandra quietened for a few years until events brought her books back to life again.

In the year Fallaci died the new Pope himself came into conflict with the force she had excoriated. Pope Benedict did not issue a Fallaci-like screed. Instead, in the course of a speech on 'faith and reason' at the University of Regensburg he merely quoted a single sentence from the Byzantine emperor Manuel II Palaiologos: 'Show me just what Mohammed brought that was new, and there you will find things only evil and inhuman, such as his command to spread by the sword the faith he preached.' Before reading this quote Pope Benedict did say that the phrase had 'a brusqueness that we find unacceptable'.[31] In doing so he reiterated that he was quoting. Nevertheless, the word went around the world that the Pope had insulted Islam. There were riots across the Muslim world and a 65-year-old Italian nun was murdered in Somalia. Protests and riots over the cartoons of Mohammed published in Denmark a few months before were already a common occurrence. Now they were joined by other riots and protests about the Pope. The fact that everybody, from Europe's most devout atheists to the head of the Catholic Church, was simultaneously falling foul of the same forces still seemed not to be enough of a warning.

9

Early-warning sirens

Other sirens were going off across Europe. In the early 2000s in Holland and then Norway the gay American author Bruce Bawer began to grow worried that increasing numbers of gay men of his acquaintance in Europe's most liberal cities (including Amsterdam) were being beaten up by Muslim men. Bawer had left his native country in the 1990s partly because of what he saw as the rise in the influence of Christian pastors who were virulently opposed to gay rights. In Europe, Bawer began to notice that there was a different type of cleric, from a different religion than the one he was used to, who didn't just think that gays shouldn't be allowed to marry but thought that they should be thrown from tall buildings. Like Pim Fortuyn, Bawer started to wonder why a society that prided itself on its liberalism seemed to be worrying about offending Muslims more than it worried about protecting gays. Islamic homophobia – an issue that had barely occurred to the gay press, much less to the mainstream press – began to get a tiny airing. But the gay-rights groups that had been so virulent in their attacks on the Catholic and other Christian churches seemed willing not only to sit out this sharper problem, but to attack people like Bawer for raising the facts. In two books and many articles he attempted to highlight the oddity of liberal societies going quiet on such bigotry just because it was coming from a community of immigrants. A set of competing victimhood narratives appeared to exist, Bawer showed, but gays were being trumped in that narrative by Muslims.

Like every other early-warning siren Bawer was considerably defamed for his trouble, often by the liberal gay press and others who might have been expected to heed his call. He was just one more demonstration of the fact that when the messenger was not actually shot, he or she was in other ways silenced as much as possible.[1] But throughout the first decade of the century it was the early-warning sirens on blasphemy and free speech that finally became most audible on the front line.

The publication of a set of cartoons of Islam's prophet in a small-circulation Danish newspaper – *Jyllands-Posten* – demonstrated one flashpoint of the era. The 'cartoon crisis' was another demonstration, like the Rushdie affair sixteen years earlier, that the issues brought about by mass migration would continue to surprise Europeans. If a Dane in the 1990s had said that the story which would bring most attention to their country in the next decade would most likely be a 'cartoon crisis' (a phrase people increasingly uttered with a straight face), people would have thought the person unhinged.

Yet that 'crisis' was kicked off in 2005 when an editor at *Jyllands-Posten* learned that a Danish children's publisher could not find any cartoonist willing to contribute cartoons for the volume on Islam in a series of children's books on the world's religions. Startled that such a taboo should exist in a free society, the newspaper tested whether that taboo was breakable. They showed that it was, but at a great cost. As well as leading to riots and embassy-burnings across the Muslim world, there were also protests by Muslims throughout Europe. In London protesters outside the Danish Embassy held signs saying 'Freedom go to hell', '7/7 is on its way' and 'Behead those who insult Islam'. After several thwarted attempts on the life of Kurt Westergaard, one of the Danish cartoonists, an axe-wielding Muslim trained by al-Shabaab in Africa entered the cartoonist's house on New Year's Day 2010 in an effort to decapitate him. A safe-room that Westergaard had been persuaded to install in his home was the only thing that saved him. This soon became the new normal in Europe. In the wake of the Danish affair, 'cartoon crises' started breaking out across Europe.

In 2006, in Norway, the editor of the Christian paper *Magazinet* chose to reproduce the Danish cartoons to show his readers what all the fuss was about. The Norwegian Prime Minister, Jens Stoltenberg, not only criticised the paper's editor, Vebjørn Selbekk, for doing so, but threatened him with prosecution. When a mob burnt down the Norwegian Embassy in Damascus the Prime Minister claimed that Selbekk was jointly responsible for the outrage. Other political and cultural figures lined up to attack the 'provocation' and lack of respect shown by the paper, while Selbekk himself was forced to go into hiding and receive police protection.

The next year a cartoon crisis broke out in Sweden when the artist Lars Vilks drew a picture of Mohammed and was chased into hiding. As with the *Jyllands-Posten* cartoonists, in the years that followed there were multiple terrorist efforts to kill him. In 2011 the offices of the French satirical magazine *Charlie Hebdo* – one of the only publications to reprint the Danish cartoons – were firebombed in Paris. In 2013 the Danish journalist and historian Lars Hedegaard – a prominent critic of Islam – was visited at his door in the morning by a gunman who fired two shots at his head. The 70-year-old survived because the assassin's gun jammed on the second bullet. Hedegaard managed to punch the man, who subsequently ran off, finding sanctuary in Turkey.

These were only some of the attacks that happened in the period from 2005 onwards. But there were many more to come. On 7 January 2015 the assassins got lucky at the offices of *Charlie Hebdo* in Paris, managed to get past the building's security, kill the bodyguards assigned by the state to protect the editor, and massacred most of the editorial team in their place of work. As well as years of threats to their lives for depicting the Prophet of Islam, the editors of *Charlie Hebdo* had also spent years being dragged through the French courts by the Muslim organisations of France. The month after the massacre at *Charlie Hebdo* – on 15 February – a meeting in support of the Swedish cartoonist Lars Vilks that convened in Copenhagen was attacked by a 22-year-old Danish-born gunman. As with the Paris attacks the previous month, the killing spree began with the cartoonists and ended up at a Jewish site – in Paris at a kosher supermarket, in Copenhagen at a synagogue.

There seemed to be no end in sight to such legal and physical attacks and so nobody flinched in 2015 at a passing mention in a piece in *The Atlantic* magazine to 'Europe's endless, debilitating blasphemy wars'.[2] Despite a couple of decades of warning, from the Rushdie affair onwards, no one in any position of authority or power had predicted this wave of events. No one who had opened up the borders of Europe to mass migration from the third world had ever thought about it as a Muslim issue. No one had prepared for the possibility that those arriving might not only not become integrated but might bring many social and religious views with them, and that other minorities might be the first victims of such lack of foresight. No one in a position of influence had expected that an upsurge in immigration would lead to an increase in anti-Semitism and gay-bashing. No one who had ever nodded through the lax immigration policies had ever predicted the emergence of Muslim blasphemy as one of the major cultural and security issues of twenty-first-century Europe. All those who had warned about it had either been ignored, defamed, dismissed, prosecuted or killed. Rarely, if ever, even after the facts changed, did the actual victims receive much sympathy.

What mainstream politicians and much of the media had in fact done, right up to and throughout the 2000s, was encourage a sense that the people in Europe who were shouting 'fire' were the actual arsonists. Efforts to silence the people who raised their voice – whether through violence, intimidation or the courts – meant that three decades after the Rushdie affair there was almost no one in Europe who would dare write a novel, compose a piece of music or even draw an image that might risk Muslim anger. Indeed, they ran in the other direction. Politicians and almost everybody else went out of their way to show how much they admired Islam.

Of course, in the aftermath of large-scale terrorist attacks – in Madrid in 2004, London in 2005, Paris in 2015 – governments had to do something and had to be seen to be doing something. Most proved able to address the specific counter-terrorism aspects of the problem. But they remained hopeless prisoners of their own and their predecessors' policies and continued to be caught in a language game entirely of their own invention. In June 2007 two car bombs were left in the centre of London by a doctor in the NHS and another Muslim who was a PhD student. The first device was left outside a popular nightclub on 'ladies night'. This nail-packed bomb was placed outside the glass frontage. The second car bomb was placed down the road from the first, to blow up people fleeing from the first blast. Fortunately, a passerby noticed smoke coming from the first car and both bombs were discovered before they could detonate. The new Labour Home Secretary, Jacqui Smith, said that it would be wrong to describe such attacks as 'Islamic terrorism' because these terrorists were in fact behaving contrary to their faith. Henceforth, she said, it would be more appropriate to describe such events as 'anti-Islamic activity'.[3]

Six years later, after another two British Muslims had hacked to death Lee Rigby, a drummer with the Royal Regiment of Fusiliers, in broad daylight in Woolwich, London, a Conservative Prime Minister (David Cameron) emerged onto the steps of Downing Street and announced, 'This was not just an attack on Britain – and on our British way of life. It was also a betrayal of Islam – and of the Muslim communities who give so much to our country. There is nothing in Islam that justifies this truly dreadful act.'[4] The next year, responding to the beheading of a British aid worker in Syria by a British-born jihadist, the same Prime Minister said, 'They claim to do this in the name of Islam. That is nonsense. Islam is a religion of peace. They are not Muslims; they are monsters.'[5]

The media also tried hard not to address what had happened. The day after Lee Rigby was murdered on the streets of London by two Koran-quoting converts, Britain's *Daily Telegraph* – the main broadsheet of the centre-right – took the Cameron line. One columnist claimed that 'The man with the bloodied knife who spoke into a video camera at Woolwich had no discernible agenda … none of it made sense.'[6] Another writer at the same paper wrote, 'For me, yesterday's barbaric act of terror in Woolwich was literally senseless. None of what happened actually made any sense ... There were knives and helicopters and guns and bodies. It just didn't make any sense.' There followed a long list of things that had happened at the scene which the author claimed also made no sense. 'He'd said "our lands". But he had a south-east London accent. And that didn't make any sense ... None of it made any sense. None of it.' The author grandiosely concluded that, 'Yesterday was the senseless day.'[7] At the other end of the political spectrum political commentary in *The Guardian* suggested that what had happened was simply 'a mundane act of violence'.[8]

Like the politicians, most of the media across Europe throughout these years showed very little desire either to understand or say publicly what might be going on. For the press the causes were obvious: a combination of fear, cowardice and an internalisation of the threat. The politicians meanwhile could not face up to the problem because they were responsible for introducing it into Europe. Throughout all the decades that had gone before almost no one had considered the ideologies or beliefs of the people who were coming or showed much curiosity in doing so. Politicians and the media in general minimised the differences between Islam and any other faith. And all the time they insisted that the solution to the problem, if it did exist, was to bind the future of European societies to the future of Islam, in backing 'the moderates' so that a 'reformed Islam' could prevail. This, the politicians insisted, would solve the problem both for Europe and for Islam as a whole. They appeared to have no awareness of the fact that from the Mu'tazilites in the tenth century to the Iranian Ali Dashti in the twentieth century, Islamic history had witnessed many reform movements and many reform-minded individuals, all of which had been defeated by the force, arguments and appeals to authority of the fundamentalists. What European politicians were doing during this period was tying the future of Europe's security to a reform movement that had failed throughout history and was at the very least likely to fail again. Still they remained undeterred in their pursuit of this argument. In a speech to the Conservative Party Conference in 2014 the then British Home Secretary, Theresa May, did what every politician was doing, which was to stress the peacefulness of Islam and to quote some of her favourite verses from the Koran. Having witnessed the forcefulness with which many Muslims were willing to defend their faith, it appeared to become the attitude of the political mainstream to pretend that the religion of Islam was at least partly true, and a source of wisdom and guidance. By 2016 one of Angela Merkel's key allies, the German Finance Minister Wolfgang Schaeuble, was calling for the creation of a 'German Islam'.

The career paths of those who took a contrary view did not flourish in the same way. In Holland, after long periods of having to live in army barracks and government safe-houses, Ayaan Hirsi Ali was finally allowed by the Dutch security service to live in a specially protected building in Holland. But her new neighbours sued to get her to move away from them, so fearful were they for their own lives with this trouble-maker so nearby. Soon afterwards, based on untrue claims made by a television station, the Minister of Immigration and Integration of Hirsi Ali's own party, the VVD, withdrew her citizenship. The country that had allowed in hundreds of thousands of Muslims without expecting them to integrate, and which harboured some of the most radical preachers and cells in Europe, withdrew citizenship from one of the only immigrants who actually showed what a fully integrated immigrant to Holland would look like. Hirsi Ali moved to America, becoming, as Salman Rushdie subsequently put it, 'maybe the first refugee from Western Europe since the Holocaust'.[9]

Europe seemed for a time to have come to the conclusion that the problems of extremism would go away if the people who pointed to them went away. Yet whether the critics were killed, chased into hiding or chased from Europe, the problem did not go away. Not least, of course, because the immigrants stayed and had no intention of going anywhere. Many heeded the explicit as well as implicit advice in the countries they had come from to remain in Europe but not to become European. At a rally in Cologne in 2008 Prime Minister (later President) Erdoğan of Turkey told a crowd of 20,000 Turks living in Germany, Belgium, France and the Netherlands:

'I understand very well that you are against assimilation. One cannot expect you to assimilate. Assimilation is a crime against humanity.' Nevertheless, he told his audience that they should get involved in politics and gain influence so that the five million Turks then living in Europe would be able to wield 'a constitutional element' and not just be 'guests'.[10]

In 2016 in Amsterdam, as in many other European cities, there are suburbs that are Muslim enclaves. On a sunny day the buildings in these areas look no worse than in any other European suburb, indeed, most of the houses are of a kind that most young couples in Western Europe would struggle to afford as a first step onto the housing ladder. This is where the Turkish guest-workers congregated from the time that they migrated to the country sixty years earlier. Today, like many other parts of the suburbs of Amsterdam and Rotterdam, these suburbs comprise mini-Turkeys and mini-Moroccos. The food shops are Halal. The women all wear some form of head covering and life goes on much as it would if the people were in Turkey or Morocco. One of the houses, in a row on a quiet, pleasant street, is where Mohammed Bouyeri lived – the house from which he set off that morning a decade ago to find Theo van Gogh and slaughter him. It is not an especially threatening area. It is simply a different area. There are election posters in many of the windows, all showing the face of Recep Tayyip Erdoğan.

10

The tyranny of guilt

In the first days of September, when the body of the three-year-old Syrian boy Aylan Kurdi washed up on a beach in Turkey, the reaction in Europe was almost unanimous. It was, as several newspaper headlines put it, 'Europe's shame'. When it was reported that the Kurdi family had been looking to join family in Canada and had already had one visa application there turned down, Aylan Kurdi's death became an issue in North America. Some campaigning for the following month's general election in Canada was suspended. Political opponents of the Stephen Harper government that was then in office made significant capital out of Canada's alleged failure to save the life of the three-year-old. The Harper government lost the subsequent election.

This general feeling of guilt and shame spread across Europe and North America and pushed aside all practical questions of precisely what could have been done for the Kurdi family or all the other families that might wish to come after them. So great was this outpouring of guilt that several pertinent facts were lost entirely. Not least among them was the fact that the Kurdi family had set out from a safe country – Turkey. The father had chosen to leave that country – where he had paid employment – to get his family into Europe. The body of his young son had washed up not on a European beach but on a Turkish beach. And though there was some media mourning in Turkey over the tragedy, there was not anything there remotely like the introspection and self-accusation indulged in by Western politicians and media.

Although parts of the wider Arab and Muslim world also lingered on the tragedy, it led to nothing like the policy challenge that this presented in the West. Indeed, the tragedy highlighted at least one extraordinary disparity not just between European and Middle Eastern reactions but between European and Middle Eastern asylum attitudes. For although Lebanon, Jordan and Turkey had taken in huge numbers of refugees from the wars in neighbouring Syria and Iraq, and received substantial financial support from the international community for doing so, the attitude of the wider Middle East to such humanitarian crises, never mind to the multiple additional human-itarian and economic crises across Africa and the Far East, stood in total opposition to that of European governments and media. Where European countries took the drowning of a three-year-old on their own consciences, the Arab world from which the boy came – and the wider Muslim 'ummah' – remained strikingly unmoved to action.

For instance, the six Gulf Cooperation countries comprising Kuwait, Bahrain, Qatar, the United Arab Emirates, Saudi Arabia and Oman had granted asylum to a grand total of zero Syrian refu-gees by 2016. Their attitude towards refugees from Eritrea, Nigeria, Bangladesh and Pakistan was not even as generous as that. Only a few months before Aylan Kurdi's death one Kuwaiti official, Fahad al-Shalami, explained in an interview on France 24 why Gulf coun-tries like his were refusing asylum even to Syrian refugees: 'Kuwait and the Gulf countries are expensive, and are not suitable for refu-gees,' he explained. 'They are suitable for workers. The transportation is expensive. The cost of living in Kuwait is high, whereas the cost of living in Lebanon or Turkey is perhaps cheaper. Therefore it is much easier to pay the refugees [to stay there]. At the end of the day, you cannot accept other people, who come from a different atmosphere, from a different place. These are people who suffer from psycholog-ical problems, from trauma.' You cannot just place them in the Gulf societies, he explained.[1]

Such an attitude is not surprising. Al-Shalami was simply trying to protect his society from the problems he believes it would inherit if very large numbers of refugees entered. What is strange is that the default attitude of Europe is to agree that the Gulf States and other societies are fragile, whereas Europe is endlessly malleable. Nobody in Europe blamed Turkey or Oman for the death of Aylan Kurdi. And while the Spanish Prime Minister Mariano Rajoy said of another migrant boat sinking in the Mediterranean, that Europe risked 'damaging our credibility if we are not able to prevent these tragic situations', few people claimed that Arab or African credibility was at stake. Indeed, throughout the Syrian portion of the refugee crisis alone, next to nobody blamed the countries actually involved in that civil war – including Iran, Saudi Arabia, Qatar and Russia – for the human cost of the conflict. There was no wide European call for Iran to take in the refugees from the conflict, anymore than there was any pressure to insist Qatar take its fair proportion of refugees.

There are many political and strategic assumptions that lie beneath such a failure. But there is also a moral self-absorption that overrides it all. And that moral self-absorption did not begin with the refugee crisis. Rather it is one of the underlying themes of all of contemporary Europe – a unique, abiding and perhaps finally fatal sense of, and obsession with, guilt.

In April 2015, after another migrant boat had sunk in the Mediterranean, the Swedish MEP Cecilia Wilkstrom stepped up her existing campaign for migrants to be given 'legal and safe' routes into Europe. The failure to do so, she insisted, would be compared by future generations to the Holocaust. 'I think that my children and grandchildren are going to ask why more wasn't done to help people running away from Isis, or violence in Eritrea or wherever, when we knew that people were dying in their thousands. People will ask the same question they did after the war, "If you were aware, why didn't you do something?" In Sweden we allowed our railroads to be used to transfer Jews to Nazi death camps. There are more refugees in the world today than during and after the Second World War. The world is on fire at the moment and we need to cope with that.'[2]

In Germany politicians did not need to be so explicit. All Germans listening would know precisely what it was that Angela Merkel was referring to during her big announcement of 31 August 2015 when she said, 'The world sees Germany as a land of hope and chances. And that wasn't always the case.' It was a reference that resonated with them and which they felt was relevant. In those crucial days of late August there had been protests outside a refugee centre and an arson attack on a facility for migrants in the east German town of Heidenau. When the Chancellor subsequently appeared in town she was roundly booed and heckled by the crowds. Other Germans watched this in horror and were ready to act to show a different side of their country. In the first days of September hundreds of thousands of people were crossing from southern Europe up through Serbia, Hungary and Austria, and into Germany. And as the Chancellor threw her country's doors open these countrymen took up the challenge. At the borders and at train stations like Munich and Frankfurt crowds of hundreds of people gathered to welcome the arriving migrants.

This footage went around the world. Here were crowds of Germans not merely offering assistance to the migrants as they arrived, but giving them what often looked like a welcome party. Migrants who had travelled across at least one continent looked dazed and often jubilant as they walked into crowds of Germans applauding and cheering them on all sides. The welcoming committees waved balloons and banners with slogans like 'Welcome' and 'We love refugees' on them. As the trains came into the stations and the migrants got off and went through the crowds some locals wolf-whistled and gave them high-fives. Human chains of volunteers handed out food and gifts, including sweets and teddy bears for the children. It was not just an expression of the *Willkommenskultur* ('welcoming culture') that Germany says it likes to practise. These migrants were not merely being welcomed. They were being celebrated, as though they were the local football team returning triumphant, or heroes returning from a war. Among the recipients of this greeting, some got into the spirit, raising their hands or punching the air as they passed through this guard of honour.

This spirit did not only affect Germans. People came from across Europe to take part in this effort and the historical parallels were explicit everywhere. Two students from Britain went to the Austrian-Hungarian border with a car to ferry migrants into Munich. Interviewed by the media one said, 'We're here because seeing scenes on television the thought belongs to the 1940s and because the historical parallels here are so reminiscent of things like the underground railway. And you just like to ask yourself what would you have done then, and I would like to say I would have helped, which is why we're here today.'[3]

This parallel was not confined to those around Germany. Second World War parallels were breaking out throughout Europe. In Denmark migrants were already pouring across the Øresund bridge to Sweden by train. They did not need passports because there was no border. But not everyone found this to be a powerful enough image. During the war, when the Nazis ordered the deportation of Jews from Denmark, local Danish resistance to the Nazis famously and heroically spirited nearly all of Denmark's 8,000-strong Jewish community across the water to neutral Sweden in the dead of night. And so it was that in September 2015 a 24-year-old Danish politician by the name of Annika Holm Nielsen began transporting migrants in her yacht across the five-mile stretch of water between Copenhagen and the Swedish city of Malmö. A man called Abdul who had come up from Germany and whom she met in Copenhagen's Central Station was ferried by her across the choppy waters in a trip that was inevitably compared in the media to the actions of the Resistance in 1943. Nielsen herself denied that this was something 'symbolic' and insisted that it simply seemed 'the safest thing to do'.[4]

Never mind that Abdul's onward journey to Sweden would have been safer, swifter and more comfortable if Ms Nielsen had simply allowed him to get on the train to Malmö like everybody else, during September 2015 'gestures' like this fitted the narrative. It was a narrative that many people forming the welcoming parties at the train stations of Germany stated explicitly: that this was in some way a remedy for what had happened in the 1930s and 1940s. The almost hysterical behaviour of the crowds radiated a sense of not just relief but ecstasy – that here were people migrating into Germany rather than migrating out of it. Instead of being a country people fled from because their lives were in danger, Germany had become a place where people escaping war and persecution were actually fleeing to.

Of course, there were several very serious problems with this. The comparison between the migrants of 2015 and the Jews of the Nazi era breaks down in several places. Firstly, the Jews who fled Hitler were desperate for any other country to live in. Germany's 2015 arrivals had walked through numerous countries – including European ones – before arriving in Germany. Secondly, although large numbers of Syrians, among other migrants, certainly were fleeing for their lives, to compare all of these migrants – including the economic migrants – with the Jews of the 1930s was not just to diminish the suffering of the exiles from Hitler's Germany. It was to insist that Europe had absolutely no choice other than to take in everybody who wanted to come. To not do so was to be a Nazi.

Whether they knew it or not, the Germans and others who crowded onto the streets and platforms of their country to celebrate these new arrivals were taking part in a historical process far beyond them. Even this emotional act came, when needed, with the same intellectual ballast as every other argument in post-war immigration. Among those interviewed on the television news a number explained that because of Germany's demographics and labour shortages it 'made sense' for the country to bring in these hundreds of thousands of new people. But these rationales appeared to be secondary. They were explanations to back up a decision that had already been taken. The original instinct of a section of the population and their political representatives was the more significant one, and just the latest and most visible expression of a historical burden that many Europeans felt themselves to be carrying.

THE STAIN OF EUROPE

Contemporary Europeans may not be the only people in the world to feel they have been born into original sin, but they certainly appear to suffer from the worst case of it. Today's Europeans expect

themselves, long before anybody else raises it, to bear specific historical guilt that comprises not only war guilt and Holocaust guilt, but
a whole gamut of preceding guilts. These include, though are by no
means limited to, the abiding guilt for colonialism and racism. And
although all of this adds up to a hefty burden, it is no longer one
we are expected to bear alone. In recent decades the same blackmail from history that has afflicted modern Europe has also been
assumed by a group of noticeably homogeneous nations. What is
striking is that all of the other countries expected to suffer for the
same sins are countries for whose creation Europe is blamed, so that
the impression appears to be that the stain of the Europeans criss-
crosses the whole world.

Whereas for contemporary Europeans, colonialism is just one
of our middle-ranking, midway sins, for Australians colonialism
has become the nation's founding, original sin. And not because
like European nations it stands accused of having plundered other
countries in its search for wealth, but because it stands accused of
plundering itself – of being a colonialist project still sitting on its
colony. For Australia colonialism is said to have started at home.
Today's Australian schoolchildren are taught that whatever its present virtues, their nation was founded on genocide and theft. The fact
that those original colonial forces were also white and European
makes the act unsurpassably worse than it would be were the story
the equally familiar one of dark-skinned peoples taking land from
other dark-skinned peoples. The conquering of one group by another
and the ill-treatment of the losers by the victors is the story of most
nations on earth. But for Australians the historic treatment of the
Aborigines and other 'first peoples' is a subject that has in recent
decades moved from the margins of public debate to the core – to
the country's deepest, founding sin. Strangely, this narrative of guilt
seems actually desired and welcomed by Australian society.

As with anything that people truly desire, some inflation of the
truth is bound to occur along the way. And so in Australia the policies
of missionaries and officials in removing some Aboriginal children
from their parents (the 'stolen generation') has even been promoted

to a 'genocide'.[5] It has been the focus of numerous popular books, films, government inquiries and repeated apologies from politicians including prime ministers.[6] Rebuttals are hard to introduce because even the most extreme claims are welcomed whereas their contradiction is only taken as evidence of the culprit's ongoing denial and racism. As a consequence, all that appears left open for discussion in Australia today is what degree of compensation ought to be distributed to Aboriginal communities for this historic hurt. The cumulative effect of this ingrained guilt has caused a palpable change in the world's impression of Australia and in the country's image of itself, from a generally sunny and optimistic place to one that has become palpably darker, not to mention mawkish about its past.

In recent years this has expressed itself in such popular acts as the 'Sea of Hands' displays in which hundreds of thousands of citizens have sponsored and signed a plastic hand in Aboriginal colours to be placed on the lawn in front of public buildings, including the Parliament in Canberra. Another ritual in which people have taken part by the thousand is the signing of names in national 'Sorry Books'. Since 1998 there has also been an annual 'National Sorry Day' in Australia.[7] Naturally, like all original sins, the one for which Australians are continually being invited to apologise could not conceivably be corrected. Many of the people who now live in Australia may be descended from Europeans and other settlers, but they themselves thieved no land and stole no generation. If they inherited any land, they did so without oppressing or usurping a soul. And although the economic and employment opportunities of the country's Aborigines may still lag behind that of other Australians – and by a very long way – this resurrects an insuperable conundrum. For now, as in the past, Australians desiring to 'correct' their policies towards the Aborigines cannot square the circle of how to 'preserve' indigenous lifestyles without encouraging or forcing them to enjoy exactly the same lifestyle as everybody else – in the process wiping out their culture.

The Australian vogue for self-blame is no longer unusual. Indeed the 2008 apology by Prime Minister Kevin Rudd to the indigenous people of Australia happened within months of a similar apology to the indigenous peoples of Canada given by that country's Prime Minister, Stephen Harper.[8] Both apologies were widely welcomed as demonstrating a statesmanlike atonement for a painful period of history. Few dissenting voices were listened to, and even the historical record seemed for a time incapable of being honestly assessed. In Canada, as in Australia and in all similar cases, the desire to talk up the scale of the crimes being apologised for should have been some giveaway. Anybody standing before a real court for real crimes who boasts of having performed worse crimes than those for which they were on trial would be deemed unfit to stand trial. Yet if one is not really in the dock or guilty oneself, but merely speaking for dead predecessors, perhaps the tendency towards hyperbole grows. For present-day politicians there are only political points to be scored from such statements, and the larger the sin the larger the outrage, the larger the apology then the larger the potential political gain for sorrow expressed. Through such statements political leaders can gain the benefits of magnanimity without the stain of involvement: the person making the apology had done nothing wrong and all the people who could have received the apology are dead.

This is a mania, clearly. A specific and common European mania. The political calculus appears to be that making such statements is an entirely cost-free exercise. Except that it isn't. Because nations whose leaders appear to be constantly offering up apologies for their country's history may finally appear (in a world in which such apologies are prodigious from some countries yet entirely absent from others) to be nations that have special cause for such guilt. If Australia is forever opening up and apologising for its own past while China remains silent, the impression may eventually be instilled, in children in Australia as much as anywhere else, that Australia is the country with more to apologise for. And while upgrading big historical mistakes into genocides may be cost-free for polemical scholars and ambitious politicians, they focus an impression of wrongdoing that may eventually burrow not only into the world's view of a particular nation but deep into that nation's view of itself.[9]

Beyond an appropriate level of historical humility what can actually be achieved by the extremes of such a tendency? Even if Australia had been born in sin, there is nothing that can be done to rectify it, other than – centuries after its founding – for everyone in Australia to be divided out by race and those believed to have descended from the earliest settlers ordered to hand over their wealth to anyone believed (after appropriate genetic testing) to be descended from indigenous peoples. The genetic codes of those of mixed race would perhaps be adjudicated by a genetics court, which – depending on the findings – might then order people to give up some wealth, get a cash windfall or keep a precise amount, depending on their DNA tests. If theft is the crime then restitution is the only possible punishment.

Absenting such an unlikely conclusion the interim agreement appears to be that Australians can continue to reside in Australia so long as they live in a state of perpetual remorse, an attitude supplemented by regular tribute to Aboriginal culture, including Aboriginal art and the generalised depiction of indigenous culture as possessing some especial purity or truth that can then be compared unfavourably with contemporary Australia. In recent years this trope has developed into Australia's version of the 'noble savage' myth.[10] This portrays what went before the present as better or purer even where it was demonstrably worse. It depicts as sympathetic those behaviours that would ordinarily cause people to abandon sympathy. It is a fashion of romantic primitivism that may have come to fruition in modern Australia, but does not only exist there. Another country that can now be blamed as an export of the Europeans is the one that, by economic standards, is also the most successful country on earth.

For several centuries after he landed somewhere in the Bahamas, Christopher Columbus's 'discovery' of America was thought to be a good thing and Columbus himself celebrated for his heroic deeds. Four centuries after his arrival immigrants to America were still putting up statues to him raised by public subscription.[11] By the five-hundredth anniversary of the event, in 1992, the calculus had changed. Columbus was no longer the discoverer of America: he was in fact the destroyer of America. America was now increasingly filled with people who seemed to wish he had never discovered the country in the first place. Columbus himself had been turned from a successful explorer and adventurer into a colonialist and, of course, a genocidist.

A rash of books published to coincide with the quincentenary made the obligatory claim that the actions of Columbus were in fact the progenitors for the actions of the Nazis. 'On the way to Auschwitz the road's pathway led straight through the heart of the Indies and of North and South America', was how one author put it.[12] Another popular author wrote a book called *The Conquest of Paradise*, which presented pre-Columbus America as literally and metaphorically a garden of Eden. It was a place in which man and nature were claimed to have lived together in perfect harmony. The country that Columbus had brought into being, by contrast, was so appalling that it now looked set to be responsible for 'the likely destruction – of the earth'.[13]

In the years that followed in America, everything to do with Columbus came up for review. Even the national Columbus Day holiday came under attack. Today numerous cities, starting with Seattle and Minneapolis, have legislated to rename 'Columbus Day' as 'Indigenous Peoples Day', presenting an opportunity to focus on the people who were in America before Columbus. As one descendant of indigenous peoples told the local radio in Oklahoma City when they were going through this debate, 'This is something that I've struggled with for a long time. The fact that our country, our state and our city celebrate this holiday around this man who murdered and enslaved and raped indigenous people and decimated an entire population.'[14] Of course, none of this had happened in her lifetime, nor the lifetime of anybody who she had ever known.

Once again both perpetrators and victims are dead and there are few if any ways to alleviate such sentiments. Although one option is, as in Australia, to play into those agrarian myths and romances that feature around the world but have such a niche in Western post-industrial societies. These see the establishment of modern civilisation as having not merely wrecked once-beautiful landscapes but as having filled hitherto unsullied human beings with the deadliest sins of human greed. It is a vision that was encapsulated, though not invented, by Jean-Jacques Rousseau, but has taken on a particular popularity in the late twentieth and early twenty-first century. According to this reckoning, it is Europeans who, when they travelled and colonised around the world, became the Eden-destroying species.

Among the sins that Europeans are now accused of having spread around the world is the sin that constitutes the founding sin of America: slavery, and through slavery, racism. To say that American presidents have been apologising for these for decades is an understatement. The country fought and won a civil war over the issue nearly two centuries ago. Nevertheless, on a visit to Uganda in 1998 President Clinton made yet another fulsome apology for the slave trade. If he or anyone among his advisors thought that this would put the matter to rest, they could not have been more wrong. Despite slavery having involved at least as many people at the Ugandan end of the chain as at the American end, the idea that people of European descent alone should feel continuous guilt for the actions of their forebears is now embedded, and helpful to everyone other than those of the guilty nation. In the last couple of decades, as the situation for American blacks has slowly improved, the rhetoric of shame has only increased. America has had black Secretaries of State of both parties, black Supreme Court Justices and a black President, but even in Barack Obama's second term there were ever louder demands for 'reparations' to be paid to all black Americans. Indeed, the argument got more mainstream than it had in generations.[15] As though to prove that nothing can ever truly be done to alleviate the sins of the past, during the sixth year of Obama's presidency it became mainstream thinking to believe that the actions of the ancestors of many white Americans should cause their descendants to give most black Americans a cash settlement for acts carried out centuries earlier. The question of reparations to other ethnic groups who had suffered historic wrongs did not become part of the ensuing debate. Only

Europeans and their descendants remember guilt. So only Europeans and their descendants have continuously to atone for it.

In America, as in Australia, such a constant drumbeat of guilt changes a people's natural feelings about their own past. It transforms feelings of patriotism into shame or at the very least into deeply mixed emotions, and troubling effects result from this. A country that believes it has never done any wrong is a country that could do wrong at any time. But a country that believes it has only done wrong, or done such a terrible, unalleviated amount of wrong in the past, is likely to become a country that is inclined to doubt its ability to ever do any good in the future. It makes a country nervous about itself whatever the wisdom of its actions. Embedding the idea of original sin in a nation is the best possible way to breed self-doubt. National original sin suggests you can do little by way of good because you were rotten from the start.

A final country also widely 'blamed' on the Europeans and so often regarded as having the same 'original sin' is the state of Israel. Since its founding in 1948, its founding 'sin' has only grown louder. Never mind that the creation of Pakistan, within the same year as the creation of Israel, brought forth unimaginable massacres and necessitated the forced movement of millions of people, the movement – and occasional expulsions – of thousands of Palestinians in order to create the State of Israel in 1948 has become the 'original sin' of the world's only Jewish state. As the years passed, an Arabic term was popularised for this: *nakba*, or 'catastrophe'. Very few states have ever been created without the movements of people. Many created in the twentieth century (Bangladesh, for instance) witnessed movements of people and bloodshed far exceeding anything seen in every succeeding decade combined since the creation of Israel. But today it is Israel that is continuously alleged to have been born into this 'original sin'. The citizens of Pakistan or Bangladesh may blame things on the British, but they themselves would never be expected to feel guilt as all Europeans and their descendants are.

Of course, in the case of Israel (the state being comparatively new) the most extreme suggestions for how to remedy this situation can seem more plausible. Whereas few people seriously call for every-one of European descent to be expelled from the Americas, it is not unusual (indeed it is policy in many Middle Eastern countries) for there to be calls for the descendants of Europeans to be expelled from Israel and for the land to be 'returned' to the sole ownership of the Arab tribes who originally lived there (and in many cases live there still). And although Middle Eastern history is perhaps even more than most a history of tribes and people usurping and replac-ing each other without recourse to any court of historical inquiry to make amends, when it comes to the Palestinian 'indigenous people' there is alleged to be an answer. And that is because the cause of the victimhood can be traced back to the Europeans. As anybody who has travelled in the region will know, the most benevolent view in the region of how the State of Israel came about is that the Europeans did something wrong in the Holocaust and now the Arabs are having to pay for it.

Australia, America and Israel are three very different countries on three wholly different continents all united by Europe. The settlers in America came from Europe. The settlers in Australia came from Europe. And although half the population of Israel are Jews who had to flee Arab lands, the Jews of Israel are widely believed to come solely from Europe. So it is not persecution-mania but simple obser-vation for Europeans to fear that the uniting 'evil' in all of these cases, among many others, is not just people in history who did bad things, but Europeans who did bad things. And who – considering a people who did so many bad things and on such a scale – could not suspect that they were in fact simply bad people?

It is understandable if modern Europeans feel themselves to have a certain toxicity. Almost alone among all the peoples of the world, Europeans seem capable not only of doing terrible things in their own continent, but of spreading their evils around the world. And as the evil metastasizes it is also generalised. There are few worse intel-lectual crimes in Europe than 'generalising' or 'essentialising' another group of people in the world. Yet generalising and essentialising are allowed to become rife when the world speaks about Europeans. A

European would be scolded for blaming every African for the crimes of every other African, or any Asian for the crimes of any Asian. But generalisations and a spreading around of historic European faults and crimes onto Europeans as a whole is normal and acceptable.

So in a debate over Western culture even in London it is not at all surprising to hear speakers telling their audiences that 'we' – not only in Europe but across the West – bear responsibility for Nazism and the Holocaust.[16] The fact that a London audience is more likely to be descended from – and may well include – people who fought against Nazi Germany (rather than bearing any complicity or responsibility) becomes background detail if not overlooked altogether. The world can generalise away about the West, and Europeans in particular, so long as the generalisation relates to the lowest points of the West's history. And while any honest student of history must conclude that every community, race and group of humans is not only capable of doing terrible things but has managed to do such things, what a particular entity or era decides to focus on tells you a great deal. Just as telling is what is not focused on and what does not get much meaningful attention.

DOUBLE STANDARDS AND THE TRIUMPH OF THE MASOCHISTS

The Ottoman Empire was one of the largest and longest sustained empires in world history. For more than six hundred years it ruled a vast swathe of land, imposed Islamic religious and cultural ideas on those whom it governed, and by its own system of laws punished those who stood against it. It pushed into south-east Europe, the Middle East and North Africa by military force, and only because of the strength of a coalition of European armies at the battle of Vienna in 1683 did Europe avoid Ottoman rule.

In the wake of the First World War, of course, the empire fell apart. But while it did so it committed one of the worst atrocities in history and the first actual genocide of the twentieth century. The destruction of the Armenian population of Anatolian Turkey saw the massacre of more than a million people in a couple of years. Hundreds of thousands more were made stateless. In 1973, five decades after Turkey's empire fell apart, Turkey invaded a European nation state, Cyprus. Occupying half of the island, its armies slaughtered Greek Cypriots and drove others from their homes. The occupation continues to this day, despite Turkey being a member of NATO and the southern Greek portion of Cyprus being a member of the EU. One might concede that Turkey, as a historical force, has been no worse, if certainly no better, than any other country in the world. Who has not carried out an actual genocide, run an empire for twice as long as the British and invaded a sovereign nation in recent decades? This is not what is striking. What is striking is that so little of this is ever raised and Turkish people are rarely if ever made to feel guilt for Turkey's historic role in the world.

In part that is because Turkey's government ensures this is the case. One of the reasons why modern Turkey is a world leader in imprisoning journalists is because under Article 301 of the country's penal code it is a crime to 'insult the Turkish nation'. Any mention of the Armenian genocide breaks that law and sees the violator sent to prison. And although a contingent of Greek Cypriots continue to complain about the ongoing occupation of the northern half of their country, this has never precluded the British government among others from continuing to call for Turkey to become a full member of the European Union.[17]

Perhaps it is unsurprising that the Turkish government has never apologised for the excesses of the Ottoman Empire. And perhaps it is unsurprising that the country still forbids by law any mention of its recent history of occupation and ethnic cleansing. What is more surprising is that so few people would use these things against the Turks as a people. If the kind of history now taught and internalised in much of Europe is intended simply to prevent a replay of the worst aspects of that history, then we should ask who else should be treated in this way. Which other nations ought to be encouraged to feel shame for their past? And if no others do, relying not only on natural pride but also outlawing historical inquiry, does Europe not find itself in the strange situation of feeling unusually guilty for being only ordinarily so?

The problem is worse. For if historical wrongs must lead to atonement in the present day, then what is the statute of limitations and to whom else may it apply? As with the 'empire strikes back' theory, it is often stated or implied that Europe must suffer any and all consequences of mass migration because it is part of a process of atonement for historical wrongs. Yet if mass migration is in part an atonement for historical wrongs such as imperialism, why do we not treat modern Turkey in such a way? Should Turkey be a country that also deserves to be altered completely? If so, where should we encourage the waves of immigration to come from? Should all Turks not happy with this process be shut down with cries of 'racist'? And when, if ever, should a halt be called to the process? Indeed, if we were at a stage of imposing 'diversity' on people for historical wrongs, why should such 'diversity' not be imposed on Saudi Arabia? Why should Iran not be forced to atone for its history by having minorities from around the world encouraged to head towards it? Since all countries, peoples, religions and races have done something terrible in their time, and since most races and cultures are not punished in this way, why should one not see a specific anti-Western and in particular an anti-European motive behind these recent movements? A curious and disturbing idea lies behind this.

For if the concept of historical guilt means anything, it means that a hereditary stain of complicity can be said to pass down from one generation to another. It is true that for many centuries, because of a single verse in the Gospels, some Christians held the Jewish people accountable in just such a way.[18] And it took until 1965 for a Catholic Pope to formally lift this historical burden.[19] But in this and almost every other such case the modern age views this descendant-blaming as morally repugnant. The case of the Jews is especially disturbing because it suggests how long such a vendetta can last. The guilt with which modern Europeans now find themselves burdened, by contrast, only began in recent decades. It is a pathology of the late twentieth century onwards. So perhaps it could – like the Christian idea of the hereditary guilt of the Jews – continue for another couple of millennia. Yet even then it is hard to see how it could be lifted.

First, because so many Europeans seem to want it to continue. Guilt, as the French philosopher Pascal Bruckner has diagnosed it in his book *La Tyrannie de la pénitence*, has become a moral intoxicant in Western Europe.[20] People imbibe it because they like it: they get high on it. It lifts them up and exalts them. Rather than being people responsible for themselves and answerable to those they know, they become the self-appointed representatives of the living and dead, the bearers of a terrible history as well as the potential redeemers of mankind. From being a nobody one becomes a somebody. In 2006 Britain threw up a particularly curious example of this type in the form of one Andrew Hawkins.

Mr Hawkins is a theatre director who discovered in mid-life that he was a descendant of a sixteenth-century slave-trader called John Hawkins. In 2006 he was invited by a charity called 'Lifeline Expedition' (which organises trips to 'heal the past') to go on a 'sorry' trip to Gambia.[21] The upshot was that Hawkins joined 26 other slaver descendants in June of that year who paraded through the streets of the capital, Banjul, with chains around their hands and yokes about their necks. As they walked to the 25,000-seater sports stadium Hawkins and the other participants also wore T-shirts with the words 'So Sorry' on them. Weeping and on their knees the group apologised in English, French and German to about 18,000 people in the stadium before being ceremonially 'freed' of their chains by the Gambian Vice-President, Isatou Njie-Saidy.[22]

It might be fair to say that to take part in such a ceremony is to demonstrate a psychological as well as a moral affliction. Mr Hawkins and his friends were lucky to meet such benevolent recipients of their apology tour as the largely bemused Gambians in front of whom they thrust themselves. Not everybody is so benign before the Western habit of self-flagellation. Many years ago, during one of the not infrequent breakdowns in peace talks between the Israelis and the Palestinians, a journalist was interviewing Yasser Arafat in his offices in Ramallah. Towards the end of the interview one of Arafat's male assistants came into the Chairman's office to announce that the American delegation was here. Wondering whether he had stumbled upon a scoop the journalist asked the Chairman who the Americans in the next room were. 'They are an American delegation who are doing a tour of the region to apologise for the crusades,' said Arafat. Then he, and his guest, burst out laughing. They both knew that America had little or no involvement in the wars of the eleventh to thirteenth centuries. But Arafat, at any rate, was happy to indulge the affliction of anyone who believed they had and use it to his own political advantage.

The desire to continue to feel yourself guilty arguably finds its end point in modern European liberal societies: the first societies in human history who, when they are hit, ask what they did to deserve it. For unassuageable historical guilt carries over into the present. It makes Europeans the guilty party even when they actually are hit, or worse. Several years before the latest surge in the migration crisis a left-wing Norwegian politician called Karsten Nordal Hauken (a self-described 'feminist', 'anti-racist' and heterosexual) was brutally raped in his own home by a male Somali refugee. His attacker was subsequently caught and convicted with the help of DNA evidence. After serving his sentence of four and a half years the attacker was scheduled for deportation back to his native Somalia.

In a subsequent piece for the Norwegian media Hauken described the guilt that he felt for this. Indeed, he said that his first instincts were that he felt 'responsible' for his rapist's return to Somalia. 'I had a strong feeling of guilt and responsibility,' he wrote. 'I was the reason that he would not be in Norway anymore, but rather sent to a dark uncertain future in Somalia.'[23] It is one thing to try to forgive your enemies. But it is another thing entirely to be brutally raped and then worry about the future living arrangements of your rapist. Perhaps masochism is a thing that always afflicts a certain number of people at any one time. Perhaps the masochists, like the poor, will always be with us. But a society that rewards those with such tendencies, and indeed tells people with such tendencies that their tendencies are not just natural but a demonstration of virtue, is a society likely to produce a higher concentration of masochists than most.

Of course all masochists, however large or small in number, have one unique problem they must always confront, which is what happens when they meet an actual sadist – when they meet someone who says, 'You think you're miserable, terrible and with no redeeming features? Well, we agree.' There may be no lack of masochists today, in Europe and in the countries for which Europeans feel partially responsible. But there is also no shortage of sadists, willing to reinforce and push upon us every idea we foster about our own wretchedness. And this is the other reason why – for the time being – existential guilt remains a one-way street. Most people do not want to feel guilty and do not want others to accuse them of being so, let alone those with ill intent towards them. Only modern Europeans are happy to be self-loathing in an international marketplace of sadists.

While the Western and European nations have been lacerating themselves and expecting the world to lacerate them for the behaviour of their ancestors, no serious authority or government has recommended that any other people should be held responsible for the hereditary crimes of their people. Not even for crimes committed in living memory. It might be because there are few sadists in the West. Or more likely it is because there are not enough masochists in other countries for such a mission to have any chance of success. The Mongol invasions of the Middle East in the thirteenth century remain among the worst brutalities in recorded history. The massacres at Nishapur in 1221, in Aleppo and Harem and the sacking of Baghdad in 1258 not only saw the slaughter of hundreds of thousands of men, women and children, but the despoliation of unimaginable quantities of knowledge and learning. If we hear much of the Crusades and little of these brutalities today it is not only because the idea of tracing Mongol descendants and blaming them would be difficult, but because no Mongol descendants would be receptive to the idea of being blamed for the atrocities of their forebears.

Only the nations of Europe and their descendants allow themselves to be judged by their lowest moments. But what makes this

self-laceration more sinister is that it should go on at the same time as
Europeans are expected to treat everybody else only by their highest
moments. While it is common enough to hear the Spanish Inquisition
or the Crusades brought up in any debate on religious extremism,
it is equally common to then hear once again about Andalusia or
the Islamic neo-Platonists. It cannot be a coincidence that these two
things – judging ourselves by our worst moments and everyone else
by their best – have gone hand in hand. It is a demonstration that
what is going on in the West is a political as well as a psychological
affliction.

Nevertheless, although modern European guilt is currently
described as though it is a terminal condition, there is no certainty
that it will be. Will young Germans, the grandchildren, great-grand-
children and eventually great-great-grandchildren of those people
who lived through the 1940s always feel the taint of their heredity?
Or is it possible that at some point there will come a moment when
young people who have done nothing wrong themselves say 'enough'
with this guilt? 'Enough' of the feelings of subservience that such
guilt forces upon them, 'enough' of the idea that there is something
uniquely bad in their past, and 'enough' of a history they were never
a part of being used to tell them what in their present and future
they can or cannot do. It is possible. Perhaps the guilt industry is
a mono-generational phenomenon, to be replaced by who knows
what?

11

The pretence of repatriation

In 1795 Immanuel Kant wrote of his preference for states over 'universal monarchy'. For as he recognised, 'the wider the sphere of their jurisdiction, the more laws lose in force; and soulless despotism, when it has choked the seeds of good, at last sinks into anarchy.'[1] This view was not shared by the politicians who ruled Europe over the last quarter of a century. 'Borders,' proclaimed the European Commission President, Jean-Claude Juncker, in August 2016, 'are the worst invention ever made by politicians.' If it was at least arguable whether politicians had actually 'invented' borders, by the time Juncker made this statement it was obvious that politicians were certainly able to make borders disappear.

In 2015, when Angela Merkel opened a door that was already ajar, the arrangements within the continent certainly favoured the views of Juncker over those of Kant. Anybody coming into Europe during that year would discover that once inside Europe there were no more borders. From 1995 onwards, twenty-six countries signed up to the Schengen Agreement that created a border-free zone. From Portugal, Spain, Italy and Greece in the south all the way up to Sweden, Finland and Estonia in the north by way of Hungary, Slovakia, Austria, France and the Netherlands, this agreement meant that more than 400 million people within Europe had the right to move freely across the continent without even having to show a passport. One condition was that the member countries had common responsibility for policing the external borders. But otherwise – with the exception of the United Kingdom, and five other smaller EU states, which refused to involve themselves in Schengen – the continent became from 1995 onwards one vast, borderless zone. It was a dream of European harmonisation and integration.

The Schengen Agreement was intended to augur a new era of peace and unity. It seemed hard to imagine the disadvantages of such 'free and unrestricted movement of people, goods, services and capital'. It was good for trade and it was good for a Frenchman who wanted to go to Brussels for the evening. Whatever the downsides, the Schengen Agreement was not just about the practical ease of travel that it ushered in but about the message it gave out. If ever there was a continent whose population could be persuaded that borders were the problem it would be Europe. One interpretation of the twentieth century is that twice in just twenty-five years the whole continent had gone to war over borders. In 1914 and again in the late 1930s the issue of borders had heralded the catastrophe of a continent. If these conflicts in which Europe twice lost a generation of its young men had indeed been caused by the existence of borders, then who would not wish to abolish them? In the same way that if the nation state is the cause of war, then who would not wish to get rid of the nation state?

Among the flaws in this argument are the misguided ideas that borders rather than German militarism caused the First World War (among a range of complex factors) and that anything but Nazi aggression caused the Second World War. It might be convenient for some, not least some Germans, to adopt alternative explanations, but blaming borders for the wars of the twentieth century is like blaming cars for all traffic accidents. If borders can sometimes cause conflict it does not follow that without borders the world would be without conflict. After all, before the wars of the nation states in Europe, the continent was wracked by wars of religion.

But the flaws in the Schengen Agreement lay not only in the presumptions it made about history. The terrible flaw in Schengen was the way in which its principles were practised. For instance, although member states committed to cooperate in policing the outer borders of the continent, in reality the task was left to the front-line states. Throughout the late 1990s and 2000s Italy, Spain and Greece were abandoned to deal with the inflow alone. Even after the creation of the EU border-force Frontex in 2004, the southern states continued to bear the burden. As an exasperated Italian Interior Minister, Angelino Alfano, had to remind his counterparts during the Lampedusa crisis in 2014, 'The Mediterranean border is a European border.'

But it was not only the burden of policing the borders for the whole continent that stretched the Mediterranean countries during this period. These were also the three (to date) iterations of the Dublin Regulation on asylum, an EU-wide agreement that was instituted from the 1990s onwards. The aim of the several versions of the Dublin Regulation was to ensure that the EU member state in which a migrant requested asylum was the state that was legally compelled to process that application. In theory it was meant to prevent multiple applications by migrants or their shuttlecocking between states. In practice the Dublin Regulation put the onus on the southern states. Given that the boatloads of people with or without documentation were arriving to claim asylum in Italy and Greece rather than Holland or Germany, the Dublin Regulation gave countries like Italy and Greece only a few potential options.

They could feel impelled to process the asylum applications of every migrant who landed. Or they could encourage migrants not to apply for asylum where they landed but instead to head north to find their way to other member states, applying for asylum once there. As of Dublin III (which came into force in 2013) the country where fingerprints and asylum claims are stored is the state compelled to see through the asylum process and offer asylum. With thousands of people arriving in southern Europe every day, by the time this iteration came in it seems extraordinary that the northern states seriously expected the southern states not to try to find ways to get around this commitment. One way in which they did so was by ensuring that the country of arrival did not take the fingerprints of all the new arrivals. If they did so then they would be compelled to see through the rest of the process and potentially offer asylum. Far easier to push the migrants north, undocumented, un-fingerprinted and unidentified. The number of people this happened to is unknown and unknowable, but front-line workers privately admit to it happening all the time. So Dublin III, which was meant to make the process clearer, in practice incentivised states not to participate in the system at all.

What is more, migrants coming in 2015 knew that if they gave their fingerprints they would have to stay in the country they were in, and so the migrants themselves increasingly refused to provide them. The Italian and Greek authorities could not force them to do so, and as the flow increased both migrants and the southern states had similar reasons not to follow the procedures. If a migrant had expressed a desire to head to northern Europe, it was better for Greece and Italy not to fingerprint them than to do so. Otherwise both migrant and country of arrival would have been faced with another asylum procedure in a country that did not want them and where the migrant did not want to be.

The Dublin Regulation, like the Schengen Agreement, turned out to be appealing when migration into the continent was at what had by then become normal levels. But they were catastrophic when migration became the biblical phenomenon it turned into in 2015. Everywhere, feelings seemed to be overriding reality. The German Chancellor, who only a few months earlier had explained to the Lebanese girl that 'politics was hard', was reported to have been 'touched' by a group of Albanians, Syrians and Iraqis filmed at the train station in Budapest on 1 September as they shouted 'Germany, Germany, Merkel, Merkel'. Later, as she went to greet arriving migrants in person, Merkel smiled, looking relaxed and happy, as she posed for selfie photos with them taken on their camera phones.

By then there were numerous possible routes. From Greece migrants would travel through Macedonia and then north on up through Serbia. From Serbia they could either keep going straight up through Hungary and then Austria until finally arriving in Germany, or make it to the same destination by going through Bosnia, Croatia, Slovenia and Austria. Those hoping to travel from Italy to Germany or the northern European states had the choice of either heading out of Italy by moving north and then west, past Genoa and through Ventimiglia and other routes along the coast to France. Or they could go to the other side of Italy and cross the Italian-Austrian border.

By early September 2015 the Hungarian authorities among others announced that they were overwhelmed by the numbers being encouraged to come and declared the situation in their country to be out of control. The Hungarian government tried to prevent the influx by stopping trains from leaving Hungary for Germany. Around 14,000 people were arriving in Munich each day. Over the course of a single weekend 40,000 new arrivals were expected. The German Chancellor had her deputy spokesman announce that Germany would not turn refugees away. And so the migrants headed off on foot along the motorways and train tracks of Hungary. The world watched as huge columns of mainly male migrants surged up through Europe. It was then, during the autumn of 2015, that the European dream of a borderless continent began to end. Having spent decades bringing the borders of Europe down for Europeans, the influx of this unknown number of non-Europeans meant that the borders of Europe began to go back up again.

Hungary, among other states, was singled out for criticism by the German Chancellor and the heads of the EU for appearing to revert back to national boundaries. But the country had been under a considerable strain not of its own making. In 2013 it had registered around 20,000 asylum seekers. In 2014 that number doubled to 40,000. During the first three months of 2015 Hungary had more people arrive in the country than in the whole of the previous year. By the end of the year the police had registered around 400,000 people. These migrants, almost all heading to Germany or Scandinavia, were entering Hungary from Serbia or Croatia at the rate of up to 10,000 a day. Most of them were people who had come through Greece and who should have been registered there. Hungarian authorities believed that perhaps one in ten of the total number of people moving into their territory had been registered in the correct way in Greece. As the Hungarians saw it, the Greeks had simply failed to comply with the Schengen Agreement and EU law.

By July the Hungarian government had begun constructing a protective fence along the Serbian border. This meant that the flow across the Croatian border increased. And so they constructed another fence along that border. The flow then moved further along, concentrating on the Slovenian border. These fences hundreds of kilometres long were the only way in which the Hungarian government could stem the numbers. They were roundly condemned by the Austrian government among others. Yet soon everybody was at it. In August, Bulgaria began building a new fence along its border with Turkey. In September, Austria imposed controls on its border with Hungary while Germany temporarily introduced controls at its border with Austria. When the German Interior Minister, Thomas de Maizière, announced on 13 September that his country would reintroduce border controls, nobody seemed to know who he was speaking for. Even people within the German government seem to be aghast at what their Chancellor had set in motion.

In the middle of September, Hungary declared a state of emergency and closed its border with Austria. Then Croatia closed its border with Serbia. Soon Austria began the construction of a barrier along its border with Slovenia. How was this Austrian fence different from what the Hungarians had put up? According to a shamefaced Austrian government, the difference was that their border fence was 'a door with sides'. Soon Slovenia was constructing a fence along its border with Croatia while Macedonia began constructing a barrier along its border with Greece. By this point the European Commission itself was urging the Macedonian authorities to seal their border with Greece on behalf of the whole EU, effectively forcing Greece unilaterally out of the Schengen area.

Every action in Berlin set off a chain reaction across the continent. The arrival of hundreds of thousands of people, many of whom had no way to provide for themselves, had wholly predictable consequences. Some of them were practical – how to house, clothe and feed all these new arrivals. In Germany the government began to threaten the owners of empty buildings with state-enforced requisition unless they were rented out to the government to house the migrants. Across the wider continent there was a growing concern about who the people coming actually were. Hungarian officials estimated that around half of their arrivals in early 2015 were from the western Balkans, notably Kosovo. Like everywhere else, most of the migrants had no papers. Around half of those waiting at Keleti railway station in Budapest claimed to be Syrian, but officials and volunteers who asked them questions about Syria often discovered that the migrants knew little or nothing about the country. Again, as with everywhere else, the vast majority of people (always more than 60 per cent) were young men.

Even Chancellor Merkel appeared now to be worrying about what she had set in motion. Both she and President Hollande of France pushed ahead with the only solution that could take some of the growing pressure off Germany. The two of them – with the European Commission – attempted to persuade every member of the EU to take in a quota of migrants. Yet from Britain to Hungary, the member states refused. One reason they did so was that they could see that the numbers they were being asked to take did not reflect the actual figures. The European Commission and Merkel were trying to persuade countries to sign up to a quota system that was already inadequate for dealing with the numbers which had already arrived.

Governments that were refusing to do the bidding of Merkel and the European Commission were also reflecting the will of their people. A solid two-thirds of Hungarians polled during this period felt that their government was doing the right thing in refusing to agree to quota numbers issued from Brussels or Berlin. And yet one of Hungary's most famous sons disagreed. The billionaire financier George Soros spent considerable sums of money during 2015 on pressure groups and institutions making the case for open borders and free movement of migrants into and around Europe. As well as a website called 'Welcome2EU', his Open Society foundation published millions of leaflets informing migrants of what to do. These informed them of how to get into Europe, what their rights were once there, and what the authorities could and could not do. The group openly advocated 'resistance against the European border regime'.

In October 2015 the Hungarian Prime Minister, Viktor Orbán, criticised Soros publicly as one of a circle of activists who 'support anything that weakens nation states'. Soros responded publicly to confirm that the numerous groups he was funding were indeed working for the ends described by Orbán. In an email to *Bloomberg*, Soros said that it was his foundation which was seeking to 'uphold European values', while he accused Orbán of trying to 'undermine those values'. Soros went on to say of Orbán: 'His plan treats the protection of national borders as the objective and the refugees as an obstacle. Our plan treats the protection of refugees as the objective and national borders as the obstacle.'[2] The dialogue ceased before anyone could ask Soros how long those European values might last once Europe could be walked into by people from all over the world.

But then the argument changed. The media across the globe were already describing Europe as 'buckling' under the strain of the new arrivals when, on the evening of Friday 13 November, Paris was rocked by three hours of coordinated terrorist attacks. Gunmen in a car using assault rifles drove by and shot at Parisians as they were eating and drinking in bars and restaurants. At the same time suicide bombers struck at the Stade de France stadium in Saint-Denis where President Hollande was among the crowd watching a football game. As well as further shootings and a suicide bombing at more restaurants, three gunmen entered the Bataclan theatre concert hall on the Boulevard Voltaire. While more than a thousand people were listening to a heavy-metal concert the attackers started firing assault rifles and gunned down as many people as they could. They lined up the wheelchair users in the disabled section of the theatre and shot them one by one. Elsewhere they roamed through the building hunting down people where they lay wounded or hiding. One young woman who survived wrote afterwards: 'As I lay down in the blood of strangers and waiting for my bullet to end my mere 22 years, I envisioned every face that I have ever loved and whispered I love you, over and over again, reflecting on the highlights of my life.' The men continued to shoot people throughout the theatre until the police arrived, at which point the gunmen detonated suicide vests.

By the end of the evening in Paris 129 people had been killed and many hundreds more were wounded.

The Islamic State in Syria claimed responsibility for the attacks. As with every previous terrorist attack in Europe, the continent held its breath and pondered the worst-case scenario. In time it transpired that the culprits were from France and Belgium. But after the attack one of the ringleaders had been able to safely return to Belgium. Of equal significance was that one of the Stade de France suicide bombers had a fake Syrian passport in the name 'Ahmad al Mohammad'. Officials admitted that a person of this name had entered Europe as an asylum seeker the month before the attacks. Fingerprints turned out to match a man who had been using that name to enter Greece in October. The person using the name had been picked up by Greek coastguards at the beginning of that month on a sinking boat filled with 70 other migrants. In November he appeared to have travelled from the Isle of Leros, through Serbia, Croatia, Austria and Hungary and finally to Saint-Denis. Although the news emerged exceptionally slowly, by a year after the attack it was clear that the majority of the Paris attackers, including the ringleaders, had not only been to Syria to receive terrorist training, but had slipped in and out of Europe whilst posing as migrants.

Any public appetite for such porous external borders began to diminish. So too, once the news of the terrorist cell's free movements in and out of France on the night of the attack, did the appetite for an entirely borderless continent within Europe. Yet two days after the Paris attacks Jean-Claude Juncker insisted at a press conference in Antalya, Turkey, 'There are no grounds to revise Europe's policies on the matter of refugees.' He went on to explain that the Paris attackers were 'criminals', not 'refugees or asylum-seekers', adding, 'I would invite those in Europe who try to change the migration agenda we adopted. I would like to remind them to be serious about this and not to give in to these basic reactions which I do not like.' Whether he liked it or not, public and political attitudes were shifting. If the advantages for a Parisian heading to Brussels for the night had always been obvious, people were now also recognising the risks of a system that allowed a Belgian Muslim to head to Paris for the evening, and return home later the same night, unharassed. The Paris attacks accelerated a process of swift reversal that was already underway. Norway hastily began to change its asylum policy, and within a fortnight of the events in Paris even Sweden announced that it would henceforth be introducing checks at its borders. From now on people entering the country would need to show some form of identification. This was announced as though nobody had ever heard of such a thing before. As Sweden's Deputy Prime Minister, Åsa Romson of the Green Party, made this announcement, she broke down in tears.

For his part, President Hollande announced that France was at war 'at home and abroad'. The country immediately stepped up its bombing campaign against Isis positions inside Syria. But the abroad part was the easy bit. The hard part was the home bit. A state of emergency was immediately declared and continued indefinitely. In the aftermath of the attacks the French police carried out 168 raids in two days across the country. A raid in Lyon turned up a rocket-launcher. A raid in Saint-Denis culminated in a woman blowing herself up with a suicide vest. One of the Bataclan bombers turned out to live in the shadow of Chartres Cathedral. As in the aftermath of the previous January's attacks on the offices of *Charlie Hebdo* and the kosher supermarket, French politicians were aware that this was a moment when there was a specific security concern on voters' minds. But they were also aware that the French public might well be dwelling on deeper issues to do with how their country had ever arrived at such a situation.

Less than a fortnight after the attacks Manuel Valls, the French Prime Minister, said that France would not accept more than 30,000 asylum seekers over the next two years. After a meeting with Chancellor Merkel in Paris, Valls pointedly announced, 'It was not France that said "Come!"' Whereas Chancellor Merkel continued to insist on the importance of sticking to a quota system for each country, Mr Valls told journalists, 'We cannot accommodate any more refugees in Europe, that's not possible.' His office later said that there had been an error in translation and he had intended to say that Europe could no longer take 'so many refugees'.

As in Britain and other European countries, the French public were right to be sceptical of such rhetoric and pronouncements. On everything to do with immigration and integration they had heard the same thing for decades. As the percentage of the population that was foreign-born continued to grow every year, French politicians like their counterparts across the continent had competed to sound tougher than each other on the matter. Throughout the 1970s and 1980s Valéry Giscard d'Estaing, François Mitterrand and their colleagues had vied with each other to sound as though they were each more stern than the other on these issues. In 1984 Jacques Chirac, then the mayor of Paris, had publicly warned, 'When you compare Europe with the other continents, it's terrifying. In demographic terms, Europe is disappearing. Twenty or so years from now our countries will be empty, and no matter what our technological power, we shall be incapable of putting it to use.'

In 1989 it was a socialist Prime Minister, Michel Rocard, who said in a television interview on the matter of asylum that France 'cannot welcome all the misery of the world'. Rocard went on to boast of the number of people he said his government had turned away and vainly promised more expulsions in the years ahead. Just like Mitterrand before him, Rocard played what was by then a clever electoral manoeuvre of the French left ahead of elections. All these pronouncements were part of a political game. Few of them had any impact in reality.

In 1985, when Jean Raspail and Gérard Dumont had written their piece asking what France would look like in 2015, the French left under François Mitterrand was in disarray. Its move from highly socialist to more free-market economic policies had been a political disaster, alienating the unionised class who formed their largest constituency. The left was already fractured between the socialists and Georges Marchais's communists, and in the run-up to the 1986 parliamentary elections it looked as though under the Fifth Republic's electoral system the left would be unable to win. President Mitterrand's experience as a minister in the Fourth Republic had trained him in electoral manoeuvring, and so in the mid-1980s he formulated a plan to neuter the right and capture the presidency in the 1988 election.

The plan consisted of getting the socialist Parliament to pass a new electoral law based on proportional representation and ensuring that immigration became a huge issue.

At this moment Jean-Marie Le Pen and his anti-immigration National Front party proved exceptionally helpful to Mitterrand who ensured that Le Pen – who had previously been kept to the farthest margins – was given as much exposure as possible. For the first time Le Pen began to get regular invitations to appear on television and was encouraged to air his views. The flip side was that a socialist-organised anti-racist movement ('*Touche pas à mon pote*') would also be given maximum exposure. In the process Mitterrand arranged that a damaged left created a damaged right. He knew that the National Front could only hurt the right and cause votes to run the other way, and that no party of the right could ever form an alliance with the National Front or even now dare to move closer to the National Front's line on immigration, national identity and patriotism. If they did so, Mitterrand knew that they too would be branded as fascists, racists and betrayers of the values of the Republic.

Mitterrand's plan worked so well in 1986 and 1988 that it remained the strategy of the left throughout the years that followed. In each election a strong showing for the National Front remained the best way to keep the right out of power and to ensure that the right could do little more than nod to concerns on immigration and identity without becoming toxic. All the while Mitterrand and his successors on the left stressed how tough they were going to be on immigration. Yet all the time the migrant communities of France grew in numbers. Eventually politicians of the mainstream right also tried to make their names by sounding tough on immigration.

In 1993, while a minister with responsibility for immigration, Charles Pasqua had announced that France would close its borders and that France would become a 'zero immigration' country. In 1993 he boasted of forthcoming crackdowns on illegal immigrants: 'When we have sent home several planeloads, even boatloads and trainloads, the world will get the message.' But it is doubtful that he believed this, even at the time. 'The problems of immigration are ahead of us and not behind us,' the same Charles Pasqua said a short time later, acknowledging that in the not too distant future the tens of millions of young people in Africa who were 'without a future' would be likely to want to head north.[3]

The French political debate throughout these years was both unique and utterly representative in Europe. Throughout those decades, in lieu of being able to deal with the larger issues thrown up by mass migration, the main parties of Western Europe concentrated on small, symbolic issues. Sometimes it was a boast. Sometimes it was a specially prepared 'crackdown' on illegal migrants. The thinking appeared to be that such issues would not only allow the politicians to look as though they were being especially tough on something, but would release a certain amount of public steam. The secular tradition of France made debates over how people dressed into particular touchstone issues.

So it was that the first headscarf debate in France emerged in 1989, when schoolgirls in the town of Creil, to the north of Paris, began to wear the headscarf to school and were banned from doing so by the school. In the ensuing debate the government of the day recommended that it was up to individual schools to decide on a policy towards headscarves. The matter returned in the 2000s when the growing visibility of the headscarf in French society and the need for government to be seen to be doing something led President Chirac (in 2004) to pass a law forbidding the wearing of conspicuous religious symbols in public buildings. The French state had not reached the decision to ban such symbols in public schools or courts because of greater numbers of French Jews wearing kippahs and Christians wearing small crosses on their necklaces. Rather, they reached this decision based on the increase in veiled women appearing in public. Recognising that the growth of the wearing of the headscarf symbolised an upsurge in conservative Muslim sentiment wherever it occurred, the French government drew the line firmly to try to stop a trend and decided that tangling up all other religions with it was a worthwhile sacrifice.

Several years later, in 2009, the people of Switzerland put down what they regarded as a worthwhile marker in a similar vein. The constitutional amendment that passed a ban on minaret construction in the country was put to a plebiscite by the Swiss government and approved by 57.5 per cent to 42.5 per cent. The following year Chirac's successor, Nicolas Sarkozy, had an opportunity to make full-face coverings into an issue. A bill was passed in 2010 that made it illegal to wear a full-face covering in public places such as streets and shopping centres. Finally, in the summer of 2016 a number of French towns banned the wearing of the so-called 'burkini' on their beaches. Although the country's highest administrative court suspended the ban, the issue of the burkini dominated the news of August 2016. One of the town halls to ban the garment (which exposes the face though not the body) was Nice. In its way this was a distillation of the French solution to the questions thrown up by mass immigration.

A month before the burkini ban in Nice, a Tunisian called Mohamed Lahouaiej-Bouhlel drove a truck into the crowds on the seafront as people celebrated Bastille Day. Eighty-six people were killed that evening on the Promenade des Anglais, and many more were wounded. Isis subsequently claimed that the terrorist had carried out the attack in a response to their call to carry out such attacks anywhere in Europe. The French government once again extended the state of emergency that had been in place in the country since the previous November, but it was typical that in the weeks after such an atrocity the loudest public debate was about an item of Islamic swimwear that had only been invented a decade earlier. It was tempting to get hooked on such comparative minutiae because all the bigger questions had become unanswerable. You may be able to stop people getting hold of Kalashnikovs but how do you stop them getting hold of trucks? And you may stop more extremists coming into your country, but what do you do with extremists who are already citizens?

12

Learning to live with it

The carnage in Nice was just the first of a set of attacks that occurred almost daily in the summer of 2016. The Monday after the Nice attack a 17-year-old asylum seeker called Mohammed Riyad pulled out an axe and a knife on a train in Bavaria, Germany, shouted 'Allahu Akbar' and started hacking at his fellow passengers. He seriously injured five people before he was shot dead by police. It transpired that the attacker had sworn allegiance to Isis. It also transpired that although he had claimed to be from Afghanistan when he had applied for asylum in Germany, recordings of him speaking suggested that he was in fact from Pakistan. If France was bad at discussing these matters, Germany proved worse than anywhere. In the public discussion that followed the train attack Germany's Green Party MP Renate Künast questioned why police on the train had killed the attacker rather than shooting to injure him.

The following day one Mohamed Boufarkouch shouted 'Allahu Akbar' ('Allah is the greatest') and stabbed a Frenchwoman and her three daughters (aged 8, 12 and 14) near Montpellier in France, apparently for dressing 'immodestly'. The perpetrator had been born in Morocco. A few days later the child of Iranian immigrants in Munich, Ali David Sonboly, killed nine people in a shooting spree beginning with seven teenagers in a McDonald's restaurant. His motives remain obscure. A couple of days later a Syrian asylum seeker used a machete to hack a pregnant woman to death in Stuttgart in what was reported to be a crime of passion. The next day another Syrian asylum seeker, Mohammad Daleel, was turned away from a music festival in Ansbach, Bavaria, because he did not have a ticket. It turned out that he was carrying a bomb packed with nails and screws, which he eventually detonated outside a wine bar. A little over 24 hours later two men shouting the name of Isis entered a church in Rouen during Mass, took the nuns and congregation hostage and slaughtered the priest, Father Jacques Hamel. A nun who was present said that the two 19-year-old killers – Adel Kermiche and Abdel Malik Petitjean – smiled as they slit the priest's throat with a knife, let him bleed to death, and recorded themselves chanting Arabic slogans over his dying body. The final words of the dying priest were 'Go away, Satan.'

Some of these attacks were carried out by people who had arrived in Europe during the migrant wave of recent years. Other attacks were carried out by individuals who had been born in Europe. The search for easy answers was as elusive as ever. Those people wishing to blame terrorism on the lack of integration strategies in Europe were at a loss to explain the sense in importing so many new arrivals to a continent so bad at integrating its earlier ones. Those who wanted to talk only about the recent migrant wave were at a loss to explain why even people born and brought up in Europe could carry out such attacks. Those who looked to explain the motives away found themselves struck by the sheer range of the targets. Those who believed that the staff of the rumbustiously secularist and anti-theist magazine *Charlie Hebdo* in some sense 'had it coming to them' in January 2015 could not explain what a priest saying Mass had done to deserve being slain at his altar eighteen months later. A 46-year old Parisian interviewed after the November 2015 Paris attacks inadvertently summed up the learning curve her society was on. In an unfortunate use of the word 'just' she said, 'Every Parisian has been touched by these attacks. Before it was just the Jews, the writers or the cartoonists.'[1]

If this was all terrible for Europe's view of itself and its future, it still had worse to discover. The terrorist attacks may have presented the public with the clearest reason for growing concern. But other equally and in some ways even more basic worries emerged over something that was perhaps even more unmentionable. Almost everybody could recognise a terrorist attack when it occurred, even though they might quibble over the causes. But alongside the growing security concerns that everyone began to agree needed addressing, another subject arose that nobody wanted to discuss and everybody was terrified of addressing.

Throughout the 2000s the question of sex attacks on local women by gangs of immigrants had been an open secret. It was something that nobody wanted to speak or hear about. There was something so base, and so rank somehow, in even mentioning it. Even to imply that dark-skinned men had a penchant for abusing white women seemed to so clearly originate from some odious, racist text that it appeared impossible firstly to even imagine that it might be happening, and secondly that it should be discussed. British officials were so terrified about even mentioning such crimes that every single arm of the state failed to respond over the course of years. When the same phenomena occurred on the continent, precisely the same concerns and problems were encountered.

Even to mention the fact in 2015 that most of the recent arrivals into Europe seemed to be young men was to court opprobrium. To question whether all these individuals might have brought modern views about women with them was unmentionable (precisely, as in Britain) because it seemed to speak to some base, racist smear. The fear of falling into a racial cliché or suffering accusations of racism prevented authorities and the European public from admitting to a problem that had spread across the continent. And the more refugees a country took in, the greater that problem became.

Even in 2014 in Germany the number of sexual assaults against women and boys was growing. These included the rape of a 20-year-old German woman in Munich by a 30-year-old Somali asylum seeker, the rape of a 55-year-old woman in Dresden by a 30-year-old Moroccan, the attempted rape of a 21-year-old German woman in Munich by a 25-year-old Senegalese asylum seeker, the rape of a 17-year-old girl in Straubing by a 21-year-old Iraqi asylum seeker, the rape of a 21-year-old German woman near Stuttgart by two Afghan asylum seekers, and the rape of a 25-year-old German woman in Stralsund by a 28-year-old Eritrean asylum seeker. While these and many other cases made it to court, many others of course did not.

Alongside the growth in cases of rapes of Germans came the increase in the number of rapes and sexual assaults in refugee shelters. During 2015 the German government was so short of accommodation to house the migrants that it was initially unable to provide segregated shelters for women. A number of women's rights groups wrote to the regional Parliament in Hesse telling it that the consequences of these shelter arrangements were 'numerous rapes and sexual assaults. We are also receiving an increasing number of reports of forced prostitution. It must be stressed: these are not isolated cases.' In the weeks that followed, rapes were recorded in refugee shelters across Bavaria. And as in Britain a decade before, the authorities were so worried about the implications of the facts that in a number of cases they were found to have deliberately covered them up. In Detmold, where an asylum seeker raped a 13-year-old Muslim girl, the local police remained silent about the assault. An investigation by *Westfalen-Blatt* claimed that local police were routinely covering up sex assaults involving migrants in case it gave ammunition to criticisms of the government's open-door policies. Nevertheless, rapes of children were recorded in numerous cities including at a facility in Bremen.

As the number of cases increased throughout 2015, the German authorities eventually could not hold back the growing number of reports of rapes against German women and boys by recent refugees. These included the rape of a 16-year-old girl in Mering, an 18-year-old girl in Hamm, a 14-year-old boy in Heilbronn and a 20-year-old woman in Karlsruhe. In a number of these cases – including the case in Karlsruhe – the police remained silent about the story until a local paper broke it. Countless other assaults and rapes were reported in Dresden, Reisbach, Bad Kreuznach, Ansbach, Hanau, Dortmund, Kassel, Hanover, Siegen, Rinteln, Mönchengladbach, Chemnitz, Stuttgart and other cities across the country.

Eventually, this unmentionable subject became so bad that in September 2015 officials in Bavaria began to warn local parents to ensure their daughters did not wear any revealing clothing in public. 'Revealing tops or blouses, short shorts or miniskirts could lead to misunderstandings', one letter to locals warned. In some Bavarian towns, including Mering, police warned parents not to allow their children to go outside alone. Local women were advised not to walk to the railway station unaccompanied. On a daily basis from 2015 onwards there were reports of rapes on German streets, in communal buildings, public swimming baths and many other locations. Similar events were reported in Austria, Sweden and elsewhere. But everywhere the subject of rape remained underground, covered up by the authorities and deemed by most of the European media not to be a respectable news story.

Unusually, in December 2015 *The New York Times* reported on the classes that Norway was offering migrants who volunteered to learn about how to treat women. These lessons were aimed at countering Norway's increasing rape problem by explaining to refugees that, for instance, if a woman smiled at them or dressed in a way that revealed some flesh, this did not mean they could rape her. These lessons to people who (in the words of one of the organisers) had never seen a woman in a miniskirt before, but only in a burka, confused some of them. One 33-year-old asylum seeker explained, 'Men have weaknesses and when they see someone smiling it is difficult to control.' In his own country of Eritrea, he said, 'if someone wants a lady he can just take her and he will not be punished.'[2] This clash of sexual cultures had been simmering across Europe for years, but it was an indelicate, noxious subject for the mainstream to discuss. Only on the last day of 2015 did it break out on such a large scale that it could no longer be ignored.

But even the events in Cologne on New Year's Eve 2015 leaked out slowly. To begin with, the mainstream media did not report the events, and only after several days and thanks to the blogosphere did the continent, let alone the rest of the world, learn what had gone on. On one of the busiest nights of the year, as the city was celebrating, crowds of up to 2,000 men sexually assaulted and robbed something in the region of 1,200 women in the main square outside the central railway station and cathedral of Cologne and in the adjoining streets. Soon it transpired that similar assaults had occurred in other German cities, from Hamburg in the north all the way to Stuttgart in the south. In the days after the attacks, as the scale and seriousness of the events sunk in, the police in Cologne and elsewhere strenuously attempted to conceal the identities of the culprits. Only when video and photographic evidence from the scenes were shared on social media and confirmed in the mass media did the police admit that the suspects were all of North African and Middle Eastern appearance. In Germany in 2016 as in Britain in the early 2000s, a fear of the consequences of identifying the racial origins of the assailants took priority over the police force's commitment to doing their job.

It was all part of a pattern that would be ongoing and seemingly interminable. Throughout 2016 the spate of rapes and sexual assaults spread to every single one of Germany's sixteen federal states. There were attacks literally every day, with most of the perpetrators never found. According to the German Minister of Justice, Heiko Maas, just a tenth of rapes in Germany are reported and of those that reach trial only 8 per cent result in a conviction. Moreover, several additional problems emerged from these cases, not least that there appeared to be a concerted official effort to suppress data about crimes where the suspects might be migrants. It was, as *Die Welt* finally admitted, a 'Germany-wide phenomenon'.[3] Just as in Britain a decade earlier, it transpired that German 'anti-racism' groups had been involved. In this case they had pressured the German police to remove racial identifiers from all suspect appeals for risk of 'stigmatising' whole groups of people.

There was also the curious problem – not confined to Germany – of some women and even girls who had been assaulted trying to conceal the identities of their attackers. One of the most striking cases involved a 24-year-old woman who was raped by three migrants in Mannheim in January 2016. She was herself half-Turkish and had claimed at the time of her attack that her assailants were German nationals. Only later did the woman – who was also a spokesperson for a German left-wing youth movement – admit that she had lied about the identities of her attackers because she did not want to 'help fuel aggressive racism'. In an open letter to her attackers she apologised to them and wrote:

> I wanted an open Europe, a friendly one. One that I can gladly live in and one in which we are both safe in. I am sorry. For us both I am so incredibly sorry. You, you aren't safe here, because we live in a racist society. I, I am not safe here, because we live in a sexist society. But what truly makes me feel sorry, are the circumstances by which the sexist and boundary-crossing acts that were inflicted on me, make it so that you are beset by increasing and more aggressive racism. I promise you, I will scream. I will not allow it, that this continues happening. I will not stand by idly and watch as racists and concerned citizens call you a problem. You are not the problem. You are not a problem at all. You most often are a wonderful human being, who deserves to be free and safe like everyone else.[4]

Germany was not the only country where such things occurred. In the summer of 2015 a young female activist working with the 'No Borders' movement at the Ventimiglia crossing-point between Italy and France was gang-raped by a group of Sudanese migrants. Her fellow 'No borders' activists persuaded her to keep the attack quiet in order not to damage their cause. When the woman did finally admit to the attack, they accused her of reporting her own rape out of 'spite'.[5]

Through all of this, in Germany as in the rest of Europe, it was often left to local authorities to try to find answers to the challenges that had come their way. They not only had to find available facilities but also to come up with suitable policies. A mayor in Tübingen addressed the problem of an upsurge of rapes of women and children in local swimming pools by appealing for more migrants to become swimming-pool attendants. As he wrote on Facebook, 'Our municipality has embraced a great prevention and integration measure. We have a Syrian lifeguard who can make known in Arabic and with authority what behaviour is allowed and what is not.'[6] The public also had to find answers to the problem that their politicians had presented them with – and in the certain knowledge that even were the policy to suddenly change, the effect on society was irreversible.

What, after all, can any government do once it realises that its policies have effects such as these? The German answer, as with the answers of governments across the continent for years, was to get on top of a specific part of the problem. Just as French governments had introduced the ban on headscarves, burkas or burkinis, the German authorities focused on the narrow issue of counter-terrorism. During the period before and after the migrant crisis their intelligence agencies maintained an impressive surveillance capability against people believed to be involved in the most radical movements. Compared to the French or the Belgians the ability of the Germans in this area was admired throughout Europe. But such success also kept the debate necessarily narrow. German politicians, as with counter-terrorism practitioners, focused on exceptionally limited questions, such as the so-called 'paths to radicalisation' that every country had discussed, but which became central to the German discussion. A bogus science grew up, while all the time policy makers missed the bigger questions beneath – questions that the general public had long been asking themselves. For the public seemed to know what the officials could not admit, which was that 'radicalisation' originated with a particular community and that as long as that community grew the 'radicalisation' would grow. There was after all a reason why the European country with the highest per-capita Muslim community – France – had suffered the largest number of attacks by 'radicals', whereas a country like Slovakia, for example, had suffered no such problems.

At such times, the gap between what the public can see and what the politicians can conceivably say, let alone do about it, became dangerously large. An Ipsos poll published in July 2016 surveyed public attitudes towards immigration. It revealed just how few people think that immigration has had a good impact on their societies. To the question, 'Would you say that immigration has generally had a positive or negative impact on your country', extraordinarily low percentages of people in each country thought that immigration had a positive effect on their country. Britain had a comparatively positive attitude, with 36 per cent of people saying they thought immigration had a very or fairly positive impact on their country. Meanwhile only 24 per cent of Swedes felt the same way and just 18 per cent of Germans. In Italy, France and Belgium only 10–11 per cent of the population thought that immigration had made even a fairly positive impact on their countries.[7]

Following such a migration surge, coming after decades of variations on the same theme, how could European governments expect to be listened to even as they spoke with great force and determination on the issues of immigration and integration? Aside from the fact that for a government like Germany's this would entail the repudiation of policies decided upon just months earlier, there is the problem that the rhetoric had long ago worn thin. It had been worn thin by politicians across Europe from both right and left – by Michael Howard and Gordon Brown, by Michel Rocard and Nicolas Sarkozy. Europeans had spent decades witnessing the gap between rhetoric and reality – the inflated claims and the simultaneous implausibility of those claims. They had even heard some 'send them back' rhetoric – ugly as it was – and realised it was no more true than any of the other claims.

Back in 1992 there had been an upsurge of illegal migrant boat-landings on the southern shores of Spain. It was government policy to return Moroccans who had entered Spain illegally, and deals with the comparatively friendly and helpful government of Morocco still held. But the government in Rabat refused to take back any non-Moroccans who had sailed from their shores. And although such illegals could be held in Spain for up to 40 days, they were then given their expulsion papers and expected to leave the country within a further 30 days. As in the years before and after, the vast majority stayed, expulsion papers or no expulsion papers. One reporter covering this in 1992 interviewed a 19-year-old from Algeria. Where would he be heading? 'I have lots of family in France,' he replied. And how would he get there? 'Across the mountains, of course.' He had mailed his passport on ahead to his relatives so it could not be confiscated on the way. Almost all the other people also being temporarily detained by the Spanish authorities were sub-Saharan Africans and all said that once they were released from detention they would head north.[8] Then as now the Spanish and Moroccan authorities announced new deals, frameworks and solutions. Then as now the ability of many officials on all sides to turn a blind eye to the trafficking, and a decision, once the migrants were in Europe, that it was easier to let them drift on up into the continent, made all such deals and solutions little better than meaningless.

The same story had played itself out across Europe. Even while he took immigration to country-changing levels Tony Blair had sometimes wanted to look tough on immigration. In 2000 there were 30,000 failed applicants for asylum in the United Kingdom – a third of the 90,000 who had applied for asylum in 1999. In that year only 7,645 failed asylum seekers had been removed from the country. The target was decided to be impossible to achieve and too divisive, politically difficult and financially costly to achieve.[9] For parties of the right – fearful as they were of the attribution of base motives – it remained even harder for them to get a grip on the problem. As a stunt in 2013 (under a Conservative majority government) the Home Office organised a number of vans with advertising posters along the sides to drive around six London boroughs where many illegal immigrants lived. The posters read 'In the UK illegally? Go home or face arrest', followed by a government helpline number. The posters immediately became politically toxic. The Labour Shadow Home Secretary, Yvette Cooper, described them as 'divisive' and 'disgraceful'. The campaign group Liberty not only branded the vans' message as 'racist' but also 'illegal'. After some months it was revealed that the pilot scheme had successfully persuaded only 11 illegal immigrants to leave the country voluntarily. The then Home Secretary, Theresa May, admitted the scheme had been a mistake and too 'blunt', and it was not repeated. Of course, the scheme had not been intended to genuinely persuade the up to one million illegal migrants in Britain to return home, but to reassure the rest of the population that their government was being tough. Subsequent efforts to arrest illegal migrant workers were met with fierce and forceful opposition on the streets by left-wing campaigners. That this was all a farce can be seen from the fact that Britain only has around 5,000 detention spaces available in the entire country and that enforced removals only ever reach around 4,000 a year: these comprise roughly equal thirds of prisoners, failed asylum seekers and immigration offenders.

Long before the height of the migration crisis officials had already given up on the idea of deportation even for most failed asylum seekers. So it was not surprising that, once the crisis was underway, even those in Europe without any legitimate asylum claim would expect to stay. As the implications of the crisis began to overwhelm them, in 2016 the governments of Germany and Sweden began to pretend that they had a system in place that would be able to process arrivals and applicants and work out who should stay and who should leave. Never mind that they had no reliable system for working out who had arrived, they did not even have success in dealing with those whose claims had been rejected. Mohammad Daleel, who carried out Germany's first suicide bombing outside the wine bar in Ansbach in July 2016, had registered as a refugee in Bulgaria and had been ordered to be returned there by the German authorities in 2014 and once again in 2016. As in Sweden where left-wing groups attempted to disrupt the removal of any failed asylum seekers, a politician from the left-wing *Die Linke* party admitted afterwards that he had intervened on Daleel's side to prevent his removal from Germany back to Bulgaria.

In August 2016 two Belgian policewomen in Charleroi were attacked in the street by a machete-wielding Algerian shouting 'Allahu Akbar'. The attacker turned out to have ties to Isis. In the wake of the assault the Belgian Secretary of State for Asylum, Migration and Administrative Simplification, Theo Francken, revealed that the attacker had been in Belgium since 2012. He had been issued deportation orders twice, but no repatriation understanding exists between Belgium and Algeria and no spaces existed in Belgium's secure detention facilities.

Such stories – of people known to be involved in terrorist attacks – are easy ones to identify. But the stories of the ordinary migrants who simply stayed and got forgotten about in the hundreds of thousands is the real story behind these headlines. In January 2016 two politicians revealed the true scale of this disaster. In an interview on Dutch television Frans Timmermans, Vice President of the European Commission, admitted that the majority of people who had come to Europe in the previous year had not been asylum seekers but economic migrants. Citing figures from the EU's Frontex border agency, Timmermans admitted that at least 60 per cent of those who arrived in 2015 were in fact economic migrants, with no more right to be in Europe than anyone else in the world. As for those from North African states such as Morocco and Tunisia, such individuals, Timmermans said, 'are people that you can assume have no reason to apply for refugee status'.

Then the Swedish Interior Minister, Anders Ygeman, admitted that of the roughly 163,000 people who had arrived in Sweden the year before, only around half had any legitimate claim to be in the country. Mr Ygeman talked about the number of planes that the Swedish government was going to need to charter and warned that it might take several years to remove these individuals. Of those immigrants into Sweden in 2015 who the government had determined should not be there he said, 'We are talking about 60,000 people but the number could climb to 80,000.' It is horrifying to think that a government can come to such a realisation only after letting so many people into their country.

The German government was eventually reduced to commissioning the private consulting firm McKinsey's to try to analyse its own repatriation programme. Perhaps it needed fresh eyes to review the mess it had created. Even what programme there was tended to fail. When the government made an attempt to deport 300 failed Pakistani asylum seekers to their country of origin, Pakistan simply refused to take them and so Germany took them back. As of the end of May 2016, Germany had over 220,000 people under deportation orders. Just 11,300 of these were deported to other countries, including their country of first entry (such as Bulgaria). Yet when the German Interior Minister, Thomas de Maizière, boasted in parliament that

'This is much more than in past years', he only revealed how paltry the efforts of previous years had been.

For if the Timmermans/Frontex figure was correct and the German government estimates of its 2015 intake were correct then this would mean that Germany ought to be preparing to deport around 750,000 people who arrived in 2015 alone. Nobody inside the bureaucracy of the German government was, or ever would be, prepared to carry out such an exercise. Anymore than the Swedish government was truly going to deport 80,000 fake asylum seekers from their country from the year 2015 alone. Everybody in Sweden and Europe knew that they would not even attempt this. Mass deportations from Europe were not on the agenda in 2015 or 2016 anymore than they were at any other time during the post-war period. What the European politicians could not admit is what every migrant crossing the Mediterranean knows, and what most members of the European public have wised up to, which is that once you are in Europe you are there to stay.

Moreover, Europe remains the world leader in not only allowing people to stay but in assisting them to fight the state even when they are there illegally. By 2016 Britain had still not even managed to deport a man wanted in India for two bombings in 1993. The Bolton greengrocer Tiger Hanif arrived in Britain illegally in 1996 and had managed to receive more than £200,000 in legal aid from British taxpayers to avoid repatriation.[10] And nor does the continent's madness stop there. When Belgian investigators looked at the perpetrators of the numerous terrorist plots carried out by Belgian nationals, they discovered that a great many of them had plotted their attacks whilst being supported by the state. Indeed, Salah Abdeslam, the lead surviving suspect of the November 2015 Paris attacks, had collected unemployment benefit to the tune of 19,000 Euros in the period preceding the attacks. He had collected his last benefits only weeks before, making European societies among the first in history to pay people to attack them.

Of course, such cases are only the most high-profile ones – the people who become known about because they engaged in terror. Of the hundreds of thousands of people who arrived in Italy in 2015 around half claimed asylum in the country. Around 30,000 expulsion orders were issued but not even half were attempted to be enforced. These are the ones Italy knows about. Nobody in Europe has any idea where the 50 per cent of people who did not ask for asylum in Italy in 2015 are today. Once the borders began to close, the pressure began to build at all of them. At the Italian-Austrian border people who were clearly not Italian were being kept out of Austria, against protocols but as a standard of the new Europe. Others continued to try to evade French forces and get into France. As these two routes were blocked, the option of crossing the mountains over into Switzerland re-emerged. But otherwise these bottlenecks continued, and continued to be Italy's problem. Greece, too, became bunged up with arriving immigrants. Where once the flow had landed and gone on up unhindered, now from Bulgaria to all points north governments were trying to reverse their policy. Yet Greece and the other reception countries were the ones most stuck with the effects of those reversals. It was Greece that could not move the migrants northwards and could not send them back home.

And what did the woman who had the most culpability for this mess have to say about it? In September 2015 the German Chancellor was receiving an honorary doctorate from the University of Bern in Switzerland. After a short speech those present were invited to ask questions. A woman of about the Chancellor's own age politely asked about something Angela Merkel had said. A minute ago the Chancellor had been talking about the responsibility that Europeans had towards the refugees. But what of the responsibility of Europeans to protect the well-being of other Europeans? The increase of the number of people from Islamic countries now coming into Europe was clearly a concern to many Europeans, the woman said. How would the Chancellor protect Europeans and European culture from this influx?

Merkel cleared her throat by saying that because of the number of fighters from Europe who had gone to join groups like Isis, Europeans could not say that all this had nothing to do with them. This was not what her questioner had asked. But the Chancellor went on, 'Fear is a bad adviser, in personal and social life.' Then, referring to her own earlier remarks about Islam being part of Germany, she said, 'We have the debate if Islam is part of Germany. When you have four million Muslims in your country I find one doesn't have to argue over this whether the Muslims are now part of Germany and Islam isn't, or if Islam is also a part of Germany.' It was what came next that was most extraordinary.

'Of course we all have the possibilities and freedoms to worship our own religions,' said the Chancellor:

And if I am missing something in all this then it isn't that I am somehow reprimanding anyone for being faithful in their Muslim faith, but rather that then we ought to be brave enough to say that we are Christians, be brave enough to say that we are entering a dialogue. But then please on the basis of also having the traditions – occasionally go to a prayer service, be versed in the Bible a little, and perhaps also know how to explain a painting in the Church. And if you were to ask for essays in Germany about what Pentecost means, I'd say that the knowledge about the Christian Occident is not as great. And to then subsequently complain that Muslims know the Quran better, I find somewhat strange. And perhaps this debate can lead on occasion to us considering our own roots and gaining a little more knowledge about this.

European history is so rich in dramatic and gruesome conflicts that we should be very careful to immediately complain if something bad happens somewhere else. We have to go against this, try and fight against it, but we have absolutely no grounds for arrogance, I must say. I say this now as the German Chancellor.[11]

In the German media Merkel was much praised for the courage and wisdom of this response.

13

Tiredness

As so often, the Germans have a word for it: *Geschichtsmüde*, meaning 'weary of history'. It is something that modern Europeans can feel at almost any time. Some may feel it continuously, whereas others get it in waves, often at surprising moments. On a recent flight to Budapest I got hit by a sudden wave of it after turning on the in-flight navigation map on the screen in front of me. We were flying over Germany and the moving map placed us over the centre of a triangle of cities: Nuremberg; Regensburg; Bayreuth.

On that occasion it was easy to identify the layers: Nuremberg obviously for the post-war trials but also the *Meistersinger*; Regensburg most recently for that careful and fateful address by Pope Benedict; Bayreuth for the culture's heights and depths. But the surge of layered thoughts brought on two things more than anything else: the reminder of how old our continent is and how many layers of history there are. Then close behind, the thing that causes the tiredness: the fear that none of this can ever be escaped and that these histories are always there, capable of not only breaking out but of dragging us under. You don't have to be German to experience this, though it helps.

It isn't an entirely new phenomenon. For centuries Europe has had terms, including pseudo-medical ones, to describe personal listlessness and fatigue, including varieties of nervous exhaustion. In the nineteenth century there was a vogue for diagnosing 'neurasthenia'. But even nineteenth-century exhaustion was not only about frayed nerves, but also existential tiredness. It was a subject in German thought and literature long before the catastrophes of the twentieth century. In the late nineteenth and early twentieth centuries Friedrich Nietzsche, Sigmund Freud, Thomas Mann and Rainer Maria Rilke all wrote about it. At that time a consensus emerged that the speed and variety of the pressures involved meant among other things that there was a draining of the spirit which was particular to modern life. Those who addressed this problem or suffered from it looked for cures as well as diagnoses and found them in a whole range of physical lifestyle changes, encompassing everything from physical exercise to the growth of the culture of the sanatorium, alterations in diet and an evangelism for the eating of muesli. Others looked abroad for a solution, identifying their listlessness as originating in a particular 'Europe-fatigue'. Some of these people looked to the Orient for the answers to their problems. There, tired Europeans could bathe their nervous souls away from the crushing weight of their own past and present.

In the decades that followed, an attention to this problem was often reframed but never went away. Today in the modern technological, global workplace one modern depiction of existential tiredness has been reframed in Germany as 'burnout'. Perhaps the term has caught on because it is more flattering than 'tiredness', absolving the sufferer from the implications of indulgence that accompanies those said to suffer from 'fatigue' or 'ennui'. After all, among other things 'burnout' suggests that the sufferer may have selflessly just given too much of themselves, with the implication that they have done so for the greater good. Yet although the term may have changed, the symptoms and causes of the old tiredness and the new burnout remain the same. They include a tiredness brought on by the peculiar speed and complexity of change in the modern world and work habits that are a result of modern capitalism and information technology. But burnout has also been attributed to the dislocation caused by contemporary secularism. In recent years so many books and articles on 'burnout' have appeared in the German press that some people have even complained of 'burnout burnout'.[1]

If it is currently accepted that a person can suffer burnout, it seems less common today to accept that societies might suffer something similar. If the burden of working for little reward in an isolating society stripped of any overriding purpose can be recognised to have an effect on individuals, how could it not also be said to have an effect on society as a whole? Or to put it the other way around, if enough people in a society are suffering from a form of exhaustion, might it not be that the society they are living in has become exhausted?

Writers and thinkers were not always as reluctant as they are today to accept such a possibility. One of the most bracingly pessimistic works of early twentieth-century German thought, Oswald Spengler's *Decline of the West*, argued precisely that. Spengler claimed that civilisations, like people, are born, flourish, decay and die, and that the West was somewhere in the latter stages of this process. Even if the standard rejection of Spenglerism – that one of the notable characteristics of Western culture is precisely that it permanently fears itself to be in decline – is true it still does not mean that at some point the self-pitying West may not be onto something. A generation earlier Nietzsche had considered the same possibility and saw some of the same warning signs. 'We are no longer accumulating,' he wrote in his late notebooks. 'We are squandering the capital of our forebears, even in our way of knowing.'[2]

With the help of such thinkers it is easier to recognise that what was already affecting Germany in the late nineteenth century was not a tiredness caused by a lack of muesli or fresh air, but an exhaustion caused by a loss of meaning, an awareness that the civilisation was 'no longer accumulating' but living off a dwindling cultural capital. If that was the case in the late nineteenth century then how much stronger is the case today, when we live on even smaller portions of that inheritance and breathe even further away from the sources that gave that culture energy.

For centuries in Europe one of the great – if not the greatest – sources of such energy came from the spirit of the continent's religion. It drove people to war and stirred them to defence. It also drove Europe to the greatest heights of human creativity. It drove Europeans to build St Peter's in Rome, the Cathedral at Chartres, the Duomo of Florence and the Basilica of St Mark in Venice. It inspired the works of Bach, Beethoven and Messiaen, Grünewald's altarpiece at Isenheim and Leonardo's *Madonna of the Rocks*.

Yet in the nineteenth century that source received two seismic blows from which it never recovered, leaving a gap that has never been filled. The effects of the wave of biblical criticism that swept through German universities in the early nineteenth century is still being felt two centuries later. When Johann Gottfried Eichhorn at Göttingen began to treat the texts of the Old Testament with the same scrutiny as would be applied to any other historical text, it had an effect that is still rarely acknowledged. Europe had knowledge of the great myths, yet the Christian story was the continent's foundational myth and as such had been inviolable.

In 1825 when a young Edward Pusey was sent from Oxford University to find out what these German critics were doing, the Englishman realised the import of the work at once. Late in his life he recalled to his biographer the impact that his discoveries in Germany had on him. 'I can remember the room in Göttingen in which I was sitting when the real condition of religious thought in Germany flashed upon me. I said to myself, "This will all come upon us in England; and how utterly unprepared for it we are!"'[3] Pusey was struck by Eichhorn's 'total insensibility' to what Pusey saw as 'the real religious import of the narrative'. In time that wave of insensibility, or sensibility, extended to the New Testament as well, not least through David Friedrich Strauss and his *The Life of Jesus Critically Examined* (1835). It finally did reach England just as it reached everywhere else. As surely as the Islamic clerics today fight to keep any element of criticism away from the foundations of their faith, in the knowledge of what it will do to the whole, so the Christian clergy across Europe tried to keep the results of such criticism away from their flock. But they could not – just as surely as the clerics today cannot wholly stem the tide of criticism coming towards them. It washed across the continent as surely as Pusey saw it would.

It was not just that the investigations of the German scholars had discovered fresh routes of scholarship. Trying to keep the Bible watertight from criticism failed not because the questions raised in the heads of the German higher critics were unique to them, but because they were questions that had occurred to many people. Now they had been voiced and the Bible was henceforth up for critical inquiry and analysis like any other text. Pulled apart by historical comparison, questions of authorship and questions of fallibility, the generation of believers after Strauss would have to find a new accommodation with these discoveries. Some pretended that these changes had not occurred, were not relevant, or had all been answered before. But much of the clergy began to realise that a fundamental shift had occurred and that they must shift too.

Of course, textual scholarship did not do this job single-handed. It was joined in 1859 by the other part of the double-whammy to the Christian faith, Charles Darwin's *On the Origin of Species by Means of Natural Selection*. And perhaps even more important than the contents of the book itself was the process that Darwin sped up. Where once divine design had explained all that was awe-inspiring, Darwin put forward an entirely new proposal: that, as Richard Dawkins has summed up, 'Given sufficient time, the non-random survival of hereditary entities (which occasionally miscopy) will generate complexity, diversity, beauty, and an illusion of design so persuasive that it is almost impossible to distinguish from deliberate intelligent design.'[4] Darwin's discovery was fiercely debated at the time, as it is now. But the backlash was doomed to failure. The condition of the argument for the divine scheme after Darwin was not good. This was not about a single discovery – it wasn't even about the filling in of one particularly large gap in man's knowledge. It was simply the first wholesale explanation for the world we inhabit that had no need for God. And though the origin of life remained a mystery, the idea that the entire mystery was solved by the claims of religion seemed less and less plausible. It was still possible to find wisdom and meaning in the Scriptures, but the Bible had at best become like the work of Ovid or Homer: containing great truth, but not itself true.

Although almost everybody in Europe now knows some version of these facts, we have still not found a way to live with them. The facts of the loss of belief and faith across a continent are frequently commented upon and indeed taken for granted. But the effects of this are less often considered. Rarely if ever is it recognised that the process described above meant one thing above all: Europe had lost its foundational story. And the loss of religion to Europe did not just leave a hole in the moral or ethical outlooks of a continent, it even left a hole in its geography. Unlike, say, the United States, the geography of Europe is of a collection of towns and villages. Leave a village and you will eventually stumble upon another. And in any low-built area the first thing you will see is the church, placed at the heart of the community. Today, where these hearts of the communities are not wholly dead and converted into housing they are dying, and the people who still congregate in them sense that they are in a dying movement.

Where faith still exists it is either wholly uninformed – as in the evangelical communities – or it is wounded and weak. In very few places does it retain the confidence it had in former times, and none of the trends favour these outposts. The tide has flowed in only one direction and there are no significant currents running the other way. Even Ireland, which in recent decades still had some of the most devout and religiously doctrinaire politics of anywhere in Europe, has become – partly because of one major scandal within the priesthood – in a little over a decade a country in which opposition to faith has become the dominant national trend.

THE DREAMS WE DREAM

Yet despite having lost our story we are still here. And we still live among the actual debris of that faith. Few people among the crowds flowing through Paris flock to Notre-Dame to pray, but yet it is there. Westminster Abbey and Cologne Cathedral may still dominate the places in which they stand, and though they have ceased to be places of pilgrimage they still signify something, though we do not know exactly what. We are able to be tourists or scholars, to study the history of these monuments as amateurs or professionals. But their meaning has been lost or mislaid. And of course the glorious debris we live among is not only physical but also moral and imaginative. The English atheist theologian Don Cupitt wrote in 2008 of the fact that 'Nobody in the West can be wholly non-Christian. You may call yourself non-Christian, but the dreams you dream are still Christian dreams.'[5]

Nowhere is the fear about the consequences of this more clearly felt than the fear of what – in lieu of faith – stand as the foundations of what are called 'European values'. It may be, as Cupitt has also said, that 'the modern Western secular world is *itself* a Christian creation'.[6] After a period of often gleeful rejection of any such notion, in recent years a significant number of philosophers and historians have returned to accepting this idea. If so, then the implications of this fact remain deeply unsettling. The post-war culture of human rights that insists upon itself and is talked of by its devotees as though it were a faith does itself appear to be an attempt to implement a secular version of the Christian conscience. It may be partially successful in doing so. But it is a religion that must necessarily be ill at ease with itself because it is uncertain of its moorings. The language is a giveaway. As the language of human rights becomes grander and grander, and its claims for itself become more and more insistent, so the system's inability to do what it aspires to do becomes plainer for all to see.

Such visible failure and a sense of lost moorings can be – for the individual as for society – not only a cause for concern but an exhausting emotional process. Where once there was an overriding explanation (however many troubles that brought), now there is only an overriding uncertainty and question. And we cannot unlearn our knowledge. Even someone who regrets their inability to connect with the faith that used to propel them cannot believe again simply in order to regain the propulsion. And as Europe learnt from philosophers such as John Locke, it is not possible to 'force' faith.[7] Nevertheless, our societies go on, largely avoiding addressing these and other gaping questions or pretending that they do not matter.

In Germany, more than most societies, the loss of God did not have nothing to replace it. There, part of the purpose of religion – in particular the pursuit of truth and the knowledge that it should be pursued – continued in some form through the nation's philosophy and culture. Yet this too crashed, even more spectacularly than the religion. From Ludwig Feuerbach and others Richard Wagner took the notion of art picking up from where religion had left off, in the belief that art could be more than a replacement for religion – it could be even better than religion. Not least because art could live without religion's 'encumbrances'. As Wagner put it at the start of his 1880 essay 'Religion and Art': 'While the priest stakes everything on the religious allegories being accepted as matters of fact, the artist has no concern at all with such a thing, since he freely and openly gives out his work as his own invention.' So Wagner professed to solve Arthur Schopenhauer's great conundrum (in his 'Dialogue on Religion') of the tragedy of the priest who cannot admit that it is all metaphor.

For Wagner the role of art was to 'save the spirit of religion'. What he attempted to speak to, in his music and essays, was the source of that other-worldly, subconscious voice that calls to us, asks questions and seeks answers. From *Tannhäuser* all the way through to *Parsifal*, his ambition and achievement created a kind of religion that could stand on its own and sustain itself. Perhaps more than any other composer he achieved that aim. Yet it was not enough, and it too foundered, of course. It failed to achieve a fully religious state for individuals – those who try to live their lives by the Wagnerian religion find themselves living very unhappy lives. And it failed more publicly because the whole world – whether justly or otherwise – could one day learn from Wagner himself that culture on its own cannot make anyone either happy or good.

There was still the philosophy. But German philosophy was almost at the very root of the problem. The sense of neurasthenia felt in the late nineteenth century was in part created by a weariness with philosophy. And not only because suddenly there was so much awareness of how much there was to think about, but because German thought was already characterised by a weightiness that too easily transferred into weariness and even fatalism. There are of course many reasons for this. But among them is the peculiarly German pursuit of continuously, relentlessly, pursuing ideas to their end point – wherever that might lead.

This tendency also has an expression in German: *Drang nach dem absoluten* ('the drive towards the absolute'). It is not a phrase that the English or English philosophy would use, but it aptly sums up that habit of pushing and pushing ideas until they reach what can then seem to be an unavoidable and even seemingly predetermined end point. Once that end point becomes clear, what can be done to avoid it? There is a reading of Hegel that can lead people to this – to the idea that history itself is a force to which we must simply submit. In this vision of philosophy – and of politics – it might be more accurate to describe not so much a drive towards the absolute as a *pull* towards the absolute. From at least the nineteenth century, German philosophy had a tendency to present certain ideas and theories as revealed truths, exercising an almost gravitational force that could not be resisted however hard it might be to live with those truths. The dogged habit of pushing ideas to their utmost point made German philosophy overtake most other philosophies of the day. It was why it swept not only across Europe but also across Russia and eventually even the universities of America. Indeed, German philosophy almost ruled the world of philosophy for a time. And it also helped to crash it.

The truths were laid down and people simply had to find a way to live with them. Martin Heidegger is often said to have provided the nadir when he used his Rector's address at the University of Freiburg in 1933 to tell his audience that the crucial decisions for the future of their country had now been made for them. Decisions were a thing of the past, in his view, because all of the important questions had now been 'decided'. All that could now be done was to submit to those decisions.

Just one of the problems with absolutes and the pursuit of them is what happens when they crash. Unlike the fudge of liberalism – which allows everybody to plausibly blame anything – an absolute, when it crashes, leaves everything in the wreckage: not only people and countries, but all dominant ideas and theories. From the rubble of those constantly crashing theories a certain ennui is not just likely but inevitable. In the nineteenth and early twentieth centuries, from Bismarck to the Great War, Germany went through such crashes repeatedly. Not least among the catastrophes of each crash was that each made the next more likely. The British writer Stephen Spender spent part of the 1930s living in Berlin and reflected on that time in his diary in 1939. Before the ultimate catastrophe had begun he mulled on the Germans he had met while living there. As he wrote, 'The trouble with all the nice people I knew in Germany is that they were either tired or weak.'[8] Why were the nice people so tired? Existential tiredness is not a problem only because it produces a list-less type of life. It is a problem because it can allow almost anything to follow in its wake.

Some people might find it unlikely that philosophy, which is never going to be a pursuit of more than the very few, could have any such widespread effects. But the failure of ideas and the systems that those ideas create do have an effect. Religious and secular ideas all start with the few, but have a way of filtering through a whole nation. A familiar attitude to questions in life is that although one may not know the answer oneself, somewhere there is someone who does. The effects when the people who know the answers, whether artists, philosophers or clergy, keep being shown to be wrong is far from energising. And while some systems may be eroded over time, as have the monotheisms in most of modern Western Europe, they may also be debunked comparatively swiftly, as eugenics and racial theories have been. Philosophical and political ideas may be dreamed up by a few but when their foundations fall away, the more popular they have been the more desolation they leave in their wake. As was the case with the most popular philosophies of all – philosophies that could be made into totalistic political visions.

Much of Europe's twentieth-century political misery came from a contemporary, secular effort to arrive at a political absolute. Indeed, one of the things that made Marxism so close to a religion was not just its reliance on sacred texts and a linear progression of prophets, but the habit of schism and intra-religious warfare. The fight to be the holder of the true flame and the truest interpreter of the faith was one of its attractions as well as one of its eventual weaknesses. But the dream of Marx and from Marx the dreams of communism and socialism were the sincerest attempts of their day to come up with and put into practice a theory of everything. The endless writings and pamphlets and evangelism in every country of Europe were one more attempt to dream a meaningful dream, capable of solving everything and addressing the problems of everyone. It was, as T. S. Eliot memorably described it, an effort at 'dreaming of systems so perfect that no one will need to be good'.[9]

As always the process of the faith's dissolution came in stages. The heresy of Leon Trotsky, the famines in the Ukraine, and the gradual realisation by many communists during the 1930s that not only were the model societies not models, they were barely societies. Efforts to purge the dissidents and other forces allegedly holding back the forces of truth were successful for a time not only in energising some of the believers but in pretending to people that there remained a pure heart to return to. By the time of the show trials masterminded by Genrikh Yagoda and others in the late 1930s the pretence that there was anything left but a will to power evaporated and persuaded the sensible communists to leave.

Those who did not would fall away after the war with the invasion of Hungary in 1956 and the crushing of the Prague Spring in 1968. These events proved to every remaining communist who had eyes and ears that the worst they had heard, and more, was true. Everything that came out from Russia and the Eastern bloc – the stories that were so continuous and similar that they could only be dismissed by the most belligerent believer – showed that if communism had been a nightmare for the world, it had been a catastrophe for the people it had claimed to govern. By 1970 in his landmark work *Ni Marx, Ni Jesus* (*Without Marx or Jesus*), Jean-François Revel could say with confidence that 'no one today, even within the communist parties of the western world, seriously contends that the Soviet Union is a revolutionary model for other countries'.[10] If the true believers were falling away gradually, they disappeared almost to a man when the

Berlin Wall fell in 1989 and the world had confirmed for them what their own warning sirens had been trying to alert them to for years. The confirmation of what their own true believers had done in their effort to dream up the perfect system was scarcely to be believed. But the millions and millions of corpses, the wasted lives – living and dead – that communism left behind as testament to its main accomplishment, were enough to give any sane believer pause. There were some true believers left, like the British historian Eric Hobsbawm, but the world generally reacted to them with the incredulity deserved for a person standing on top of a pile of corpses promising that with just a few more deaths he could make the whole thing right.

Throughout the stages of its collapse, communism had not only revealed its own horrors, it also revealed the foolishness of several generations of people meant to be among the cleverest and most informed people in the continent. From the era of Marx right through to 1989 many of the cleverest people of the age contaminated themselves by their approval of the communist system. From George Bernard Shaw to Jean-Paul Sartre almost all the secular prophets turned out to have been apologists for the worst systems of their time.

If there was a half-decent explanation for why many of them stayed around and the whole experiment had been able to survive for so long, it was in part because of the political force against which it had seemed for a time to stand. The fascist dream, like its communist cousin, began as a sincere effort to answer the severe problems of the age – in particular to address unemployment and want in the devastation of Europe following the First World War. It never carried the intellectual class as communism did, but it was able to enrapture some romantics and sadists in a similar manner. And though it crashed sooner than its communist counterpart, largely with that counter-part's assistance, the devastation it left was as great.

Italy was able to survive the catastrophe, partly because its fascism had been a slightly different beast from that of Germany, partly because the truest believers had never reached as great a depth in as great numbers as their allies to the north. It was also possible to downplay Italian fascism as a response to the country's pervasive chaos, a chaos that those who planned the post-war Italian state made sure would continue. But while the Italians had drawn deeply at the well of Italian and Roman history to justify their state and their role, the whole well of their history did not seem to have been contaminated, or poisonous from the start as it seemed to much of Germany. The famous and often-asked question of Germany, namely how the most sophisticated artistic culture in the world could have become the most barbaric, was a question with a sting in its tail. For always afterwards would come the possibility that it was that very culture and sophistication that had made the ensuing barbarism possible: that German culture and philosophy were not the things that had been contaminated by Nazism but were the very things that had watered it. The well had always been contaminated.

Countless stings remained, some of which became clear only with time. For example, now that decades have elapsed it is easier to understand the twentieth-century struggle between two competing totalitarian visions for a disbelieving world. But it is also easier than it has ever been to feel a fear not only of these ideologies but of any ideologies. If two apparent opposites (as they seemed at the time) could lead where they did, then perhaps anything can lead there. Perhaps all ideology and certainty are the problem?

It is possible that the intellectual and political pollution of Europe's twentieth century will never go away. Perhaps it is not a sin that can be washed out. But the number of forces that it polluted along the way are still being counted. Some cannot be missed. Most obvious among these are the racial theories that had fascinated some European writers and geneticists up to the 1940s but lost their appeal after Bergen-Belsen. Other forces caught in the slew included things that Europeans might have had need of in the years ahead. They include the very concept of the nation state and the feeling of nationhood as well as the ideologies of nationalism. As a form of hyper-nationalism, Nazism took all of these down with it. Somewhere downriver from there it also swallowed up the possibility of patriotism. The catastrophe of the First World War had already made patriotism look unforgivable and senseless. The catastrophe of the Second World War made it clear that patriotism could be the source of wickedness itself.

What else did these conflicts and the clash of ideologies destroy? If not the last vestiges of religion then certainly the last refuge of the idea of a merciful God. If this had not been achieved in the mud of Flanders then it was completed in the trial of God as described by Elie Wiesel at Auschwitz. The Jews could continue their traditions as a people and could believe in the people even if they had lost faith in their God. But Christian Europe had lost faith not only in its God but in its people as well. Any remaining faith that man had in man was destroyed in Europe. From the period of the European Enlightenments onwards, as belief and trust in God had waned, so belief and trust in man had partially replaced this. The belief in autonomous man had accelerated after the Enlightenments that had stressed the potential wisdom of mankind alone. Yet those who let reason be their guide now looked as ridiculous as everyone else. 'Reason' and 'rationalism' had led men to do the most unreasonable and irrational things. It had been just another system used by men to control other men. Belief in the autonomy of man had been destroyed by men.

So it was that by the end of the twentieth century Europeans could be forgiven for possessing or inheriting a certain weariness. They had tried religion and anti-religion, belief and non-belief, the rationalism of man and a faith of reason. They had originated nearly every one of the great political and philosophical projects. And Europe had not just tried them all and suffered them all, but – perhaps most devastatingly – seen through them all. Between them these ideas had left hundreds of millions of people dead, not just in Europe but around the world wherever versions of these ideas were tried. What could anyone do with such regrets, or such knowledge? An individual responsible for such mistakes would have either to deny them or to die of shame. But what does a society do?

In the first decade of the present century it seemed for a moment that this European ennui might find some relief in the form of what was termed a 'muscular liberalism': a concerted and sometimes even violent defence of liberal rights around the globe. Britain in particular signed up for this, as did a number of other European countries, including, on occasion, France. But after interventions in Iraq, Afghanistan and Libya, all in the name of defending human rights, we noticed that we had left a trail of failed states behind us. Before we had fully realised that fact a minister of the German government once told me that his country too must one day face up to the fact that there are some values that it may be willing not only to fight for and to die for, but to kill for. A striking admission in a country that is still so violently anti-military. Could I quote him on that? Even off the record without attribution? 'Certainly not' came the reply, leaving me to ponder the efficacy of a policy where a people may proclaim themselves potentially willing to fight, die and kill for their beliefs – but only off the record. The moment of muscular liberalism came and went, and by the time that Syria fell apart without Western intervention we appeared to have recognised that the global situation was beyond our control and that if we were to be blamed when we acted as well as when we did not it was best to do nothing. Everything that Europeans touched turned to dust.

ICARUS FALLEN

After the fall of the Soviet Union the French philosopher Chantal Delsol came up with the most haunting analogy for the state in which modern Europeans now found ourselves. In *Le Souci Contemporain* (1996), translated into English as *Icarus Fallen*, she suggested that the condition of modern European man was the condition that Icarus would have been in had he survived the fall. We Europeans had kept trying to reach the sun, flew too close and hurtled back down to earth. We may certainly have failed, and we may be dazed, but we somehow survived: we are still here. All around us we have the wreckage – metaphorical and real – of all our dreams, our religions, our political ideologies and a thousand other aspirations, all of which in their turn have proved false. And though we have no more illusions or ambitions left, yet we are still here. So what do we do?

There are a number of possibilities. The most obvious is that the fallen Icaruses could give themselves over to lives devoted solely to pleasure. As Delsol observed, this is not a rare resort among people who have lost their gods. 'The great collapse of ideals often draws in its wake a kind of cynicism: if all hope is lost, then let us at least have fun!' As she points out, it is what, among others, the Soviet leaders did once they lost faith in their particular utopian ideal. When they saw that the system they were meant to have absolute faith in, and had devoted their lives to, was not just unworkable but a lie, an elite caste within the Soviet Empire coped, despite the unimaginable wretchedness outside, by enjoying an existence devoted to their own personal comfort and enjoyment. Yet as Delsol points out, our situation is beyond even that of the Soviet leaders who chose to live only for pleasure once their god had failed. 'For us it is not only the impossibility of achieving our various certainties that led us to abandon them,' she stresses. We have not become 'absolute' cynics, but we have become deeply 'suspicious' of all truths.[11] The fact that all of our utopias failed so terribly did not only destroy our faith in them. It destroyed our faith in any and all ideologies.

It does seem, living in any Western European society today, that this particular world-view has caught on. Not only the entertainment industries but also the information industries speak to populations intent only on a fairly shallow kind of personal pleasure. In the words of a famous atheist bus campaign slogan in Britain: 'There's probably no God. Now stop worrying and enjoy your life.' The question of how we are to enjoy that life is answered only with, 'However you see fit.' Who knows what will step into this void, but for the time being the consensus appears to be that the answer lies in enjoying our consumerist culture, frequently buying things that do not last and then buying newer versions of the same to replace them. We can go on holiday, of course, and generally try to have as nice a time as possible.

Whatever its advantages, such a lifestyle is reliant on a number of things. One is the maximum possible number of people in a society feeling fulfilled by it, and seeking no other meaning. Another is that it must go on indefinitely, for it is almost certainly sustainable only so long as the economic tide is rising. If one of the prerequisites for avoiding political extremism is to ensure that the economics do not go wrong, then Europeans are going to have to work exceptionally hard to ensure the economics go right. This is one explanation for why the argument of mass migration as a net economic gain is so popular. If migrants do keep us in the style to which we have become accustomed, by providing us with a constant supply of young and cheap labour, then we may be willing to put up with a lot of potential downsides. If the economics do not go well and the standard of living for Europeans drops, then any wise political leader must know the number of depths that could be visited or revisited. However, for the time being, skating on top of these fears and trying to enjoy ourselves is one answer, if not exactly the most interesting our species has come up with.

It may be a terrible generalisation to say this, but beneath this surface existence everything else in European thought and philosophy is a mess. So much so, that even whilst seeing where some of those nineteenth- and twentieth-century thinkers went wrong, it is possible to look back on their ideas with something like envy. How certain they were. How infinitely surer still seemed their predecessors. The vastness of the gap between them and us strikes at sudden moments. Consider Izaak Walton's life of John Donne (1640). At the end of this brief work Walton speaks of his friend's last days and describes his body 'which once was a temple of the Holy Ghost and is now become a small quantity of Christian dust'. And then the last line: 'But I shall see it reanimated.'

We sometimes behave as though we had the certainties of our ancestors, yet we have none of them, and none of their consolations. Even the bleakest philosophers of nineteenth-century Germany look plagued with certainty and consolation beside their descendants today. Today German philosophy, like the philosophy of the rest of the continent, has been ravaged not just by doubt (as it should be) but by decades of deconstruction. It has pulled itself and everything else apart, without having any notion of how to put anything – let alone itself – back together again. Instead of being inspired by the spirit of truth and the search for the great questions, the continent's philosophers have instead become entranced by how to avoid questions. Their deconstruction not only of ideas but of language has led to a concerted effort never to get beyond the tools of philosophy. Indeed, avoidance of the great issues sometimes seems to have become the sole business of philosophy. In its place is an obsession with the difficulties of language and a distrust of all fixed things. The desire to question everything in order never to get anywhere appears to be the point, perhaps in order to defang both words and ideas for fear of where both might lead. Here too there is a vastness of self-distrust.

It was some years ago, during a conference at the University of Heidelberg, that the full catastrophe of modern German thought suddenly came upon me. A group of academics and others had gathered to discuss the history of Europe's relations with the Middle East and North Africa. It soon became clear that nothing would be learned because nothing could be said. A succession of philosophers and historians spent their time studiously attempting to say nothing as successfully as possible. The less that was successfully said, the greater the relief and acclaim. No attempt to address any idea, history or fact was able to pass without first being put through the pit-stop of the modern academy. No generality could be attempted and no specific could be uttered. It was not only history and politics that were under suspicion. Philosophy, ideas and language itself had been cordoned off as though around the scene of a crime. To any outsider the edges of that scene were clearly visible. The job of the academics was to police the cordons, all the while maintaining some distractions in order to at all costs prevent wanderers from stumbling back onto the terrain of ideas.

All relevant words were immediately flagged and disputed. The word 'nation' was an obvious problem. 'History' was another word that caused immediate interruption. When someone was so unwise as to use the term 'culture', events ground to a halt. The word had too many different connotations and disagreements around its use to be able to be used. The word itself could not be allowed to signify anything. The aim of this game – for game it was – was to maintain the pretence of academic inquiry while making fruitful discussion impossible. As in so many academies and colleges across Europe this game continues to the satisfaction or relief of its participants, and the frustration or indifference of everybody else.

If there remains any overriding idea it is that ideas are a problem. If there is any remaining commonly held value judgement it is that value judgements are wrong. If there remains any remaining certainty it is a distrust of certainty. And if this does not add up to a philosophy it certainly adds up to an attitude: shallow, unlikely to survive any sustained onslaught, but easy enough to adopt.

Yet most people in their lives seek some form of certainty. Religion, politics and personal relations remain among the very few ways to try to create such certainty before the chaos we see all around us. Most people outside Europe – or the cultures we have influenced – share none of these fears, distrusts or doubts. They do not distrust their own instincts or their own actions. They do not fear acting in their own interest or think that their own self-interest or the self-interest of their kind should not be furthered. They seek to further their own lives, aspire to standards of living they see others having attained. And they have, in the meantime, a whole range of ideas, often just as numerous as Europe's, which draw them to other conclusions.

What is the effect of people coming into Europe in very large numbers who have not inherited the doubts and intuitions of Europeans? Nobody knows now, and nobody ever did. All we can be certain of is that it will have an effect. Putting tens of millions of people with their own sets of ideas and contradictions into a continent with its own set of ideas and contradictions is bound to have consequences. The presumption of those who believed in integration is that in time everybody who arrives will become like Europeans, a presumption made less likely by the fact that so many Europeans are unsure whether they want to be Europeans. A culture of self-doubt and self-distrust is uniquely unlikely to persuade others to adopt its own stance. Meantime it is possible that many – at least – of the incomers will either hold fast to their own certainties or even, quite plausibly, attract Europeans in the generations to come with these certainties. It is also plausible that many of those who come will enjoy the lifestyle, will take part in the aspirations and the fruits of the economic uplift so long as it continues, and yet despise or disdain the culture into which they have come. They may use it – as President Erdoğan so memorably said of democracy – like a bus, and get off whenever it has taken them to their desired destination.

Surveys of social attitudes consistently show migrant communities from outside Europe to have views on the social liberalism, not to say libertarianism, of Europe that would terrify Europeans if those views came from within their own communities. The liberalism of modern Europe also provides these arrivals with some ostensible justifications for their stance. The Muslim father does not want his daughter to become like Western women, because he sees some Western women and knows what they do. He does not want his daughter to become obsessed with consumerist culture when he sees all that it produces. That which he would refute is in the society all around him. Perhaps in time, rather than become more like the society into which they have moved, such people will become more entrenched in their own ways precisely because of the society into which they have moved. At the same time the evidence to date suggests that it is unlikely Europeans will much defend their own values before such people. In a country like Britain it has taken decades for opposition to female genital mutilation to be mainstream. Despite being illegal for three decades, and despite more than 130,000 women in Britain having suffered this barbaric treatment, there have still been no successful prosecutions for the crime. If Western Europe finds it so difficult even to confront something as straightforward as FGM, it seems unlikely it will ever be able to defend some of its subtler values in the years ahead.

Yet even if all the incomers were a clear threat, even if Europeans regarded all further migration as composed entirely of people who would grow to dislike them, even then the fatigue returns. For if that is the case then an attitude will have to be taken towards it and a reaction, even a rebellion, will have to take place. Before this there is a weariness Europeans have felt before – most obviously after the Great War. Can it be possible that having lost so much, another problem of perhaps an even greater scale can emerge? Surely such sacrifice and disaster earns us some time off in the grand calendar of history?

The lack of questions and discussion about the change that is happening in Europe may in large part come down to this: it is better off not to ask the questions because the answers to them are bad. Certainly that would help explain the otherwise extraordinary levels of opprobrium heaped on dissenting voices in the era of mass immigration. In particular it explains the adamant belief that if the people shouting fire are silenced or stopped then the problem they are identifying will go away. After the offices of *Charlie Hebdo* were fire-bombed in 2011, Foreign Minister Laurent Fabius attacked the magazine. 'Is it really sensible to pour fuel on the fire?' he asked. Nobody asked him, in reply, who had turned French society into a fire.

An era that was unafraid of the consequences of its decisions would not have tried to silence every one of the voices that even said 'pause'. Yet the burden of tiredness can fall even, or especially on those who have sounded critical alarms. In an interview with an Italian paper in 2016 Ayaan Hirsi Ali was asked about the situation back in her formerly adopted country of Holland. After she had left, what had happened to the people who spoke out on the issues she warned about before she was chased out? The writers, artists, cartoonists, intellectuals and journalists. Had they all just fallen silent? She replied: 'The people in the Netherlands who write and talk about Islam and these issues are tired.'[12]

WHY THE EAST IS DIFFERENT

Yet all of this raises another question. Why is Eastern Europe so different? Why has its attitude throughout the migrant crisis, towards borders, national sovereignty, cultural cohesion and many other points besides been so wholly at odds with that of Western

Europe? Throughout the crisis, as in the years before, it was unimaginable that a right-wing Western European leader would have said half of what a left-wing Eastern European leader would. From the summer of 2015 up to the present whatever the threats and imprecations from the German government and the European Commission, the Visegrad Group of Slovakia, Poland, Hungary and the Czech Republic took a line entirely contrary to that of Angela Merkel and Brussels. They criticised the Chancellor's shortsightedness and they held firm in their refusal to take in migrant quotas dictated from Berlin and Brussels.

In January 2016, when the Swedish authorities, European Commission and others began publicly to acknowledge that the majority of the people they had taken in the previous year had no right to claim asylum in Europe, Jean-Claude Juncker continued to insist on the Commission's proposed quota system to share out the migrants between each country. Slovakia continued to refuse to have any part in what its government described as a 'nonsense' and 'complete fiasco'. While volunteering to add 300 guards to the Schengen area's external borders, they nevertheless continued to insist that they would not take in any quotas of migrants. The left-wing Slovakian Prime Minister, Robert Fico, said in despair, 'I feel that we in the EU are now committing ritual suicide and we're just looking on.'[13] The other Visegrad countries held the same view as Fico. The difference from their Western European partners could not have been more stark. What was it that made the East and West of the same continent think so differently on such central issues?

Chantal Delsol noticed the seeds of this difference in the mid-1990s. Spending time in Eastern Europe after the fall of the Berlin Wall, she saw that Eastern Europeans 'increasingly considered us as creatures from another planet, even while at a different level they dreamed of becoming like us. I later became convinced that it was in these eastern European societies that I should seek some answers to our questions ... the divergences between us and them led me to the belief that the last fifty years of good fortune had entirely erased our sense of the tragic dimension of life'.[14] That tragic dimension of life had not been erased in the East. And nowhere have the consequences of this been more clearly displayed than in the attitudes of Eastern Europe's leaders, with the support of their publics, to the migration crisis.

All these countries wished to join the European Union and all wanted the greatest possible integration of European countries, with free movement and all the economic benefits that membership entailed. But when Chancellor Merkel opened up the external borders of Europe all of these countries rebelled – and not just rebelled but made a stand. On 15 March 2016 the Prime Minister of Hungary used his ceremonial speech for the National Holiday to explain the East's wholly different approach to migration, borders, culture and identity. Viktor Orbán told the people of Hungary that the new enemies of freedom were different from the imperial and Soviet systems of the past, that today they did not get bombarded or imprisoned, but merely threatened and blackmailed. But 'the peoples of Europe may have finally understood that their future is at stake,' he said:

At last, the peoples of Europe, who have been slumbering in abundance and prosperity, have understood that the principles of life that Europe has been built on are in mortal danger. Europe is the community of Christian, free, and independent nations; equality of men and women; fair competition and solidarity; pride and humility; justice and mercy.

This time the danger is not attacking us the way wars and natural disasters do, suddenly pulling the rug from under our feet. Mass migration is a slow stream of water persistently eroding the shores. It is masquerading as a humanitarian cause, but its true nature is the occupation of territory. And what is gaining territory for them is losing territory for us. Flocks of obsessed human rights defenders feel the overwhelming urge to reprimand us and to make allegations against us. Allegedly we are hostile xenophobes, but the truth is that the history of our nation is also one of inclusion, and the history of intertwining of cultures. Those who have sought to come here as new family members, as allies, or as displaced persons fearing for their lives, have been let in to make a new home for themselves. But those who have come here with the intention of changing our country, shaping our nation in their own image, those who have come with violence and against our will have always been met with resistance.

For the most powerful country in Europe this vision from Hungary could not be accepted. It stood not just in opposition to the policy of the German government of the day, but of each German government's immigration policies since the Second World War. The pressure from Berlin was unrelenting. Yet the irreconcilably different outlooks between East and West remained. That May, just a month before his country took over the Presidency of the European Union, Robert Fico, defended Slovakia's refusal to take in quotas of migrants as dictated by Brussels and Berlin. Despite the threat of huge fines for every migrant not taken, the Slovakian Prime Minister dug in: 'Islam has no place in Slovakia', he said. Migrants change the character of our country. We do not want the character of this country to change.'[15]

These countries had drunk from the same wells as the Western European countries for most of their histories, yet a different attitude had clearly settled here. Perhaps they did not feel or otherwise had not absorbed the guilt of Western Europe and did not think that all the faults of the world could be attributed to them. Or perhaps they had not suffered the enervation and tiredness that had afflicted the Western European countries. Or perhaps, having had no mass immigration during the post-war period (despite having much else), they had retained a sense of national cohesion that the Western Europeans were struggling to imagine or remember. Perhaps they were looking at what was happening in Western Europe and simply decided that they did not want the same things to happen in their countries.

Perhaps it was all of these things. And perhaps underlying them was the fact that the Visegrad countries had suffered the effects of Western torpor once before. Certainly they alone of the European nations had within living memory all experienced the tragic dimensions of life that their Western allies had forgotten. They knew that everything they had could be swept away from one direction and then just as easily swept away from another: that history does not give any people time off even when they feel they deserve it.

Meantime the rest of the continent remained as much prisoners of history as ever. By the summer of 2016 the Austrian and French authorities had tried to shut their borders to further waves of migrants coming up through Italy from their arrival points on Lampedusa and Sicily. As these restrictions came in, more migrants intent on heading north began to resort to the Swiss option. During the winter these mountainous passes can be lethal, though during the summer the remote, thin trails across the Italian-Swiss border are passable. That summer the Italian paper *La Stampa* spoke to locals in the village of Dumenza that lies between Lake Maggiore and the Swiss border. They noted the trails that were being used, and one old local commented in passing, 'These are the same paths that Italian Jews used to flee during the war.'[16]

To think about the migrants was to think about the migrants before. To consider those heading these ways into Germany was to think of those migrants heading the other way once before. To think about the migrants of today was to think about the Jews of yesterday: a pass that cannot be avoided.

14

We're stuck with this

On 19 March 2016 Belgian police shot and arrested the Belgian-born French citizen of Moroccan ancestry who was a ringleader of the previous November's attacks in Paris. After those attacks Salah Abdeslam had travelled to Belgium where his fingerprints were found in at least two apartments in the heavily Muslim Molenbeek area of Brussels. He was finally arrested in another residence in Molenbeek where he had been living with a local family. In the immediate aftermath of the arrest Belgian riot police had to head to the area to deal with local 'youths' who were hailing Abdeslam as their hero and hurling stones and bottles at the police in protest at his arrest. Three days later three suicide bombers blew themselves up in the Belgian capital. Najim Laachraoui and Ibrahim el-Barkaoui exploded their suicide vests at the departures gate of Brussels airport, while Ibrahim's brother, Khalid el-Barkaoui, exploded his at Maelbeek Métro station, just by the headquarters of the European Commission. All three perpetrators were once again 'locals'. Their victims included thirty-two people of a wide range of ages and nationalities.

Across the continent the traditional search for explanations began. Some blamed the attacks – carried out by Belgian nationals from the Molenbeek district – on town planning, others on a lack of 'gentrification' in the area. Still others blamed Belgian foreign policy, Belgian history including Belgian colonialism, or the 'racism' of Belgian society. After the first round of this public debate *The New York Times* carried an unremarkable article, pointing the finger for the attacks at various Belgian policy failures. They interviewed one Yves Goldstein, a 38-year-old child of Jewish refugees who was now a councilman in Schaerbeek and chief of staff for the minister-president of the Brussels Capital Region. He insisted that it was wrong to blame the attacks on Islam but criticised the failure of people like himself to prevent this rising 'radicalism among youths'. He said, 'Our cities are facing a huge problem, maybe the largest since World War II. How is it that people who were born here in Brussels, in Paris, can call heroes the people who commit violence and terror. That is the real question we're facing.'

Then in passing Mr Goldstein let slip the thing of interest. Friends who taught high-school students in the predominantly Muslim areas of Molenbeek and Schaerbeek told him that when it came to their students' views of the terrorists who had just bombed their city, '90 per cent of their students, 17, 18 years old, called them heroes'.[1] Elsewhere, in an interview with De Standaard, the Belgian Security Minister, Jan Jambon, said that 'a significant section of the Muslim community danced when the attacks took place'. As is the norm, Jambon was criticised for this by his parliamentary colleagues and the media. He replied that he had the information from several of the Belgian security services. But what he said, as with the revelation from Mr Goldstein, is in fact a glimpse beneath the surface that is afforded the public in stories following every act of terrorism in Europe. These stories are at least as responsible as the attacks themselves for the decisive shift that is occurring in the mood of Europe. Because although the bombs, gun and knife attacks are all of utmost concern, a secondary concern (but one that in the long run is greater) is the question of the relationship between the tiny number of extremists who carry out such attacks and the rest of the populations from the same background.

A poll taken in Britain in 2006, the year after the Danish cartoons were published, showed that 78 per cent of British Muslims believed the publishers of the cartoons should be prosecuted. A slightly smaller number (68 per cent) felt that anyone who insulted Islam should be prosecuted. The same poll found that almost a fifth of

British Muslims (19 per cent) respected Osama bin Laden, with 6 per cent saying they 'highly respected' him.[2] Nine years later, when two members of al-Qaeda in the Arabian Peninsula walked into the offices of *Charlie Hebdo* in Paris and massacred the publication's staff for printing caricatures of Mohammed, 27 per cent of British Muslims said they had 'some sympathy' for the motives of the attackers. Nearly a quarter (24 per cent) said they believed violence against people who publish images of Mohammed can be justified.[3] The BBC, for whom this poll was carried out, ran it with the good-news headline 'Most British Muslims "oppose Muhammad cartoons reprisals".'

The combination of very high-visibility events and an awareness that what lies beneath the terrorism constitutes an even bigger problem means that in recent years the views of the European publics have increasingly diverged from those of their leaders. After nearly every terrorist attack the political leaders of Europe informed their publics that this had nothing to do with Islam, and that Islam was in any case a peaceful religion. The publics appeared to disagree.

In June 2013 the polling company ComRes carried out a poll for BBC Radio 1 asking a thousand young British people about their attitudes towards the world's major religions. When the results were released three months later they caused a small furore. Of those polled 27 per cent said that they did not trust Muslims and 44 per cent said they thought Muslims did not share the same views as the rest of the population. The BBC and other media in Britain promptly set to work to try to discover what had gone wrong and how Britain could address the fact that so many people thought this way. The overwhelming response to the poll was one of concern that young people should be thinking such thoughts and a debate over how to turn such perceptions around. There were more surprising things about the results, not least the fact that 15 per cent of those polled said they did not trust Jews, 13 per cent said they did not trust Buddhists and 12 per cent said they did not trust Christians. The question of precisely what Buddhists had done in recent months to annoy so many young British people went unaddressed. But rather than run a re-education programme on the nation's youth, one clue as to why young British people answered as they did may have laid with the timing of the poll. The fieldwork was carried out 7–17 June 2013.[4]

It had only been a few weeks earlier that Drummer Lee Rigby, a young soldier on leave from Afghanistan, had been hit by a car in broad daylight outside an army barracks in South London. Michael Adebolajo and Michael Adebowale got out of the car, dragged their young victim into the middle of the road and hacked at his body with machetes. They attempted to decapitate him, but were unable to completely remove the head. Waiting for armed police to arrive, his hands covered in blood and still holding a machete, Adebolajo railed to a camera about why they had done this deed. After Adebolajo's arrest police found a letter (by then smeared in blood) on him. It was addressed to his children and provided a justification for his actions. This letter was produced at the subsequent trial. Among other things it said, 'My beloved children. Know that to fight Allah's enemies is an obligation.' It went on 'Do not spend your days in endless dispute with the cowardly and foolish if it means that it will delay your meeting Allah's enemies on the battlefield.' The letter finished with a footnote containing almost two dozen references to passages in the Quran, which Adebolajo obviously intended as scriptural backup to the contents of his letter.[5]

Perhaps it is possible that rather than being bigots who make assumptions about vast swathes of people without any evidence, the young people who answered the Radio 1 poll were simply guilty of reading the news. After all, how much higher would the polling numbers have been regarding levels of distrust of Jews or Christians if two extremist Jews or fundamentalist Christians had slaughtered a British soldier in broad daylight only days earlier? Much though it might be lamented, the people who were asked their opinions in that poll and who connected Islam and Muslims with violence did so because on their streets Islam had very recently been associated with extreme violence.

A similar story emerged shortly afterwards when a school in Dundee in Scotland asked some of its pupils to list words they associated with Muslims. Among the words volunteered by the children were 'terrorists', 'scary' and '9/11'. The shocked teachers responded by calling up a local Muslim centre and asking someone to come and correct the pupil's answers. Soon a charity was up and running that sent Muslim women around Scottish schools to 'correct' schoolchildren's views on Islam and Muslims. A report of one such occasion noted that two headscarf-wearing Muslim women explained to the children that the 9/11 hijackers had 'nothing to do with Islam'.[6]

Unfortunately for those involved in re-educating the public, such efforts have been dwarfed by the growing public awareness of a problem. Almost the entire European political establishment and media have failed to persuade the public that the problem has been exaggerated. This is partly because the internet has diversified the sources of information, but mainly because of the simple passage of events. When you consider what Europe's political leaders say and do with what their public now think, the divide is startling.

A poll carried out in the Netherlands in 2013 revealed that 77 per cent of respondents said that Islam does not enrich their country. Some 73 per cent said that 'a relationship exists' between Islam and terror attacks and 68 per cent responded that they thought there was 'enough' Islam in the Netherlands. The view was not confined to voters for any one particular party but was shared by a majority of voters from all Dutch political parties.[7] The same views have emerged across the continent. In France in the same year – that is two years before the Paris terror attacks in 2015 – 73 per cent of people polled said that they viewed Islam negatively[8] and 74 per cent said that they regarded Islam as intolerant.[9] It is worth remembering that around 10 per cent of the French population are Muslim.

In these same polls 55 per cent of Dutch voters said they didn't want any more Muslims in their country, 56 per cent of Germans said they associated Islam with a striving for political influence and 67 per cent of French people said that they believed Islamic values to be 'incompatible' with the values of French society.[10] By 2015 one poll showed that only 30 per cent of the general public in Britain agreed that the values of Islam are 'compatible' with the values of British society.[11] Another poll carried out around the same time found that only a fifth (22 per cent) of the British public agreed with the statement that Islamic values and British values were 'generally compatible'.[12]

It is the same everywhere. A poll carried out in Germany in 2012 showed that 64 per cent of respondents associated Islam with violence while 70 per cent associated it with fanaticism and radicalism. Only 7 per cent of Germans associated the religion with openness, tolerance or respect for human rights.[13] As the American scholar of contemporary Islam, Daniel Pipes, has noted, opinion polls on these issues show a constant upward trajectory. Polling of the European public never reveals their concerns about these subjects diminishing. It is a one way street. So in 2010 not yet a half (47 per cent) of Germans said that they agreed with the statement that 'Islam does not belong in Germany'. By May 2016 the number of Germans who agreed with this statement had risen to 60 per cent.[14]

All of this has gone on despite the entire Western European governing class telling the people that they are wrong. In fact, to date the most common response of Western Europe's governing leaders has been that people who think in such a way have clearly not experienced enough diversity, in particular they haven't experienced enough Islam, and that if they did they would think differently. The polls in fact show the opposite. The more Islam there is in a society the more dislike and distrust there is in that society towards Islam. But the response of the political classes has had something else in common, which has been their insistence that in order to deal with this problem they must deal with this expression of public opinion. Their priority has been not to clamp down on the thing to which the public are objecting but, rather, to the objecting public. If anybody wanted a textbook case on how politics goes wrong, here is one.

In 2009 the Royal Anglian Regiment, on their return from Afghanistan, was given a homecoming parade through the town of Luton. This is one of the towns in England in which 'white British' are in a minority (45 per cent) and the town has an especially large Muslim community. Many locals turned out for the parade and were angered by the sight of extremists from the Islamist group al-Mu-hajiroun heckling and protesting the soldiers as they marched through the town centre. Among other things the group called the soldiers 'murderers' and 'baby killers'. Enraged members of the public attempted to confront the protesters, but the British police protected the protesters and threatened the enraged locals with arrest. In the weeks that followed, some of these locals tried to organise a protest opposing the Islamists, but they were prevented from getting to the same Town Hall to which al-Muhajiroun had previously walked. And while al-Muhajiroun had handed out their flyers of protest in mosques with impunity, the locals opposed to the Islamists were prevented by police from handing out any leaflets.

Appalled at the double standards they perceived, in the weeks that followed a group formed that became known as the English Defence League (EDL). In the years that followed they organised protests in numerous cities across the United Kingdom that often descended into violence. This was, by the admission of the main organiser (called 'Tommy Robinson'), partly because of the people that such protests attracted and also because everywhere they went organised groups of 'anti-fascists', often comprising large numbers of Muslims, turned up and began violent confrontations. These 'anti-fascist' groups all had the support of leading politicians, including the Prime Minister. They had also previously held 'anti-fascist' rallies where one of the killers of Lee Rigby had addressed the crowd on the 'anti-fascist' side. But the most important thing about the EDL was not so much its activities as the attitude of the authorities towards them. At no stage did the local police or local government, the national police or government, consider that the EDL had a point. As well as ally-ing with groups that opposed the EDL even when those groups were themselves involved in extremism and violence, the upper echelons of government had clearly issued an order to shut the EDL down and prosecute its leadership.

On one occasion the EDL's leader was arrested for trying to walk, with one companion, through the heavily Muslim area of Tower Hamlets in London. On another occasion he was arrested after an organised protest overran its running time by three minutes. And from the outset the authorities did everything they could to make life difficult if not impossible for the leadership of the group. From the moment Robinson started the organisation his bank accounts were frozen. He and all of his immediate family had their homes raided by police and files and computers were taken away. Eventually, a mortgage irregularity was found and Robinson was tried, convicted and sent to prison for this offence.[15] At the same time there were constant threats from Islamist groups. As well as repeated assaults by Muslim gangs on the EDL's leaders, there were also serious efforts to kill them. In June 2012 the police stopped a car containing part of a cell of six Islamists. The vehicle contained bombs, sawn-off shotguns, knives and a message attacking the Queen. The men were heading back from an EDL demonstration where they had planned to carry out the attack but due to a small attendance that day the protest had finished early. As on other occasions there was little public sympathy due to a general feeling that the EDL had brought any such attacks upon themselves. In response to the problematic light in which their town was shown by the emergence of Muslim gangs as well as the EDL, the local council put on an event called 'Love Luton'. This was a celebration of the 'diversity' and 'multiculturalism' in Luton that included a range of foods and also stilt-walkers.

In different versions this same story has been replayed across Europe. In Germany in 2014 a movement calling itself Pegida formed in Dresden. Their agenda was similar to that of the EDL and other popular protest movements across Europe. They expressed themselves opposed to radical Muslims and mass immigration, though stressed their openness to immigration in general (especially in the case of Pegida to legitimate asylum seekers). As with the EDL their numbers included prominent members of ethnic and sexual minorities, though these were rarely if ever mentioned in the press. Pegida's protests centred on an objection to indiscriminate Muslim immigration and an objection to hate-preachers, Salafists and other extremists. As with the EDL, the group's founding symbols were not only anti-Islamist but anti-Nazi, attempting to distance themselves at the outset from any connection to such horrors of the past. Although such connections were consistently made in the media, by December 2014 the number of attendees at Pegida protests grew to more than 10,000 and had begun to spread across Germany. Unlike the EDL, which had attracted an almost exclusively working-class contingent in Britain, Pegida seemed able to appeal to a wider range of citizens in Germany including middle-class professionals. Eventually (though in much smaller numbers) the movement spread to other parts of Europe.

The reactions of the German authorities was the same as their British counterparts. Despite – or perhaps because of – opinion polls showing that as many as one in eight Germans would join a Pegida march if it occurred in their town, the entire German state came down on the movement. At its height, around 17,000 protesters came out on the Monday before Christmas to join Pegida in Dresden. Extraordinarily for a movement that had attracted such a comparatively small proportion of the German public to its protests, the Chancellor used her New Year's message to respond to Pegida. The year 2014 had been an extraordinary one for Germany, though not as extraordinary as the year Merkel was about to usher in. Yet the official figures for asylum seekers in 2014 were already (at 200,000) around four times the number they had been just two years earlier, and already represented a two-decade high.

The Chancellor used her New Year's message not to waylay these fears but to criticise those who felt them. 'It goes without saying,' she said, 'that we help them and take in people who seek refuge with us.' And she warned the German public about Pegida. According to Merkel, movements such as Pegida discriminated against people because of the colour of their skin or their religion. 'Do not follow people who organize these,' she warned the German people, 'for their hearts are cold and often full of prejudice, and even hate.' The following Monday, Pegida held a protest in Cologne. The cathedral announced in advance that it would turn off its lights in protest at the gathering in the city. Few people in Cologne would miss the symbolism of the fact that almost exactly a year later the cathedral's lights were blazing as hundreds of local women were molested, raped and robbed by migrants in the same streets in which the cathedral authorities had objected to Pegida protesters walking, standing or congregating.

This habit of attacking the secondary symptoms of a problem rather than the primary problem has many causes. Not the least of them is that it is infinitely easier to criticise generally white-skinned people, especially if they are working class, than it is to criticise generally darker-skinned people whatever their background. And not only is it easier, but it elevates the critic. Any criticism of Islamism or mass immigration – even criticism of terrorism and rape attacks – can be seized upon by anyone else as a demonstration of racism, xenophobia or bigotry. The accusation, however untrue, can come from anywhere and can always carry some moral taint. By contrast, anybody who criticises someone as a racist or a Nazi is somehow elevated to the position of judge and jury as an anti-racist and anti-Nazi. Different standards of evidence also apply.

So, for instance, the chairman of the Luton Islamic Centre, Abdul Qadeer Baksh, is also the headteacher of a local school, associates with local politicians including MPs, and works with local officials on the 'Luton Council of Faiths' interfaith network. He also believes Islam to be in a 1,400-year war with 'the Jews', that in an ideal society homosexuals would be killed, and he has defended the chopping off of hands of thieves and lashing of women under Islamic 'hudud' punishment laws. Yet none of these facts – all easily available, all known or knowable – made him a pariah or an untouchable. The local police never raided the houses of his relatives looking for any excuse at all to arrest him. By contrast, from the moment that Tommy Robinson emerged, the desire was to pin the accusation of 'racism' and of being a 'Nazi' to him, whatever he did. The Islamists against whom the EDL and similar movements protested were innocent even when found guilty, whilst those who reacted to them were guilty even when they were innocent. European governments tried to avoid finding the Islamists guilty but went out of their way to find movements that reacted to them guilty. Most of the media demonstrated a similar order of priorities, the most striking example of which was the desire to prove anti-Semitism on the part of any reactive movement whilst ignoring actual anti-Semitism in the primary movement to which the secondary movement was objecting. So although the entire German media rushed to try to prove Pegida's leaders or members anti-Semitic, it has shown itself to be almost as slow as the German government when it comes to identifying the anti-Semitism among the Salafists and others to whom Pegida says it objects. Only after the government had let in the migrant flow of 2015 did members of the government and media in Germany start to concede that anti-Semitism among migrants from the Middle East in particular might be a problem.

But this is not just a political failing, it is a public one also. When it comes to anti-fascism in most of Western Europe, there would appear for now to be a supply-and-demand problem: the demand for fascists vastly outstrips the actual supply. One of the few bedrocks of post-war politics was anti-fascism, a determination never to allow fascism to emerge again. And yet in time this became perhaps the sole remaining certainty. The further fascism receded into history and the fewer visible fascists there were on display, the more self-proclaimed anti-fascists needed fascism to retain any semblance of political virtue or purpose. It proved politically useful to describe as fascist people who were not fascists, just as it proved politically useful to describe as racist people who were not racist. In both cases the terms were allowed to be applied as widely as possible. In both cases a huge political and social price was paid by anybody accused of these evils. And yet unjustly accusing people of these evils carried no social or political price whatsoever. It was a cost-free exercise, which could bring only political and personal advantages.

Nonetheless, while it may also be noted that no similar 'anti-communist' fervour was ever sustained in Western Europe, or was dismissed where it was suspected as akin to 'witch-hunting', anti-fascists in Europe were not always onto nothing – a fact that applies yet another layer of complexity onto Europe's social problems. In the United States a popular protest movement of any kind, including one to do with immigration or Islam, is likely to attract some eccentric or even crazy people with kooky signs. But it will rarely consist early on, let alone firstly, of actual Nazis. When the Dutch MP Geert Wilders split off from the Dutch Liberal Party (VVD) in 2004 over the VVD's support of Turkey's entry into the EU, he formed his own party. The Party for Freedom (PVV) gained nine out of 150 seats in the Dutch Parliament at its first election in 2006. Opinion polls in 2016 showed the party to be the most popular party in Holland. Despite a growing number of MPs, Wilders remains to date the sole actual member of his party. When the party was first incorporated, Wilders himself ensured that this was the case. Neither members of the public nor in the end his own party's Members of Parliament were able to join the party. In the process Wilders forfeited large amounts of state funding (which increases in Holland with the size of the political party). The single reason why Wilders chose to operate the party in this manner was, he explained privately at the time, that if he were to make it a membership party the first people to join could be the small number of skinheads that exist in Holland and because of them the next groups of people would not join.[16] He was not willing to allow a tiny fringe of actual neo-Nazis to destroy the political prospects of an entire country.

This points to a deep problem in modern Europe and poses a severe challenge to any movement of people committed to challenging the issues that are at the forefront of European concerns. The same story is replicated in parliamentary parties and street movements. When Tommy Robinson set up the EDL he was shortly afterwards told that an actual Nazi, based abroad, insisted on coming in and taking the movement over. Robinson refused, at some risk to himself, and much of his time in the EDL was spent trying to keep such people out of the movement, not that he was ever given any credit for these moves. Nor was it often noted that a conviction for assault in 2011 was caused by him head-butting a person he said was actually a neo-Nazi. If the media and politicians claim that a movement is far to the right, it will of course attract what far-right people there are, even if the organisers are sincerely trying to rid the movement of such people.[17] But it is also the case that there are small movements of actual racists and fascists in European countries.

All of which raises numerous questions for Europe. The short-term answer to those objecting to the consequences of mass immigration has been to ostracise them from any place in the discussion, by calling them racists, Nazis and fascists. If it was recognised that at least some of the people so designated did not warrant the label, then this was clearly thought a price worth paying. But what does a political class and the media do when they discover that the views they have tried to make beyond the political pale are in fact the views of the majority of the public?

15

Controlling the backlash

One route to an answer would be to consider what if anything might be said or done by 'ordinary' people who object to the mass immigration into their societies and some of the negative consequences that this brings with it. What would a decent movement that expressed such concerns look like? Would it be allowed to have any working-class people? Ought everybody involved to have university degrees, or are non-university-educated people allowed to have concerns about the direction their country is headed in without being 'Nazis'? In 2014 Chancellor Merkel could have started such a process herself. Instead of using her New Year message to condemn Pegida for having coldness in their hearts, she could instead have told the German people that the Salafists and other radicals to whom Pegida professed themselves opposed have the most appalling coldness in their hearts – a problem for which Germans must find an answer without themselves in turn shunning all the world's refugees. It was the same with the response of the German political establishment to the recently created Alternative für Deutschland. Concentrating on attacking the AfD's views and supporters while massively increasing the causes of their concerns was a deeply short-term policy. Yet attacking all expressions of concern and failing to address or in any way stem the cause of them – to attack the secondary problem and not the primary problem – became a European habit in these years, and a sign of significant further problems to come.

The mainstream European media has the same affliction. Having internalised the Rushdie fatwa, the Danish cartoons and *Charlie Hebdo* lessons as much if not more than anyone, Europe's media know that alone among subjects there is a physical as well as reputational risk to delving into Islamic matters. While they hide behind 'good taste' defences on such issues, all the time there are easier themes for them to revert to. The 'rise of the far-right' in particular is such a trope in journalism that the far-right is said to be rising even when it is collapsing, as it did in Britain during the last decade. Nevertheless the powerful trope is often given further colour, such as when the right or far right are also said to be 'on the march'. The headline claim that 'The far right is on the march across Europe' has been used promiscuously in recent years, whether the people in question are right wing or not. As the writer Mark Steyn pointed out at the time of the rise of Pim Fortuyn in 2002, 'Gay professors on the march' just doesn't have the same ring to it.[1]

At the same time an obsession with the alleged prevalence of European racism means that any day's news is dominated by such questions. Any ordinary day, picked at random anywhere in Europe, will include headlines such as that on the front page of the Dutch daily *de Volkskrant* in the summer of 2016, 'Hoe racistisch is Nederland' ('How racist is the Netherlands?').[2] The answer is usually 'very', and puts the onus for any failures of integration or assimilation squarely at the door of Europeans. So Europeans are blamed for what is happening to them, are denied any legitimate way to object, and the views of the majority are made to appear not just dangerous but marginal. Of all the countries in Europe attempting this experiment, Sweden is one of the most interesting, not least for having the most rigidly enforced political and media consensus of any country in Europe. Despite or because of this, politics is shifting in that country faster than anywhere.

On first glance the situation in Sweden can appear to be different from that of other European countries. The only country to have had comparable rates of immigration to Germany in 2015, Sweden unlike Germany does not seem to be bowed down with the weight of its history. On the contrary, it presents itself on the terms of its political class: as a liberal, benevolent 'humanitarian superpower'. With its population of under 10 million this most northerly outpost of Europe is famed for its social-welfare spending, high taxes and high quality of living. But the problems it has encountered with immigration are the same as everywhere else.

Like everywhere else in Europe, in the aftermath of the Second World War Sweden began to take in migrant labour. Occasional waves of refugees during the years of communist rule in Eastern Europe (notably in 1956 and 1968) persuaded many Swedes that they could not only take in these people but that they were successful at integrating them. Throughout this period Sweden's reputation as a safe haven for the world's asylum seekers grew and helped burnish the country's self-image as well as its image around the world.

Yet beneath the veneer lies another truth. For although at first glance Sweden can look as though it might be taking in migrants for genuine and unalloyed reasons of good-heartedness, the guilt of Europe only runs more subtly through Swedish society than it does through its southern neighbours. Having had a minimal colonial history, the country does not suffer any serious legacy of colonialist guilt. And having remained neutral during the Second World War, it does not suffer guilt for military action. Yet guilt still hangs around those years. Although Sweden presents its neutrality as an example of the moral high ground, the further one moves from the 1940s the more shameful that studied neutrality becomes. And the clearer it also becomes that Sweden did not remain as neutral as it maintains. Not only because it permitted trains with Nazis and supplies to travel across its territory during the occupation of neighbouring Norway, but because it provided Germany with raw materials that allowed the Nazis to continue fighting.

The aftermath of the war brought further bruises to the country's self-image. The extradition from Sweden of soldiers from the Baltic states who had fought against the Soviets was one small but significant episode. The lesson for the Swedes was that refugees returned can act as a moral taint as much as refugees not taken in the first place, whereas refugees staying in Sweden once there must be an unalloyed good. Or so the Swedes thought for a time.

Sweden's pride over its ability to be a safe haven for the world's asylum seekers began to shift in the 1990s when the country took in tens of thousands of refugees fleeing the wars in the Balkans. For the first time these refugees brought significant social problems. Bosnian gangs became a regular feature of the Swedish news. Despite this warning sign migration rates in the first decade and a half of the twenty-first century accelerated exponentially. The swift increase in the Swedish population – including population growth solely accounted for by immigration – led to the usual strains on public services. The official figures show a population of 8 million in 1969 and a projected population of 10 million by 2017, with (on current growth rates) the population reaching 11 million by 2024. This requires Sweden at normal levels of population increase to be building 71,000 new residences a year to meet the needs of the country by 2020, or 426,000 new residences in total by that date.[3]

Although there is a presumption that the Swedish people, like their political elites, were always in favour of such migration, the facts suggest otherwise. In 1993 the newspaper *Expressen* broke one of the great taboos of Swedish politics and published a rare opinion poll on the country's actual views. Under the headline 'Throw them out' the paper revealed that 63 per cent of Swedish people wanted immigrants to go back to their home countries. An accompanying article by the paper's editor-in-chief, Erik Månsson, noted that, 'The Swedish people have a firm opinion on immigration and refugee policies. Those in power have the opposite opinion. It does not add up. It is an opinion bomb about to go off. That is why we are writing about this, starting today. Telling it just like it is. In black and white. Before the bomb goes off.' As though to prove the point he was making, the only result of this opinion poll was that the owners of *Expressen* fired the paper's editor-in-chief.

When migration to Sweden began to swell significantly in the 2000s the public discussion was kept in check not only by the uniformity of the political class but also by the political uniformity of the

Swedish press. Perhaps more than any other country in Europe, the Swedish media viewed discussions related to immigration with a sense of disdain as well as danger. Research into the political sympathies of Swedish journalists has revealed that in 2011 almost half (41 per cent) were sympathetic to the Green Party. The only parties to come close to them in the affections of journalists were the Left Party (15 per cent), the Social Democratic Party (14 per cent) and the liberal conservative Moderate Party (14 per cent). Only around 1 per cent of journalists expressed sympathy for the Sweden Democrats, which is within the margin of error.[4]

Yet in 2016 this party that was so reviled by the journalistic class was the highest-ranking party in the Swedish polls. The story of how it got there reads like a cross section of modern Europe's dilemmas. When the party was founded in the 1980s it was an unarguably racist as well as a nationalist movement. Its alliances and policies were in line with genuine far-right movements across Europe, including those advocating racial white supremacy. It was regarded in the way that the British National Party is viewed in the United Kingdom and never had any meaningful voice in politics. In the 1990s there was a conscious effort to reform the party, with the throwing out of people involved in neo-Nazi movements. Then in the 2000s a group of four young men, mainly born in the 1970s, looked for a way to break the Swedish status quo.

Jimmie Akesson and his colleagues had the choice of either forming a new party or taking over a party that already existed. They chose the latter option and throughout the 2000s worked to expel remaining far-right elements from the Sweden Democrats and make it into a nationalist but non-racist movement. No credit was given to them for doing so. The media and other politicians continued to describe the Sweden Democrats as 'far-right', 'racist' and 'xenophobic', and continued to portray them as neo-Nazis. In the 2010 general election the party won more than 5 per cent of the vote and entered Parliament for the first time. The other parliamentary parties were aghast and treated the new MPs as pariahs, refusing to have any dealings with them, cooperate with them or even talk to them.

Yet in the years after that election the issues of immigration and identity that the Sweden Democrats were raising came to the fore. Up until then the country had experienced the same symptoms as the rest of Europe, although arguably worse than anywhere else. Its culture of self-negation was especially strong. In 2006 the country's Prime Minister, Fredrik Reinfeldt (from the conservative 'Moderate' party) had proclaimed, 'Only barbarism is genuinely Swedish. All further development has been brought from outside.' The Churches in Sweden reinforced all mainstream political views. For instance, the Archbishop of the Church of Sweden, Antje Jackelén, among other prominent clergy insisted that the country's migration policies must keep in mind that 'Jesus himself was a refugee'.

With a weary predictability this era also witnessed an exponential rise in anti-Semitic attacks in Sweden. As the Muslim immigrant population in the city of Malmö grew, so the number of Jews in the city (which had once been a haven) began to dwindle. Jewish buildings, including the chapel of the Jewish cemetery in the city, were fire-bombed and by 2010 when the city's Jewish community had fallen to under a thousand, as many as one in ten local Jews were harassed in a single year. Non-Jewish locals took to escorting kippah-wearing Jews to and from services and other communal events.

Despite the same warning signs as everywhere else, from 2010 migration into Sweden accelerated rapidly. Potential migrants from around the world saw Sweden as especially desirable, with new arrivals not only given housing and welfare provisions but an especially attractive family reunification programme. In the 2014 election the Sweden Democrats more than doubled their share of the vote, becoming the third largest party in the country with almost 13 per cent of the vote. And just as everybody could see what was going on, the Swedish press accelerated their effort to avoid all stories that could feed the narrative of the Sweden Democrats and bolster their support. The results were predictably tragic.

In the summer of 2014 the 'We Are Stockholm' music festival took place as normal. Except that at the event dozens of girls as young as 14 were surrounded by gangs of immigrants, particularly from

Afghanistan, molested and raped. Local police covered up the case, making no mention of it in their report on the five-day festival. There were no convictions and the press avoided any mention of the rapes. Similar organised rapes by migrant gangs occurred at music festivals in 2015 in Stockholm and Malmö among other cities. The figures were extraordinary. Whereas in 1975 there were 421 rapes reported to the Swedish police, by 2014 the annual number of rapes reported had risen to 6,620.[5] By 2015 Sweden had the highest level of rapes per capita of any country in the world after Lesotho. When the Swedish press did report these events they wilfully misreported them. For instance, after the gang rape of a girl on a ferry from Stockholm to Abo, Finland, it was reported that the culprits were 'Swedish men' when they were in fact Somalis. It was the same story as in all of the neighbouring countries. Research published in Denmark in 2016 showed that Somali men were around twenty-six times more likely to commit rape than Danish men, adjusted for age.[6] And yet in Sweden as everywhere else this subject remained unbroachable.

It took the 2015 New Year's Eve attacks in Cologne and the scandal of that cover-up to be unearthed for the Swedish media to even report on what had happened for years at Swedish music festivals and other events. Not only was a cover-up by the police finally exposed, but the cover-up by the Swedish press was revealed as well, thanks to the work of a number of web magazines and blogs. All of this was happening against a background of daily new arrivals, even in 2014, which meant that in August of that year the Prime Minister admitted that with asylum seekers coming into the country at such a rate, 'We will not be able to afford much else.' 'But,' said Reinfeldt, refusing to change his government's policy, 'it's really people fleeing for their lives.' That Christmas Eve the then ex-PM gave a television interview in which he said that the Swedish people themselves are 'uninteresting', that borders are 'fictional' constructs, and that Sweden belongs to the people who have come to make a better life there rather than to the people who have lived there for generations.

Even by such standards, what Sweden went through in 2015 is unheard of in the country's history. With as many as 10,000 people entering Sweden on some days in September 2015 after Chancellor Merkel's announcement, for a period the country was almost paralysed. Although 163,000 people claimed asylum in that year alone, an unknown number of people entered and disappeared into the country without trace. People visiting laundry rooms of their buildings in the tenements of Malmö found migrants living there. The city already had the lowest tax-base of anywhere in the country, with areas such as Rosengard already with few non-immigrants and some areas with as few as 15 per cent of residents in employment. Yet these are not unpleasant areas. They are better provided for than working-class areas in numerous other European cities, and until these areas became almost entirely immigrant-based, many working Swedes had saved to buy houses in them. But any prospects for integration were already dire. Even before 2015 in Rosengard, not one child in the local school had had Swedish as their first language for fourteen years. Even before 2015 the emergency services refused to enter these areas without police escorts because residents attacked the ambulances or fire engines.

Becoming alarmed at the large concentration of migrants in some cities, in 2015 the Swedish authorities tried another tactic. They decided to shift recent arrivals to remote towns and villages, particularly in the north of the country. They put 200 migrants in the village of Undrom in the Sollefteå region (a village with 85 inhabitants). They put 300 migrants in the village of Trensum, in the Karlshamn region (a village with 106 residents). Other remote villages tripled in size overnight. Of course, the migrants had not come to Sweden to live in such isolated and strange areas and police often had to drag them out of the buses used to transport them. Yet Swedish politicians insisted that their country had plenty of space to house migrants. Only once they had accelerated their migration policy did they recognise the pitfalls of this idea. The next year's budget anticipated the cost of migration to be in the region of 50.4 billion Swedish kroner in direct costs alone (and so constituting only a portion of the true final cost). To put that in context the Justice Department budget for 2016 was 42 billion kroner and the Defence budget 48 billion kroner. Sweden is a rare country in this respect. During times of global downturn it has been able to run a budget surplus. Now, in a period of growth, Sweden faces the possibility of having an economy with a deficit.

Faced with such realities, even the clearest humanitarian justifications for this began to wither. Among the new arrivals in 2015 there was a particularly large number of undocumented, unaccompanied minors. Although there were children among them, social workers said that perhaps three out of five of these 'children' claimed that their birthdays were on 1 January. And of course the vast majority of these (92 per cent) were male. It was the policy of Swedish officials to ignore these facts even when they were staring them in the face. But in August 2015 an asylum seeker whose application had been turned down murdered two Swedes with a knife in an Ikea store in Västerås. As the months passed, the patience of some Swedish people began to snap.

In October 2015, asylum centres in Munkedal, Lund and a dozen other places across the country were set alight by locals. The government moved to have all such locations kept secret in future. But the following January when a young female social worker was stabbed to death in an asylum shelter by a child migrant who turned out to be an adult, public opinion further soured. The issue of so-called 'no-go zones' became a major issue within the country, with officials furiously denying that there were areas of Sweden where the authorities could not enter even though local residents and emergency services who regularly came under assault in such areas knew this to be the case.

That August an eight-year-old boy from Birmingham, England, whose family were from Somalia, was killed in a gang-related grenade attack whilst visiting relatives in Gothenburg. As with a Gothenburg car bomb a year earlier, which had killed a three-year-old girl, ethnic gang violence of this kind had become routine. In 2016 it transpired that as much as 80 per cent of the Swedish police force were considering quitting because of the dangers that their jobs now entailed in dealing with the increasingly lawless, migrant-dominated areas of their country.

As with every other country, these migrants had been portrayed by the Swedish government and media as consisting almost entirely of doctors and academics. In reality a huge number of low-skilled people who did not speak the language had been imported into a country with very little need for low-skilled workers. And while the government reluctantly tightened up its border procedures, political and community leaders continued to insist that there should be no borders and that immigration could be limitless. Archbishop Jackelén insisted that Jesus would not approve of government restrictions on immigration.

In the summer of 2016, whilst in Sweden, I went to a regional conference of the Sweden Democrats Party, held in Västerås, in the centre of the country. In the manner of an academic conference, several hundred party members gathered to hear a day of speeches. Party leaders mingled with the party members, and although everybody was in agreement that they were nationalists there was not the remotest sign of racism or extremism. There was much talk among party members and leaders of how to halt the government's immigration policies, but the mainly young leadership were striking in private and public for their moderation. In private they wanted to know their visitor's thoughts on Viktor Orbán and other European leaders who – like them – objected to mass migration. How savoury were they? Which were allies, and which were actually 'extreme'? This party that the media in Sweden and abroad continue to portray as 'far right' and 'fascist', seemed as worried about the actual far-right and fascists as everybody else.

Whatever their views, the party's recent success is hardly surprising. The country's politics have swiftly changed because the demographics have so swiftly changed. According to the Swedish economist Dr Sanandaji (himself of Kurdish-Iranian origin), in 1990 non-European immigrants counted for just 3 per cent of Sweden's population. By 2016 that figure had increased to around 13–14 per cent and is now growing at between one and two percentage points a year. In Malmö – Sweden's third-largest city – non-ethnic Swedes already constitute almost half of the population. According to Sanandaji, within a generation other cities will follow and ethnic Swedes will be a minority in all the major cities: partly as a result of immigration, partly as a result of higher birth rates among immigrants, and partly as a result of ethnic Swedes abandoning areas where immigrants dominate. Not the least interesting aspect of surveys of Swedish attitudes is that even while so-called 'white flight' goes on, the average Swede still says it is important to live in a multicultural neighbourhood. Indeed, those who have moved away from 'multicultural' areas are disproportionately likely to say how important it is to live in them.[7]

A gap clearly exists in Sweden as elsewhere across the continent between what people think and what they believe they are meant to think. And while the attitudes of Europeans are continuing to move in the same direction, at varying speeds, their political leaders still continue to take decisions that will make those views change faster still. Sweden is merely an extreme demonstration of a trend.

Throughout 2016, as Europe's political and societal plates moved, the leadership of Europe continued on the same inexorable course. By the summer of that year the deal with Turkey had slowed the migration through the Greek route with the result that there was an upsurge of movement into Italy. That August 6,500 migrants were rescued by the Italian coastguard in the waters off Libya on a single day. The coastguard carried out more than 40 rescue missions just 12 miles from the Libyan town of Sabratha. The passengers on the boats – mainly from Eritrea and Somalia – cheered as they were picked up. By now the people smugglers did not even bother to fill their boats with sufficient fuel to get even halfway to Lampedusa. Knowing that they would be intercepted earlier by European rescue vessels, the people smugglers were filling the boats with enough fuel only to reach the rescue vessels. The Europeans took over from there.[8]

The politicians continued to pursue the same policies and import more and more people into what they themselves had recognised as a failed model. But everywhere in Europe the public attitudes had begun to change. In July 2016, less than a year after Chancellor Merkel's grand gesture, a poll found that less than a third of native Germans (32 per cent) still believed in the concept of the *Willkommenskultur* and continuing mass immigration into their country. A third of Germans as a whole said that the country's very future was threatened by the migration and a third believed that the majority of migrants were economic migrants rather than actual refugees. Even before the country's first suicide bombing and other terror attacks in the summer of 2016, half of all Germans strongly feared terrorism as a result of the influx. Perhaps most interesting was the finding that among foreign-born Germans just 41 per cent wanted to see a continuation of mass immigration, with 28 per cent wishing it to end completely. In other words Merkel had even lost the approval of migrants for her migration policy.[9]

By the following month her approval rating had slipped from 75 per cent (where it had been in April 2015) to just 47 per cent.[10] A majority of Germans now disagreed with their Chancellor's policies. In September's regional elections in Pomerania, Alternative für Deutschland (AfD), though only three years old, beat Angela Merkel's party into third place. Such results were reported as metaphorical earthquakes, but they were in fact the smallest tremors and did not necessarily signify any major change. The European publics had been opposed to mass immigration from the moment it had started to happen. But none of their political leaders from any political persuasion had ever cared to reflect on the fact or change their policies as a result of it. Although Chancellor Merkel had sped up a process, it was only part of a continuum that the continent had been on for decades. The effects of all this occasionally became startlingly clear.

On 19 December 2016, in the final shopping days before Christmas a 24-year old Tunisian named Anis Amri hijacked a lorry, killed the Polish driver, and drove the vehicle through a crowded Christmas market by the Kurfürstendamm, West Berlin's main shopping street. Twelve people were killed in the ensuing carnage and many more injured. After escaping from the lorry Amri then made his escape across Europe. Despite being the most wanted man on the continent he managed first to travel to Holland. Then he managed to enter and travel through France – a country still meant to be on heightened alert during its second year in a state of national emergency. Then Amri travelled to Italy where two policemen in Milan asked to see his identity papers. He reached for a gun and shot one of the Italian police officers before the other officer shot Amri dead. It transpired that Amri – who had pledged allegiance to Isis before the attack – had landed as a migrant in Lampedusa in 2011. Turned down for an Italian residency permit, he was later imprisoned on Sicily for setting fire to a government-provided shelter. In 2015, after leaving prison he entered Germany and registered as an asylum-seeker under at least nine different names. The failure of local German authorities to communicate with each other, added to Europe's lax external and absent internal borders systems had served Amri well. The same systems had served the shoppers at a Christmas market in Berlin less well.

While large-casualty atrocities like this caught the headlines and galvanised the European press for a couple of news cycles, all the time the facts on the ground were changing the continent as a whole. The German authorities recorded an additional 680,000 arrivals into their country in 2016 alone. Such continuing mass immigration, high birth rates among immigrants and low birth rates among native Europeans all ensured that the changes underway would only accelerate in the years ahead. The German people had demonstrated at the polls that politically speaking even Merkel was mortal. But she had helped to alter a continent and change an entire society, with consequences that would play out for generations to come.

16

The feeling that the story has run out

It is as well to admit when your enemies are onto something. Today the antagonists of European culture and civilisation throw many accusations at the continent. They say that our history has been especially cruel, whereas it has been no crueller than any other civilisation and less cruel than many. They claim that we act only for ourselves, whereas it is doubtful if any society in history has become so unwilling to defend its own or more ready to assume the opinions of its detractors. And we remain among the only cultures on earth so open to self-criticism and the recording of our own iniquities that we are capable of making even our greatest detractors rich. But on one single thing it is possible that our critics are onto something. They do not identify it well, and when they do identify it they prescribe the worst possible remedies. But it remains a problem worth identifying, not least in order to raise ourselves to answers.

The problem is one that is easier to feel than it is to prove, but it runs something like this: that life in modern liberal democracies is to some extent thin or shallow and that life in modern Western Europe in particular has lost its sense of purpose. This is not to say that our lives are wholly meaningless, nor that the opportunity liberal democracy uniquely gives to pursue our own conception of happiness is misguided. On a day-to-day basis most people find deep meaning and love from their families, friends and much else. But there are questions that remain, which have always been central to each of us and which liberal democracy on its own cannot answer and was never meant to answer.

'What am I doing here? What is my life for? Does it have any purpose beyond itself?' These are questions that have always driven human beings, questions that we have always asked and ask still. Yet for Western Europeans the answers to these questions that we have held onto for centuries seem to have run out. Happy as we are to acknowledge that, we are far less happy to acknowledge that with our story of ourselves having run out we are nevertheless still left with the same questions. Even to ask such questions today has become something like bad manners, and the spaces where such questions can be asked – let alone answered – have accordingly shrunk not only in number but in their ambition for answers. If people no longer seek for answers in churches, we simply hope that they might find sufficient meaning in the occasional visit to an art gallery or at a book club.

The German philosopher Jürgen Habermas addressed an aspect of this in 2007 when he led a discussion at the Jesuit School of Philosophy in Munich titled 'An Awareness of what is Missing'. There he attempted to identify a gap at the centre of our 'post-secular age'. He related how, in 1991, he had attended a memorial service for a friend at a church in Zürich. The friend had left instructions for the event that were closely followed. The coffin was present and there were speeches by two friends. But there was no priest and no blessing. The ashes were to be 'strewn somewhere' and there was to be no 'amen'. The friend – who had been an agnostic – had both rejected the religious tradition and was also publicly demonstrating that the non-religious view had failed. As Habermas interpreted his friend, 'The enlightened modern age has failed to find a suitable replacement for a religious way of coping with the final rîte de passage which brings life to a close.'[1]

The challenge that Habermas's friend posed can be quietly heard around us in contemporary Europe, as can the results of the questions going unanswered. Perhaps we are wary of this discussion simply because we no longer believe in the answers and have decided on some variant of the old adage that if we have nothing nice to say then it is better to say nothing at all. Or it is possible that we are aware of the existential nihilism which underlies our society but find it embarrassing. Whatever the explanation, the changes that have happened to Europe in recent decades and sped up exponentially in recent years mean that these questions can no longer go unaddressed. The arrival of large numbers of people with wholly different – indeed competing – attitudes towards life and its purpose means that there is a new urgency about these questions. This urgency is motivated not least by the certainty that societies, like nature, abhor a vacuum.

Occasionally, a mainstream politician seems to acknowledge some of the fears that have begun to bubble up beneath the surface, giving all these questions some urgency. But these acknowledgements come in the form of a terrible, exhausted fatalism. For instance, on 25 April 2016, a month after the attacks in Brussels, the Belgian Minister of Justice, Koen Geens, told the European Parliament that Muslims would 'very soon' outnumber Christians in Europe. 'Europe does not realise this, but this is the reality,' he told the Parliament's Justice and Home Affairs Select Committee. His cabinet colleague Jan Jambon, Minister of the Interior, added that although in his estimation the 'overwhelming majority' of Belgium's 700,000-strong Muslim community shared the values of Belgium, 'I've said a thousand times, the worst thing we can do is to make an enemy of Islam. That is the very worst thing we could do.'

Somewhere underneath all this is the sense that unlike other societies – including for the time being the United States – this could all very easily change in Europe. Having been for some years, as the English philosopher Roger Scruton has put it, downstream from Christianity, there is every possibility that our societies will either become unmoored entirely or be hauled onto a very different shore. At any rate, very unsettling questions lay dormant beneath the surface of our societies even before they began to change as rapidly as they are now doing.

There is, for instance, the dilemma that Ernst-Wolfgang Böckenförde posed in the 1960s: 'Does the free, secularised state exist on the basis of normative presuppositions that it itself cannot guarantee?'[2] It is rare to hear this question even raised in our societies. Perhaps we sense the answer is 'yes', but we do not know what to do if this is the case. If our freedoms and liberties are unusual and do in fact arise from beliefs that we have left behind, what do we do about it? One answer – which dominated in Europe for the final years of the last century – was to deny this history, to insist that what we have is normal and to forget the tragic facts of civilisation as well as life. Intelligent and cultured people appeared to see it as their duty not to shore up and protect the culture in which they had grown up, but rather to deny it, assail it, or otherwise bring it low. All the time a new orientalism grew up around us: 'We may think badly of ourselves but we are willing to think exceptionally well of absolutely anyone else.'

Then at some point in the last decade the winds of opinion began gently at first to blow in the contrary direction. They began to affirm what renegades and dissidents suggested in the post-war decades and admit, grudgingly, that Western liberal societies may in fact owe something to the religion from which they arose. This admission was not made because the evidence changed: that evidence was there all along. What changed was a growing awareness that other cultures now increasingly among us did not share all of our passions, prejudices or presumptions. The attempt to pretend that what has been believed and practised in modern Europe is normal has taken repeated blows. Across some rather surprising learning moments – a terrorist attack here, an 'honour' killing there, a few cartoons somewhere else – the awareness grew that not everybody who had come to our societies shared our views. They did not share our views about equality between the sexes. They did not share our views on the primacy of reason over revelation. And they did not share our views on freedom and liberty. To put it another way, the unusual European settlement, drawn up from ancient Greece and Rome, catalysed by the Christian religion and refined through the fire of the Enlightenments, turned out to be a highly particular inheritance.

While many Western Europeans spent years resisting this truth or its implications, the realisation came anyway. And although some people still hold out, in most places it has become possible to acknowledge that the culture of human rights, for instance, owes more to the creed preached by Jesus of Nazareth than it does, say, to that of Mohammed. One result of this discovery has been a desire to become better acquainted with our own traditions. But whilst opening up a question, it does not solve it. For the question of whether this societal position is sustainable without reference to the beliefs that gave birth to it remains deeply relevant and troubling to Europe. Just because you are part of a tradition does not mean you will believe what those who originated that tradition believed even if you like and admire its results. People cannot force themselves into sincere belief, and that is perhaps why we do not ask these deeper questions. Not only because we do not believe the answers we used to give in reply to them, but because we sense that we are in some way in an interim period of our development and that our answers may be about to change. After all, how long can a society survive once it has unmoored itself from its founding source and drive? Perhaps we are in the process of finding out.

A recent survey by Pew showed that affiliation to Christianity is falling away in Britain faster than in almost any other country. By 2050, the Pew projection suggests, religious affiliation to Christianity will have fallen by a third in the United Kingdom from almost two-thirds in 2010 and will thus become a minority affiliation for the first time. By the same date, Pew indicates, Britain will have the third-largest Muslim population in Europe, higher than France, Germany or Belgium. The left-wing demography expert Eric Kaufmann wrote in 2010 that even in Switzerland by the end of the century 40 per cent of the country's 14-year-olds would be Muslim.[3] Of course, all such predictions are rife with possible variations. For instance, they assume that Christians will continue to become non-religious whereas Muslims will not, which may be the case or may not. But such statistics also fail to take into account ongoing mass immigration, let alone an upsurge of the kind in recent years. In any case, these are movements – like those across Europe and the United States (where Muslims will by 2050 outnumber Jews among the American population) – that cannot fail to have significant repercussions. Demographic studies show ethnic Swedes becoming a minority in Sweden within the lifespan of most people currently alive, which raises the fascinating question of whether Swedish identity has any chance of surviving this generation. This question will also have to be faced by every other Western European country. Europe was proud of having 'international cities', but how will the public react to having 'international countries'? How will we think of ourselves? And who and what will 'we' be?

Addressing or even acknowledging questions of meaning has become so uncommon that the absence seems at least partly deliberate, as though our problems have fuelled a habit for distraction as well as ennui. Despite the unparalleled opportunity, our media and social media cannot help purveying endless rounds of reaction and gossip. To immerse oneself in popular culture for any length of time is to wallow in an almost unbearable shallowness. Was the sum of European endeavour and achievement really meant to culminate in this? All around us we see other demonstrations of shallowness. Where once our forefathers built the great structures of Saint-Denis, Chartres, York, San Giorgio Maggiore, St Peter's and El Escorial, the great buildings of today compete only to be taller, shinier or newer. Municipal buildings seem designed not to inspire but to depress. Skyscrapers in European cities steal the glances of people from the nobler skylines that are now all but dwarfed. In London the great building to commemorate the turn of the millennium wasn't even a structure built to last, but a vast empty tent. If it is true that the best test of a civilisation are the buildings it leaves behind, our descendants will take a very dim view of us. We look like a people who have lost the desire to inspire because we have nothing to inspire anyone with.

At the same time the highest ends of our culture seem content to say – at best – that the world is complex and that we must simply embrace the complexity and not look for answers. At worst it says openly that all this is quite hopeless. Of course, we live in an age of extraordinary prosperity, which allows us to be comfortable even when we are despairing. But it might not always be like this. Even today, when the sun of economic advantage still shines upon us, there are people who notice a gap in our culture and are finding their own ways to fill it.

For some years now I have been especially struck by numerous accounts I have heard first hand and also read from people who have chosen to convert to Islam. Partly these stories are striking because they are so similar. They are almost always some variant of a story nearly any young person could tell. They generally go something like this: 'I had reached a certain age [usually their twenties or early thirties] and I was in a nightclub and I was drunk and I just thought, "Life must be about more than this."' Almost nothing else in our culture says, 'But of course there is.' In the absence of such a voice young people search, and they discover Islam. The fact that they choose Islam is a story in itself. Why do these young men and women (very often women) not reach out and find Christianity? Partly it is because most branches of European Christianity have lost the confidence to proselytise or even believe in their own message. For the Church of Sweden, the Church of England, the German Lutheran Church and many other branches of European Christianity, the message of the religion has become a form of left-wing politics, diversity action and social welfare projects. Such churches argue for 'open borders' yet are circumspect about quoting the texts they once preached as revealed.

There is another cause, too. The critical analysis of and scholarship around the roots of Christianity has not yet occurred to the same degree with the roots of Islam. A worldwide campaign of intimidation and murder has been exceptionally successful in holding back that tide. Even today in the West the very few people who work on the origins of the Koran and engage in serious Koranic scholarship – such as Ibn Warraq and Christoph Luxenberg – publish their work under pseudonyms. And just as anyone deemed to have blasphemed the religion of Islam in the Muslim-majority world will find their life in danger, so across Europe the people who have engaged in criticism of the sources and the founder of Islam will find themselves under sufficient threat that they either stop, go into hiding or – like Hamed

Abdel-Samad in Germany – live under police protection. This has certainly had an effect in protecting Islam for a time and slowing the tide of criticism of its origins and beliefs that is coming its way. Since 1989 the texts, ideas and even images of Islam have become so heavily policed and self-policed even in Western Europe that it would be understandable if a young person becoming politically and religiously aware in the last few decades might have arrived at the conclusion that the one thing our societies really do hold sacred and impervious to ridicule or criticism are the claims and teachings of Mohammed.

But the work of the blasphemy police cannot stop the tide of critical progress forever. A greater appetite for critical scholarship of Islam's origins has begun and the internet among other tools has made it easier to spread and disseminate this than at any period in history. The Danish former extremist Morten Storm, for instance, abandoned his belief in Islam as well as his membership of al-Qaeda when in a rage one day he opened his computer and typed into the search engine 'contradictions in the Quran' and began reading. He later wrote, "The whole construction of my faith was a house of cards built one layer upon the next. Remove one, and all the others would collapse.'[4] Storm was by no means a typical Muslim, but the fear he had of inquiring into the origins and meaning of Islam, and the need to satisfy that urge, is something many Muslims sense. Many are fighting this urge and will hold it back, and will have to try to hold back others, because they know what it would do to their faith. You can glimpse this fear when the leading cleric Sheikh Yusuf al-Qaradawi said in an interview in 2013 that if Muslims had got rid of the death penalty for leaving the religion, 'Islam would not exist today'. Such leaders know what is coming their way and they will fight with everything they have for everything they believe. If they fail – as they probably will – then the best that can be hoped for is that Islam will at some point in the future be brought to the same state as the other religions: deliteralised, wounded and defanged. This would solve one problem, but whilst alleviating Western Europe's problems it would not in turn solve them.

The desire for radical change and the sense of emptiness of people like those converts would continue. There would still be a desire and search for certainties. Yet still these clearly innate desires run against nearly all the assumptions and aspirations of our time. The search for meaning is not new. What is new is that almost nothing in modern European culture applies itself to offering an answer. Nothing says, 'Here is an inheritance of thought and culture and philosophy and religion which has nurtured people for thousands of years and may well fulfil you too.' Instead, a voice at best says, 'Find your meaning where you will.' At worst the nihilist's creed can be heard: 'Yours is a meaningless existence in a meaningless universe.' Any person who believes such a creed is liable to achieve literally nothing. Societies in which that is the case are likewise liable to achieve nothing. While nihilism may be understandable in some individuals, as a societal creed it is fatal.

And we look in the wrong places for answers. Politicians, for instance, seeking to tell our thoughts back to us and address the broadest possible range of people, speak so widely and with such generalities as to mean almost nothing. They too speak as though there are no issues of significance left to discuss, and apply themselves to matters of organisation. Some aspects of that organisation, such as education, are important. But few politicians raise any deep vision of what a meaning-filled life is or even might be. And perhaps they should not. Yet although the wisdom of our time suggests that education, science and the sheer accessibility of information must surely knock any deeper urges out of us, these questions and the need to answer them have not been knocked out of us, however much we pretend otherwise.

The way in which science, the dominant voice of our time speaks to us and of us is itself revealing. At the opening of his 1986 work *The Blind Watchmaker* Richard Dawkins wrote: 'This book is written in the conviction that our own existence once presented the greatest of all mysteries, but that it is a mystery no longer because it is solved. Darwin and Wallace solved it.' Right there is the gulf that now exists between the accepted secular-atheist world view of our culture and the reality of how people live and experience their lives. Because although Dawkins may feel that our mystery has been solved – and although science has indeed solved part of it – most of us still do not feel solved. We do not live our lives and experience our existence as solved beings. On the contrary we still experience ourselves, as our ancestors did, as torn and contradictory beings, vulnerable to aspects of ourselves and our world that we cannot understand.

In the same way, while no intelligent person could reject what we now know to be our kinship with the animal kingdom, few people rejoice in being referred to as mere animals. The late atheist writer Christopher Hitchens often used to describe himself in front of audiences as a 'mammalian'. Yet while it may shock and even stimulate us to recall our origins and the materials we are made from, we also know that we are more than animals and that to live merely as animals would be to degrade this thing we are. Whether we are right or wrong in this, it is something we intuit. In the same way that we know that we are more than mere consumers. It is unbearable for us to talk about ourselves as though we are mere cogs in an economic wheel. We rebel not because we are not these things, but because we know that we are not only these things. We know we are something else, even if we do not know what that else is.

Of course religious people find talk like this frustrating because for real believers the question will always be, 'Why do you not just believe?' Yet this latter question ignores the most likely irreversible damage that science and historical criticism have done to the literal-truth claims of religion and ignores the fact that people cannot be forced into faith. Meantime the non-religious in our culture are deeply fearful of any debate or discussion that they think will make some concession to the religious, thereby allowing faith-based discussion to flood back into the public space.

This may be an error, not least because it encourages people to go to war with those whose lives and outlooks – whether they like this or not – descend from the same tree. There is no reason why the inheritor of a Judaeo-Christian civilisation and Enlightenment Europe should spend much, if any, of their time warring with those who still hold the faith from which so many of those beliefs and rights spring. Likewise there is little sense in those from a Judaeo-Christian civilisation and Enlightenment Europe, who between them maintain a different understanding, deciding that those who do not literally believe in God are therefore their enemies. Not least because we may yet face far clearer opponents not only of our culture but of our whole way of living. Perhaps this is why Benedetto Croce said halfway through the last century, and Marcello Pera reiterated more recently, that we should call ourselves Christians.[5]

Unless the non-religious are able to work with, rather than against, the source from which their culture came, it is hard to see any way through. After all, though people may try, it is unlikely that anyone is going to be able to invent an entirely new set of beliefs. In the absence of anyone coming up with a wholly new faith system, it is not just that we lose our ability to talk of truths and meaning. We even lose our metaphors. Popular culture is replete with talk of 'angels' and love that will last 'forever'. Candles and other flotsam of religion also drift through. But the language and ideas are empty of meaning. It is the metaphor absent of the things to which it refers: symptoms of a culture running on empty.

Yet it is not only the religious tributary into our culture that has become a conundrum without answer. For many years it was the presumption of people who might describe themselves as some form of liberals that the lessons of the Enlightenment – the glories of reason, rationality and science – were so attractive that they would eventually succeed in persuading everyone of their values. Indeed, for many people in late twentieth- and early twenty-first-century Europe the nearest they had to a creed was a belief in human 'progress' – a belief that mankind was on an upwards trajectory, propelled not only by technological progress but by an accompanying progress of thought. The presumption grew that because we were more 'enlightened' than our ancestors and knew more about how we got here and what the universe around us consisted of, we could also avoid their errors. The attractions of knowledge acquired through science, reason and rationalism were expected to be so self-evident that, like liberalism, it was assumed that life would be a one-way street. Once people began to walk that way and enjoyed the benefits for themselves it was impossible to believe that anybody (least of all anybody acquainted with its pleasures) would choose to walk back down that street.

Yet in the era of mass migration the people who believed this began to notice before their eyes, in ones and twos and then in larger movements, that there were indeed people walking back down that street. A whole current of people were flowing the other way. People who thought that the battle to acknowledge the fact of evolution was over in Europe discovered that whole movements of people had been brought in who not only did not believe in evolution but were determined to prove that evolution was untrue. Those who believed that the system of 'rights', including women's rights, gay rights and the rights of religious and minorities were 'self-evident', suddenly saw ever-larger numbers of people who believed not only that there was nothing self-evident about them but that they were fundamentally wrong and misguided. So the liberal awareness grew that it was possible that one day there would once again end up being more people walking against what was presumed to be the current of history than walking with it, and that as a result the direction of travel might in time change for everyone and that liberals would be outnumbered. And what then?

If that fear did ever arise, it did next to nothing to still the instincts of many liberals. Indeed, while liberals in the Western European democracies spent years discussing increasingly niche aspects of the women's rights and gay rights movements, they continued to argue for the importing of millions of people who thought such movements had no right starting in the first place. And while in the second decade of the present century the question of non-binary, transgender rights began to preoccupy those who thought in terms of social progress, those same people campaigned to bring in millions more people who did not think that women should enjoy the same rights as men. Was this a demonstration of belief in enlightenment values? A belief that the values of liberalism are so strong, so all persuasive, that they must in time convert the Eritrean and the Afghan, the Nigerian and the Pakistani? If so, then the daily news from Europe in recent years must stand at the very least as a rebuke to their presumption.

A recognition of this must cause immense pain for those through whom it runs. And that itself could lead in various directions. It could result in a denial of these realities (for instance, through the claim that all societies are in fact at least equally 'patriarchal' and oppressive). Or it could result in the insistence '*Fiat justitia ruat caelum*' ('Let justice be done though the heavens fall'): a noble sentiment right up until the moment that the first debris descends. There are also those of course who so hate Europe – what they are and what they have been – that they are willing for literally anyone to come in and take over. In Berlin during the height of this crisis I spoke with a German intellectual who told me that the German people were anti-Semitic and prejudiced and that for this reason if no other they deserved to be replaced. He would not consider the possibility that some of the people being brought in to replace them could make many mid-twentieth-century – let alone modern – Germans look like paragons by comparison.

More likely is a growing acceptance that people are different, that different people believe different things, and that our own values may not in fact be universal values. This is an acknowledgement that could lead to even more pain. For if the rights movements that sprang from the social progress of the twentieth century, and the movement towards reason and rationalism that has spread throughout Europe since the seventeenth century, are not the preserve of all mankind, then it means that these are not universal systems but a system like any other. This means not only that such a system may not triumph, but that it may in fact be swept away in turn like so much else before it.

It is no overstatement to say that for many people the collapse of this dream is, or will be, just as painful as the loss of religion is to those who lose it. The liberal post-Enlightenment dream always had about it a slight aura of religion. Not that it made the same claims for itself, but that it adopted some of the same tropes. It had its own creation myth, for insistence (a 'big bang' of intellectual awakening as opposed to the long and messy emergence of particular schools of thought). And most importantly it had its own myth of universal applicability. Many people in Western Europe today have been taught these myths or taken them on because of their quasi-religious attraction. They provide not only something to believe in and to campaign for but something to live for. They give a purpose and an organisation to life. And if they cannot provide the afterlife promised by religions they can at least suggest – almost always erroneously – a veneer of immortality suggested by the admiration of your peers.

In other words the liberal dream may prove as hard to wrench out of people's hands as religion was, because it shares the same irreplaceable advantages. In an age of peace and tranquillity such people's religion might be deemed harmless and those who do not believe in it may still permit the others to believe it unmolested. But the moment when such beliefs harm the lives of everyone else is perhaps the moment when a less generous and ecumenical attitude towards such believers will arise. In any case, the vast hole already left by religion may yet be opened up still further by the gap left by Europe's last non-religious dream. And after that, deprived of any dream, but still searching for answers, all the urges and questions will still remain.

THE LAST ART

Today the most obvious answer to this – the nineteenth-century answer – is most notable by its absence. Why can art not take over, without the 'encumbrances' of religion, from where these religions left off? The answer lies in the work of those who still aspire to this calling. It nearly all has the aura of a destroyed city. Such felled predecessors as Wagner seem to have made the idea of any similar aspirations seem futile when not dangerous.

Perhaps it was the realisation of this that persuaded so many contemporary artists to stop aiming to connect to any enduring truths, to abandon any attempt to pursue beauty or truth and instead to simply say to the public, 'I am down in the mud with you'. Certainly there was a point in twentieth century Europe when the aim of the artist and the expectations of the public changed. It was evident in the way in which the public approach to art moved from admiration ('I wish I could do that') to disdain ('Even a child could do that'). Technical ambition significantly diminished and often disappeared altogether. And the moral ambitions of art travelled on the same trajectory. One might blame this on Marcel Duchamp and his sculpture *Fountain* (a urinal), but enough of the continent's artistic culture fell in behind him to suggest that he had merely led where others wished to follow. Today, if you walk through a gallery like Tate Modern in London the only thing more striking than the lack of technical skill is the lack of ambition. The bolder works may claim to tell us about death, suffering, cruelty or pain, but few have anything actually to say about these subjects other than pointing to the fact that they exist. Certainly they provide no answers to the problem they present. Every adult knows that suffering and death exist, and if they did not then they will hardly be persuaded in an art gallery. But the art of our time seems to have given up any effort to kindle something else in us. In particular, it has given up that desire to connect us to something like the spirit of religion or that thrill of recognition – what Aristotle termed anagnorisis – which grants you the sense of having just caught up with a truth that was always waiting for you.

It may be that this sense only occurs if you tap into a profound truth and that the desire to do so is something of which artists, like almost everyone else, have become suspicious or incapable. Go to any of the temples of modern culture and you can see great crowds of people wandering around looking for something, but it is unclear what they are after. There are strands of art that can remind people of something greater. Once, while wandering somewhat aimlessly and underwhelmed through an art gallery, I heard the strains of *Spem in Alium* and made my way towards the sound. Suddenly I realised another reason why the earlier galleries had been so depopulated. Everybody had migrated towards the same 'sound installation' by Janet Cardiff, consisting of 40 speakers arranged in an oval, each relaying the voice of a singer in the choir. In the centre people stood mesmerised. Couples held hands and one pair sat embraced. This was before Thomas Tallis's work featured in the sadomasochist novels of E. L. James, or who knows what might have happened.

It was deeply moving, though also striking that people thought the achievement was Janet Cardiff's rather than Thomas Tallis's. But that was anagnorisis happening right there. One could not be certain how many of the crowd knew either the words or meaning of the piece that the 'sound installation' was taken from. But something strange and out-of-time was occurring. One of the few contemporary works that have a comparable effect is the sculpture by Antony Gormley called *Another Place*, consisting of 100 cast-iron, life-size human figures looking out to sea on Crosby Beach, near Liverpool. The whole installation – which was made permanent at the request of local residents – is best appreciated when the tides are receding or when the figures are facing into the setting sun. The reason is partly the same. Here is an image experienced in the everyday that reignites the memory of a story (in this case resurrection) from the heart of our culture. It may not answer it, but it remembers it.

Such works are, however, no more than the artistic wing of Ernst-Wolfgang Böckenförde's problem. What resonates does so because of something that happened before, not because of anything intrinsically great about the work. Indeed when such works succeed they arguably do so because they are parasitic works of art. They get what meaning they have from a tradition they themselves cannot profess or sustain. Yet works like this do at least seek to address the big issues that religion seeks to address. Their answers may be more blurred and their confidence more timid than what came before, but they do at least try to speak to the same needs and the same truths. The more original strain in European art is the one that deals with the continent's underlying trauma. This is part of an ongoing tradition, but it is also one that constitutes a full stop.

Even before the First World War there was a strain in European art and music – in Germany more than anywhere – that was turning from ripeness to over-ripeness and then into something else. The last strains of the Austro-German Romantic tradition – exemplified by Gustav Mahler, Richard Strauss and Gustav Klimt – seemed almost to have destroyed itself by reaching a pitch of ripeness from which nothing could follow other than complete breakdown. It was not just that their subject matter was so death-obsessed, but that the tradition felt as though it could not be stretched any further or innovated any more without snapping. And so it snapped: in modernism and then post-modernism. There is a sense that ever since then successful European art, and German art in particular, has only been possible by existing in the debris that are the result of that explosion. Other than that no one has found a way out.

The major visual artists of post-war Germany have spent their careers working in the rubble of their culture's catastrophe. Whether they are celebrated because they tackle it, or tackle it in order to be celebrated, it is noticeable that Germany's most renowned artists remain immersed in that disaster. The career of Gerhard Richter for instance, born in 1932, really began in the 1960s with a series of oils on canvas repainted from photographs. Some were easier to begin to interpret than others. Among the most obvious and famous is the haunting painting from a photograph of a slightly lopsided man in an ill-fitting Nazi uniform titled *Uncle Rudi* (1965). Others were clearly of equally ominous subject matter even when the viewer didn't know precisely what that subject was. *Herr Heyde* (1965) only shows an oldish man heading into a building with a policeman beside him. But even if we knew nothing of the names, we hardly need to be told that Werner Heyde was an SS doctor who was captured after nearly fifteen years on the run and hanged himself in prison. Others, such as *Familie Liechti* (1966), further blur the lines. Are we looking at a family of perpetrators or victims? They lived through those years. Something must have happened to them. Beyond the technical skill, Richter's accomplishment is in capturing through these often marginal shots the fact that a pall hangs over everything from the era they depict and the era in which they were created. A layer of guilt and blame lies over the whole culture like a fog.[6]

The same goes for the work of Anselm Kiefer. Born thirteen years after Richter, in the year the Second World War ended, his work is even more obviously devoted to recording a great culture in the wreckage of its self-destruction. His vast *Interior* (1981), like Richter's work of the 1960s, obviously records the horror. In this case the first-time viewer can probably guess, by the grandiosity of the room and the dilapidation of the image – the shattered look of the glass ceiling, the ripped walls in the grand hall – that this is a Nazi room. Further reading shows that it is in fact one of the offices in the New Reich Chancellery designed for Hitler by Albert Speer. But the sense that this is a grand vista (the painting is about nine square metres) of a room in which something terrible happened is as obvious as a guilty-looking man in a police line-up. More recent works like *Ages of the World* (2014) are also carefully created depictions of societal ruin. In that case, discarded canvas is piled on discarded canvas, amid rubble and twisted metal. It is as though after the catastrophe, little can be done with it other than to dwell on the fact that everything is ephemeral, everything can be destroyed, next to nothing can be saved.[7]

What comes after this full stop in a tradition, nobody can tell. One of the reasons why it seems so difficult for artists to move beyond the catastrophe is not just because there is a knowledge that the continent's politics and art went wrong, but the fear (almost certainly self-aggrandising) that the politics went wrong partly because the art went wrong. Of course that would result in a certain reticence as well as fear about the matter that we are dealing with.

For now the world of higher culture remains a part of the wider European crime scene. Artists and others might pick over the debris to work out what happened. But they know that any continuation of that tradition risks at some point kindling the embers and causing the crime to reoccur. The only answer is to conclude that what happened occurred in spite of the art and that art in other words had absolutely no impact on the culture. If that is so and art does indeed make nothing happen, then in the final analysis culture is of absolutely no importance. This is one explanation at least for why the art world currently plays the same games of facile deconstruction that the academy has engaged in. And why the partly New York-imported art of tongue-in-cheek, naïve, ironic or jokey insincerity, fills so many galleries and sells for such huge sums of money.

These three movements in contemporary art – the parasitic, the haunted full stop and the studiedly insincere – are not aberrations in the culture. They represent the culture all too well. The first cannot sustain itself, the second comes with such an oppressive weight that anybody might eventually wish to throw it off, and the last has no point. We can witness the results of this all about us. Go to any of the towns or cities mentioned in this book and you will find that act of throwing off. Although some concerts go on in some places as usual, everywhere there is the attempt to accommodate the changes going on all around. In Malmö one night the only concert in town is a fusion concert that has something to do with falafel, which is only right in its way. The culture should reflect the society and the society has changed. The programmes in the concert hall reflect this as much as the emptying synagogue does. Both are demonstrations of what is happening and adequately suggest the times we are living in.

The fact of this transition, from one culture into something else, is the greatest possible refutation of the presumptions of recent generations. Contra all the assurances and expectations, the people who came into Europe did not throw themselves into our culture and become a part of it. They brought their own cultures. And they did so at the precise moment that our own culture was at a point that it lacked the confidence to argue its own case. Indeed, it was with some relief that many Europeans welcomed such alleviation from themselves, happily changed with the times, and watered themselves down or changed completely.

DEPRESSIVE LUCIDITY

Nobody knows, of course, what comes next. It could be that this stage goes on for a very long time to come. Or it could be that it all changes and that something steps into this spiritual and cultural vacuum exceptionally swiftly. One of the reasons why Michel Houellebecq may turn out to be the emblematic writer of our age is not just that he is a chronicler and exemplar of the fullest-blown nihilism, but because he has also forcefully and persuasively suggested what may follow after it.

For Houellebecq and his characters, life is a solitary and pointless labour, devoid of interest, joy or comfort aside from the occasional – generally prostitute-acquired – blow-job. The fact that the chronicler of such an existence can have been celebrated by his peers with the Prix Goncourt among other awards is perhaps less surprising than the fact that such a writer has proved so popular. For almost two decades his books have been best-sellers in their original French and in translation. When books sell this well – especially when they are also quality, rather than pap, literature – it is because they must speak to something of our times. It may be an extreme version of our present existence, but even the bracing nature of Houellebecq's nihilism would not be so sufficient an attraction without his readers getting at least a disgusted flicker of self-recognition.

His first major novel, *Atomised* (1998), laid out what became a signature scene, depicting a society and a set of lives with no purpose whatsoever. Familial relations are poisonous where they are not absent. Death, and the fear of it, fills the space that was once absorbed by the business of God. At one point the protagonist Michel takes to his bed for two weeks, and repeatedly asks himself as he stares at a radiator, 'How long could Western civilisation continue without religion?' No revelation comes from this, only more looking at the radiator.

In the middle of what is described as 'depressive lucidity' there are – apart from sex – no moments of pleasure. Christine, with whom Bruno has been having a halting, meaningless conversation, interrupts a silence by suggesting they go to an orgy on a nudist beach. The philosophical state of their culture has washed across them and submerged them under in its own pointlessness. At one stage we read, 'In the midst of the suicide of the West, it was clear that they had no chance.' Although the joys of consumerism are certainly not enough, they can prove diverting. As Bruno is meant to be arranging for the burial or cremation of his mother's body he plays Tetris on his Gameboy. 'Game over,' it says and plays 'a cheerful little tune'.

While the themes and characters of *Atomised* are repeated in *Platform* (first published in English in 2002), they also find something to centre on. Again, graphic sex, repetitions and variations of the same, are the only light in the gloom. Valerie, a woman who is willing to do absolutely anything sexually with the main character, Michel, is a good find and a source for hope. Even so, the genitals, it is made clear, are 'meagre compensation' for the misfortune, shortness and pointlessness of life. However, in *Platform* another world view imposes itself on Houellebecq's characters.

Having given up his job as a civil servant, Michel takes Valerie on holiday to Thailand. He loathes the decadence of the tourism and the people who take part in it even whilst taking part in it himself. One day Islamist terrorists – who also loathe the decadence on show but have a view of their own on what to do about it – storm the beach and massacre many tourists, including Valerie. After the 2002 Bali terrorist attacks this particular scenario was seen to have been prescient. But whatever respect Houellebecq might have garnered from this was mitigated by the trouble the book helped get him into in France. After the massacre his contempt for Islam builds to a paragraph in which he reflects:

It is certainly possible to remain alive animated simply by a desire for vengeance; many people have lived that way. Islam had wrecked my life, and Islam was certainly something which I could hate; in the days that followed, I devoted myself to trying to feel hatred for Muslims. I was quite good at it, and I started to follow the international news again. Every time I heard that a Palestinian terrorist, or a Palestinian child or a pregnant Palestinian woman had been gunned down in the Gaza Strip, I felt a quiver of enthusiasm at the thought that it meant one less Muslim. Yes, it was possible to live like this.

For this passage and others deemed offensive both in interviews and in *Atomised* (where a character describes Islam as 'the most stupid, false, and obscure of all religions'), Houellebecq found himself the target of legal proceedings in France. Whether for this reason, or his oft-cited desire to minimise his taxes, Houellebecq left France to live in Ireland.

Perhaps it was the stupidity that chased him away. After all, anybody who actually read Houellebecq – as opposed to just the excerpts they hoped to be offended by – could see that the characters in his novels are infinitely harsher in their criticism and contempt of the modern West than they are of the precepts and claims of Islam or Muslims. Houellebecq's contempt fires in all directions – including at homosexuals, heterosexuals, the Chinese and most other nationalities. Dragging Houellebecq to court for being rude about Muslims was a demonstration of a gross game of sensitivity trump-cards, but it also showed a literary ignorance. Not just in hauling an author to court for his expressions, but in the fact that Houellebecq's derision or contempt so clearly goes beyond the whines and pleadings of special-interest groups: his is a rage and contempt aimed against this age and species as a whole.

Yet however great the acrobatics and pyrotechnics in a literature of this type, it is always the case that it must at some point either mature or fizzle out. The evidence that Houellebecq wasn't going to fizzle out came with *The Map and the Territory* (2010), the story of an artist who makes himself fabulously wealthy through his deeply occasional work. The wealth allows him to seclude himself from a France doomed to become in the near future little more than a cultural theme-park for the new Russian and Chinese super-rich. The work is not only an exploration of the traditional Houellebecq themes (dysfunctional family life, empty sex, solitude) but a profound satire on modern culture. It includes a hilarious and devastating self-portrait – a reminder of the truth that the most savage critics always also turn their gaze on themselves. The artist visits the drunken writer Michel Houellebecq in his remote and unattractive Irish retreat.

The self-portrait is remarkably accurate. Dissolute, alcoholic, depressive and meandering, the portrait of Houellebecq in *The Map and the Territory* shows an almost affrontingly desiccated life. It is also a life that produces enemies. A curious detail is that at one point in the novel 'Houellebecq' is found dead – decapitated, flayed and mutilated. In 2016 that scene assumed less amusing overtones.

Submission, was due for publication on 7 January. Even before publication it had caused critical and political controversy. The plot takes French politics forward to the 2020s. President François Hollande is coming to the end of a disastrous second term. The National Front party of Marine Le Pen is ahead in the polls. The moderate right of the UMP (Union pour un Mouvement Populaire) collapses, as do the Socialists. But another party has come together over recent years – a Muslim party led by a moderate Islamist who enjoys the support of France's growing Muslim population. As the run-offs get closer it is clear to the other mainstream parties that the only way to keep the National Front from power is to unite behind the Islamist party. They do so, and the Islamist party wins. Using some pliant old French left-wingers for cover, the Islamists set about transforming France, not least by taking control of education and transforming (with the help of substantial Gulf funding) all public universities, including the Sorbonne, into Islamic institutions. Gradually even the novel's main character – a dissolute scholar of the nineteenth-century novelist J. K. Huysmans – sees the sense of converting to Islam.

In the few public comments he made about the book, Houellebecq was at pains to stress his admiration for Islam – another demonstration perhaps that the browbeating and threats of the thought-police do work. It was to be expected that such pleas would be drowned out, if not for the reasons that transpired. Among those to attack and ridicule Houellebecq for a plot many claimed was wilfully provocative was a satirical weekly magazine called *Charlie Hebdo*, then little known outside France. The magazine – which has a long tradition of left-wing, secular, anti-clerical iconoclasm – had come to limited international attention in recent years after repeatedly showing itself willing to depict Islam's prophet (a willingness it was almost alone in demonstrating after the 2005 Danish cartoons affair). Despite assaults, legal threats and a firebomb attack on their Paris offices, the publication held firm, as it had over earlier critiques of the Pope, Marine Le Pen and others.

In expectation of the launch of the new novel a typically ugly caricature of a hideous, gnome-like Houellebecq was on the cover of the magazine on that January morning when two Islamist gunmen forced their way into *Charlie Hebdo*'s Paris offices and shot dead ten of the magazine's staff and two policemen. As the Yemen-trained French Muslim gunmen left the offices they were heard shouting, 'We have avenged the Prophet Muhammad' and 'Allahu Akbar'. Among the victims of their assault on the magazine's morning editorial meeting was the economist Bernard Maris, a close friend of Houellebecq.

Houellebecq's publishers announced that his publicity tour was cancelled and the author himself went into hiding. Ever since he has been accompanied by bodyguards. Yet although the French state is helping to protect him, it has by no means thrown itself behind him. In the immediate aftermath of the *Charlie Hebdo* attacks the country's Socialist Prime Minister, Manuel Valls, chose to make an address in which he said, 'France is not Michel Houellebecq ... it is not intolerance, hatred and fear.' Obviously – unless he had got hold of an early proof – the Prime Minister had not read the novel. Although it should be no concern of a Prime Minister even if the novel was provocative, as it happens, *Submission* is no mere provocation. And it is an infinitely subtler and more sophisticated book than Jean Raspail's *The Camp of the Saints* or other dystopian novels.

The life of the main character, François, is not only dry in the usual Houellebecquian way, it is also painfully in need of relief. As French culture and society decay all around him, two particular revelations stand out. The first comes as a result of his Jewish girlfriend's choice to leave France and join her family in Israel. After a sexually athletic final meeting she asks him what he will do, especially now that the university looks as if it will close when the Muslim party comes to power. 'I kissed her softly on the lips, and said, "There is no Israel for me." Not a deep thought; but that's how it was.' In fact that is a very deep thought indeed.

But the deeper spiritual point in the novel lies precisely in François's meditations on his scholarly interest. Houellebecq (like a lot of his literary critics) assumes that his readers will be unfamiliar with the work of Huysmans, but a significant portion will have read or at least heard of *A Rebours* (*Against Nature*), one of the central texts of late nineteenth-century French decadence. By the point at which the novel starts François is tiring of his enthusiasm for Huysmans, in the way that many academics are after their first love is overlaid by years of identical lectures and questions. But the choice of Huysmans as a constant presence in the novel is important, because as it develops, François not only rediscovers part of his passion for Huysmans but also confronts one of the central challenges of Huysmans's life. Like many of his contemporary decadents across Europe, Huysmans ended up being received into the Roman Catholic Church. It is a journey that François tries to emulate as everything falls apart around him – while intimations and then sporadic and shocking outbursts of violence become commonplace across France.

François even heads back to the monastery in which Huysmans found his faith and in which the young François spent some time in search of his literary idol while a younger man. He sits in front of the same Madonna and his meditations strain towards the same goal. But he cannot do it: he may have returned to the source, and he may even be open to the moment, but he cannot perform the necessary leap of faith. And so he returns to Paris, and there the university authorities – now Islamic – explain to François (who they have generously pensioned off) the logic of Islam. And not just the logic that he will get his career back at the Sorbonne if he converts, but the logic it will make in other corners of his life. He will have wives (up to four, and younger – if he wishes – even than his usual tastes). And of course he will be part of a community of meaning for the first time. He will be able to continue enjoying most of the few pleasures he has had and will gain much more than he had thought possible in the way of comforts. Unlike the leap required to become a Catholic, the logic of Islam is practical and, in a society ripe for submission, becomes irrefutable.

Even before its publication the question around *Submission* was whether or not the novel's vision was remotely plausible. Since its publication part of that question seems to have been answered. Endless small details rhyme. For instance, in the run-up to the crucial election the French media and mainstream politicians deliberately obscure stories of real interest. French readers will be reminded of the events in December 2014 in France when Muslim extremists kept driving into crowds of people while shouting 'Allahu Akbar', only for the politicians and media to dismiss these events as meaningless traffic incidents. Then there is the portrait of the Jewish community leaders who remain around to flatter their enemies and negotiate for themselves even as everything signals their community's destruction. And of course the novel's truest conceit is the depiction of a class of politicians across the political divide so keen to be seen above all as 'anti-racist' that they end up flattering and ultimately handing over their country to the worst and most swiftly growing racist movement of their time.

But more important than the political analysis is the societal diagnosis. If there is a reason why Houellebecq towers over most contemporary novelists it is because he recognises the depth and sweep of the questions now facing Western Europe. The most propitious coincidence of his career is that his work came to artistic maturity in time to capture a society tipping from over-ripeness into something else. But what precisely? More decadence and barbarism, or salvation? And if salvation, then what kind, and whose?

17

The end

A year on from Chancellor Merkel's big decision, politicians, media stars, celebrities and others continued to insist that Europe must continue to take in the world's migrants. Those people, including the general public, who continued to question this policy, were repeatedly dismissed as cold-hearted and probably racist. And so even a year after the situation in Europe was agreed to be a catastrophe, the naval patrols in the southern Mediterranean were continuing to pick people up in their thousands. Indeed, according to the EU's own agencies, the number of migrants arriving into Italy in July 2016 was 12 per cent up on the numbers in July 2015. A year on from what was meant to be the peak, more than ten thousand people were picked up off the North African coastline in just 48 hours. Whenever the media did report these events they described the migrants as being 'saved' or 'rescued' from the Mediterranean. Most of the time the European vessels simply went ever nearer to the North African shore and picked people up from the boats they had been pushed off in not many minutes earlier. But the implication was really that they were being 'saved' and 'rescued' from terrible situations that had caused them to set out on the boats in the first place. And as before, none of the details mattered.

Among the absent details was the fact that the flows of migrants into Italy hardly included any Syrians from the civil war. Instead, they were nearly all young sub-Saharan African men. Another point which could have been of some interest was that whatever they were fleeing from was quite possibly no worse than what hundreds of millions of others might wish to flee from in the months and years ahead. Once the migrants had been 'saved', the benevolent Europeans who called for this policy to continue lost interest in their newest arrivals. When the 2015 crisis was at its height many individuals in Britain from the leader of the Scottish Nationalist Party to the Labour party's Shadow Home Secretary, with numerous actors and rock stars in between, had said they would take in a refugee family. More than a year later not one of these people had actually done so. As with the generosity and benevolence throughout the crisis, it was easy to expect others to be benevolent on your own behalf once you had signalled that you were on the side of the earth's poor and oppressed. The consequences of your benevolence could be left to others.

The actual details remained as troubling and badly arranged as ever. In September 2016, a month after I was last on Lesbos, migrants inside Moria burnt the camp down. The spark could have been almost anything. People had been left there for almost half a year as the other European nations that still insisted on the importance of the rescue missions closed their borders and left Greece to deal with the consequences of the rescue. Rumours had been flying around the camp's occupants of an imminent repatriation to Turkey. Others said that the riots that led to the torching of the camp were due to arguments over the food queues. It could have been because of this or the inter-ethnic violence that simmered. A video taken of the camp burning down includes shouts of 'Allahu Akbar'.

The week after Moria was burnt down I was in Germany again. Everywhere the consequences of the previous year's decision by the Chancellor were visible. The television schedules included a stand-up comedy show starring migrants who entertained a small audience of Germans for the cameras. The migrants were giving a human face to the flow and their audiences were desperately leaning in to love the experience. But TV stardom was not the reality for the overwhelming number of newcomers. In the basement of one Evangelical-Lutheran church in the suburbs of Berlin I found 14 refugees living on bunk beds. All male and in their twenties, mainly from Iran, they had come in 2015. One admitted to paying $1,200 to cross the sea to Greece and had first made his way to Norway but did not like it there. These men said they had converted to Christianity, which was why the church was giving them shelter. Although their claim might have been sincere, the Christian conversion business had also become a well-known racket by this point. To claim conversion to Christianity almost ensured an asylum claim was approved.

In the Bundestag I had an opportunity to speak with a Member of Parliament who was a major supporter of Chancellor Merkel and her stand throughout the crisis. He presented the issue as a solely bureaucratic one. The lack of housing, for instance, was 'not a catastrophe, but a task'. How might the country ensure better integration? The migrants currently get 60 hours of courses on German values. The MP thought this perhaps should be increased to 100 hours. Most striking, as I had heard in Germany for years, was his belief that German citizens were the ones with problems. Those concerned with a change in their area, he said, 'spend too much time on blogs and not enough time in reality'. And when asked about the criminal activities of migrants he unloaded himself of his opinion that 'The refugees are less criminal than the average German inhabitant.'

As for taking in one million people in a year: it was, the MP said, 'not a big deal'. Imagine, he said at one point, that there were 81 people sitting in this room and there was a knock on the door. It turns out to be someone telling us that if he remains in the corridor he will be killed. What do we do? Of course we let him in. And what do you do, I wondered, if after letting an 82nd person into the room there comes a knock at the door once again. Must the 83rd person also be let in? Certainly, the MP says. There seems to be no point at which the door cannot continue to be opened. So we change tack. In 2015 Germany gave priority to the asylum claims of Syrians. Why, I asked, putting the point that the Afghans on Lesbos had put to me, should the Syrians be given priority? Why should Germany not also make a priority of bringing Afghans into Germany. And what of the others? There was no doubt that the situation in Eritrea and many other countries in Africa was bad. What about the people I had met from the Far East, from Burma and Bangladesh and elsewhere? Why should Germany not be making a priority of bringing these people in too?

The MP was getting exasperated with what he clearly thought to be a theoretical point. This situation, he insisted, was not a real one and so required no response. Besides, people were not coming to Germany in these numbers any more, so it was not necessary to consider such scenarios. This was – I must admit – a lightning-bolt moment throughout all my travels. For this German MP speaking in late 2016 must have known what anybody reading a newspaper must know, which is that the flow of migrants has not slowed because the need had slowed. It had slowed because the governments of Europe – and the government of Germany in particular – had changed the facts on the ground. If there was a reason why in 2016 the numbers had fallen by several hundred thousand from the year before it was because of two things. Firstly because of the deal that the EU (led by the German government) did with the Turkish government earlier in the year, paying the Turks to keep migrants inside their country and preventing boats from setting off for Greece. And secondly because, quietly in some cases but more noisily in others, the borders of Europe had gone back up. And not all of these decisions had been discouraged by the Germans. The enforcement of the Macedonian border was particularly helpful for the German government, creating a bottleneck of migrants who had arrived in Greece, but ensuring that they did not have the opportunity to flow up in such numbers as the year before to Germany or beyond.

Unsatisfied with his casuistry, I pushed my MP. He must know, and his colleagues must know, that the reason why the flow had diminished was because of these two factors. If Germany really did care as much as it claimed about all the oppressed, beleaguered and war-torn of the world, then there were obvious solutions to their plight. Germany did not need to keep making Greece pay the price. Why did Germany not lay on a fleet of airplanes to bring migrants from the Greek islands and fly them straight up into Berlin? If the dominant country in Europe really did abhor the re-erection of borders – as it officially claimed to do – then it should not permit those borders to be a hindrance to their humanitarian activism. Massive numbers of chartered flights from the extremities of Europe to its heart were clearly the answer.

My interlocutor would not grant this, and that is where the realisation struck that even these people – even the most pro-Merkel, pro-migrant, MPs – have their snapping point. And here we were right at the edge of it. He was willing to plead the plight of all migrants, also condemn all the borders, and simultaneously be willing to pretend that the flow had slowed of its own volition. This was the way in which his conscience and his survival instinct had found room for an agreement. By pretending that the migrants simply weren't coming whilst supporting a policy that had stopped them from coming, it was possible to remain a humanitarian and remain in power. He had made a pact with himself that many other Germans were also beginning to make.

News from Germany strangely no longer travels very far. The cost of foreign-reporting, even of having a single correspondent full-time in another European city, is one explanation. As is an apparently diminishing public appetite for news rather than gossip and entertainment. Elections are still covered, of course, as are unavoidably huge events. But in a continent that likes to pretend it is wholly interconnected, the real news of what is going on rarely travels from one country to another. Yet as anybody who knows Germany will know, any normal day's news, that rarely travels further than the German-language press, reveals a country teetering ever nearer to disaster.

A single day's news in September 2016 might suffice. The front pages – like the rolling news channels – covered the fire-bombing of a mosque in Dresden. No longer an uncommon event, no one had been injured and the mosque building had not been badly damaged. Bad as it still is, this is the sort of story the media know how to deal with. It remains suggestive of the results of bigotry of any kind and anti-migrant bigotry in particular. Inside, and given far less coverage, are other now even more routine stories. There had been violent clashes in a small village between a gang of German bikers and a gang of migrants. The migrants had overwhelmed the biker gang before the police got there. Serious violence was narrowly averted.

Another story related events at an asylum centre the day before. On the evening of 27 September a migrant called police from a Berlin centre to say that he had seen another migrant abusing a child in some bushes. Three policemen arrived to find a 27-year-old Pakistani man still in some bushes where he was raping a six-year-old Iraqi girl. One of the policemen began to take the girl away as the two others handcuffed the Pakistani man and began to put him in the back of their police car. As they did so the abused girl's father – a 29-year-old Iraqi – came running out of the asylum centre towards the car, holding a knife. The police shouted 'stop', but clearly intent on revenge he would not stop. The policemen shot the father dead. Articles covering this occurrence raised the bureaucratic questions of whether the police had acted appropriately.[1] But none noted that these stories of lives irrevocably and haphazardly changed now constituted just another day in the new Germany.

Not that this new Germany was in a continent unrecognisable from the old. That same month of September, ahead of the Jewish holidays of Rosh Hashanah and Yom Kippur, a new survey of attitudes among European Jews was released. The work, carried out by two Jewish organisations, surveyed attitudes in Jewish communities from Britain to Ukraine. It found that despite increased security measures at synagogues across the continent, 70 per cent of European Jews said they would avoid attending synagogue. In 2016 fear of anti-Semitism and terror attacks would keep a majority of the continent's Jews away from practising their faith.[2]

In September the German public finally had an opportunity to vent their feelings about what their Chancellor had done to their country. Voters in Berlin gave the CDU the lowest electoral results in the capital, winning just 17.5 per cent of the vote. Meanwhile the AfD entered the state capital's Parliament for the first time after receiving a 14.1 per cent share of the vote. This meant that the new party was represented in most of the country's regions. The AfD's particularly strong showing in the former East Germany tended to be ascribed to the comparatively lower socio-economic conditions there. Other factors – such as the possibility that like the rest of eastern Germany its inhabitants remembered something their Western compatriots had forgotten – were rarely even discussed in the media at large. What the Chancellor had done was somehow deemed to be right, and anyone who thought otherwise – including the public – must have some strange temporary reason for not yet seeing this.

These results did, however, manage to wrest a rare concession from the former East Germany's most famous daughter. That month she made what was hailed across the world's media as a 'mea culpa'. In fact, the words she used after her party's collapse in Berlin were some way short of that. 'If I could, I would rewind time by many, many years,' she said, 'so that I could better prepare myself and the whole government and all those in positions of responsibility for the situation that caught us unprepared in the late summer of 2015.' But of course the situation had not caught them unprepared. Germany – like every other European country – had been experiencing mass immigration for years. It had been experiencing for decades a breakdown of its border controls, a laxness in repatriations of failed asylum seekers and a failure to integrate new arrivals. So much so that Merkel herself had conceded as much in 2010. If the 'multiculturalism has failed' speech had been anything other than words, it should have given Germany a head start in preparing for the integration tsunami that would come five years later. But it didn't, because it had indeed only been words.

In September 2016 Merkel did concede that her phrase from the year before, 'Wir schaffen das' ('We can do it'), was 'a simple slogan, almost an empty formula', and one that had significantly underestimated the scale of the challenge. But this was also wordplay, as one of her own MP colleagues in the CDU admitted to the press. This MP insisted that 'The government has been on the right track with its policies for some time now. But our communication must be better. The Chancellor seems now to have accepted this.' The 'mea culpa' claim was merely electorally useful for the CDU. But there was no serious remorse for what had been imposed on the country. For what Merkel also said at the same press conference and which was less widely quoted, was that it had been 'absolutely right' to take in the more than one million migrants of the year before. Nevertheless, 'We have learnt from history. Nobody, including me, wants a repeat of this situation.'[3]

Yet it seemed as though the only lessons Germany had learned from history were the usual ones, and those from eight decades earlier. On the eve of the AfD's success in the Berlin elections the mayor of Berlin Michael Müller, from the left-wing SDP, warned that a double-digit result for the AfD would 'be seen around the world as a sign of the return of the right wing and the Nazis in Germany'. Everywhere else in Europe the same warning kept being issued from every direction after every event.

In the same month as the regional elections in Germany, one year after Germany had opened its doors, the British government announced that it was going to have to build a further security wall in Calais near to the large migrant camp there. The one-kilometre wall was designed to further protect the entry point to Britain, and specifically to prevent migrants from trying to climb onto passing lorries on their way to the United Kingdom. Responding to this proposal the French senator and vice-chair of the Senate Foreign Affairs Committee, Nathalie Goulet, said, 'It reminds me of the wall they built around the Warsaw Ghetto in World War Two.' And behind the perennial slur that borders were associated with the Nazis came the familiar presumption that borders were also part of history. 'Putting up walls has happened throughout history,' explained Ms Goulet. 'But eventually people find a way around them or they fail. Look at the Great Wall of China – now tourists walk on it and take pictures.'[4]

In Britain the issue of Calais remained the foremost one in the discussion. Given that there were fewer than 6,500 people in the camp most of the time, a solution to Calais always seemed straightforward. All that was needed – activists and politicians from all sides tried to argue – was a one-time generous offer and the camp could be cleared. This was Europe's big failing in microcosm. If only these people could be admitted to the United Kingdom then the problem would be solved – or so it seemed. Rarely was any thought given to the fact that after the camp emptied it would simply refill again. For 6,500 people was an average day's migration into Italy alone. In the meantime, while the British and French governments argued over who was responsible for the current situation at Calais, both day and night migrants threw missiles into the motorways and at cars, trucks and lorries heading to Britain in the hope that the vehicles would stop and they could climb aboard as stowaways for the journey across the Channel.

Everything about the discussions over Calais, like everything else for decades, was short-sighted and short-term. When the British government agreed to take in a certain number of unaccompanied child migrants from the camp, photographs of the young arrivals appeared in the newspapers. Some of the 'children' looked distinctly adult. Some were in their thirties. One backbench Tory MP, David Davies, pointed this out and suggested the use of dental tests. The entire media and political class descended on him. Television hosts used the opportunity to invite Davies onto their show and shout him down. Other MPs said they were disgusted to sit in the same Parliament as him. Suddenly the debate shifted onto whether it was 'racist' to check people's teeth. An age-test used across the continent was suddenly condemned as unimaginably barbaric. The consensus remained that the good thing to do was to invite all migrants in. The bad thing was to suggest any limitations on their numbers. Or even the enforcement of laws already in place. As so often in the past the government weighed up the pros and cons of holding the line and decided not to hold it.

For of course the migrants who ended up in Calais trying to break into Britain had already broken all the EU's laws to get there. They had not applied for asylum in their first country of entry, had not abided by the Dublin Treaty but pushed on through up to the north of France. In taking them in, the British government thought it was doing a good deed. In fact, it was rewarding the people who had broken the most rules and leap-frogged over all other more deserving migrants. This was a precedent that had been set for years, but it was an unwise precedent nonetheless. Everywhere it remained the same story. To be on the side of the incomers was to be on the side of the angels. To speak for the people of Europe was to be on the side of the devil. And all the time there existed that strange assumption that Europe was simply letting one more person into the room. Whether that person was genuinely about to be killed in the corridor became immaterial. If he was cold, poor, or just worse off there than the people inside the room, he too had the right to come in. Europe could no longer be bothered to turn anyone away. And so the door just remained open to anyone who wanted to walk through it.

18

What might have been

With the right political and moral leadership this could all have worked out differently. Chancellor Merkel and her predecessors would not have been unsupported or unaided had they taken a different set of steps from the beginning.

They could have started by asking themselves the question Europe never did: should Europe be a place to which anybody in the world can move and call themselves at home? Should it be a haven for absolutely anybody in the world fleeing war? Is it the job of Europeans to provide a better standard of living in our continent to anybody in the world who wants it? To the second and third of these questions the European publics would have said 'no'. About the first question they would have felt torn. That is why the supporters of mass migration – who would have said 'yes' to all three – found it convenient to elide the boundaries between those fleeing war and those fleeing something else. What, after all – such people asked – is the huge difference between being at risk from bombs and at risk from hunger?

Had Chancellor Merkel, her contemporaries and her predecessors thought this all through before transforming their continent, they could have consulted Aristotle among other great philosophers of Europe. From him they would have learnt why these questions seemed so complex. They were trying to weigh up the balance not between good and evil but between competing virtues: on this occasion 'justice' and 'mercy'. When such virtues appear to be in contravention, Aristotle suggests, it is because one of them is being misunderstood. Throughout this era of uncontrolled migration 'mercy' has consistently appeared to triumph. It is the virtue towards which it is easiest to pay homage, the one with the swiftest short-term benefits and the one more admired in the society in which those benefits are received. Of course, it was rarely asked how 'merciful' it really was to encourage people to cross the globe to reach a continent with few houses and few jobs where they would be ever less wanted. Yet justice – which took such a back seat even as all the laws of the continent were trampled upon – also had a claim. And if the appeal to justice to enforce the Dublin III Treaty or the laws on the repatriation of failed applicants had seemed like so much paperwork, still there ought to have been an appeal to a greater justice. When justice did emerge in the argument it emerged only as the justice demanded by or for those arriving. The absent party in all this, for whom justice was never considered, were the peoples of Europe. They were people to whom things were done, whose own appeals – even when they could be voiced – were not listened to.

In the great migration movements the decisions of Merkel and her predecessors had overridden all their rights to justice. Those on the liberal wing of Europe's political spectrum had reason to feel aggrieved about the way in which their customs and laws had been trodden upon and about the seemingly endless changes to their liberal societies: changes that endangered the carefully balanced ecosystems of which such societies were comprised. Liberals in Europe might rightly have wondered whether societies that are the product of lengthy political and cultural evolutions could be sustained with immigration at such rates. That the front lines of the mass migration era continually involved threats to sexual, religious and racial minorities should have alerted far more liberals than it did to the possibility that in pursuit of a 'liberal' immigration policy they might lose their liberal societies.

An appeal to justice of a different sort could just as well have come from those of a more conservative mindset. Such people might, for instance, have taken the view of Edmund Burke, who in the eighteenth century made the central conservative insight that a culture and a society are not things run for the convenience of the people who happen to be here right now, but a deep pact between the dead, the living and those yet to be born. In such a view of society, however greatly you might wish to benefit from an endless supply of cheap labour, a wider range of cuisine or the salving of a generation's conscience, you still would not have the right to wholly transform your society. Because that which you inherited that is good should also be passed on. Even were you to decide that some of the views or lifestyles of your ancestors could be improved upon, it does not follow that you should hand over to the next generation a society that is chaotic, fractured and unrecognisable.

By 2015 Europe had already failed the easiest part of the immigration conundrum. From the post-war period up until the seismic movements of the present century it had set about fundamentally changing the nature of European society out of personal comfort, lazy thinking and political ineptitude. So it is not surprising that it also failed the harder test, which was the migration conundrum that Chancellor Merkel confronted in her live televised discussion with the solitary Lebanese teenager but then buckled under when it came to the untold millions (a buckling that was precisely the opposite way around to most people, who abhor the crowds but pity the individual). She had misunderstood the virtues. Merkel could have been merciful to those in need whilst not being unjust to the peoples of Europe. How could this have been achieved?

The first way would have been to go right back to the basics of the problem: principally the question of who Europe is for. Those who believe it is for the world have never explained why this process should be one way: why Europeans going anywhere else in the world is colonialism whereas the rest of the world coming to Europe is just and fair. Nor have they ever suggested that the migration movement has any end other than the turning of Europe into a place belonging to the world, with other countries remaining the home of the people of those countries. They have also only succeeded to the extent they have by lying to the public and concealing their aims. Had the leaders of Western Europe told their publics in the 1950s or at any point since that the aim of migration was to fundamentally alter the concept of

Europe and make it a home for the world, then the people of Europe would most likely have risen up and overthrown those governments.

Even before the migration crisis of recent years the greatest challenge was always over genuine refugees. Like their publics, political leaders held consistently conflicted views on those refugees – conflicted views expressed not just one to another, but within themselves. Nobody could allow a child to drown in the Mediterranean but nor could it be viable to allow the world in if the world was on our shores. In the summer of 2016 I got talking with two Bangladeshi men in Greece. One of them, a 26-year-old, had come through India, Pakistan, Iran and Turkey to get to Lesbos. On his journey, he said, 'I saw dead bodies everywhere.' He spent 15,000 Euros on this journey and said that he had to leave Bangladesh because he was involved with the political opposition. 'My father is a bank manager,' he said. 'It is not about money. It is about life. Everyone loves their mother country', but 'nine out of ten people are here because they want to live'. The evidence suggests otherwise, namely that the economic attractions are the main lure. Yet even if everyone coming to Europe was coming in the face of imminent death back home, there is no practical way that Europe could take in those untold millions. So even a refinement of the errors of European migration is itself based on an error.

Some people say that the crisis is primarily not Europe's but the world's – that even talking about this represents a Eurocentric way of looking at things. But there is no reason why Europeans should not be, or feel, Eurocentric. Europe is the home of the European peoples, and we are entitled to be home-centric as much as the Americans, Indians, Pakistanis, Japanese and all other peoples are. The follow-on claim that we should therefore focus our energies on 'solving' the problems of the world is a diversion. It is not in Europe's power to 'solve' the situation in Syria. Much less is it within our gift to simultaneously raise living standards in sub-Saharan Africa, solve all world conflicts, protect liberal rights universally and rectify all problems of political corruption across the world. Those who present these as problems that can be solved by Europe should start by explaining their detailed plan for solving the problem of Eritrea. Or finding it on a map.

Anyone in power with a genuine desire to help migrants could enact a number of policies. They could, for instance, prioritise a policy of keeping migrants in the vicinity of the country from which they are fleeing. Migration experts including Paul Collier and David Goodhart have – even before the current crisis – explained the importance of such a policy.[1] It avoids the cultural challenges that arise from encouraging people to travel to the far end of a different continent. It also allows people to return home more easily when whatever the disaster they are fleeing from comes to an end. Throughout the Syrian crisis Turkey, Lebanon and Jordan have taken in huge numbers of refugees. Britain and other nations have contributed huge sums in aid to relieve the situation in refugee camps and other places in which Syrian refugees are living. Policies like those suggested by Collier of European countries paying migrants to do work in Middle Eastern countries (where for reasons of local sentiment current labour laws often preclude refugees from entering the workforce) would be constructive. Such ideas would be predicated on the view that it is better for a Syrian to be able to work in Jordan than to be unemployed somewhere in Scandinavia.

What is more, the money that a country like Sweden now pays to house immigrants in Sweden is spendthrift even if the concerns of immigrants and potential immigrants were the only concerns of the Swedish government. The housing shortage in Sweden – which, as in the United Kingdom, is largely caused by immigration – creates huge problems for the Swedish government. Not least financial problems. In southern European countries such as Italy or Greece a temporary solution for migrants is to house them in tents. Because of Sweden's cold climate it costs between 50 and 100 times more to house a migrant in a tent there than it does in the Middle East. As Dr Tino Sanandaji has pointed out, it costs more for 3,000 migrants to be housed in temporary accommodation tents in Sweden than it does to fund outright the largest refugee camp in Jordan (housing around 100,000 Syrian refugees).[2]

One other policy upon which European leaders could have embarked from the beginning was to ensure that asylum claims were processed outside Europe. For legal and organisational reasons, it makes no sense to begin the process of working out who is a legitimate asylum seeker and who is not once migrants are inside Europe. This was the policy of the Australian government when they experienced over the last decade a flow of migrant boats setting off for their country mainly from Indonesia. As with the situation in the Mediterranean a number of the boats sank and there were huge outpourings of public sympathy for the migrants. But asylum centres in Australia were full and the processing became a legal nightmare once migrants were in Australia. Although the stretch of water is far wider than the Mediterranean and the numbers were never of a comparable size, the Australian government instituted an emergency policy that swiftly saw a decline in the number of boats setting out. They used Nauru and Manus Islands, off the coast of Papua New Guinea, as holding centres and processed the asylum claimants there. Australian government vessels also increasingly located and turned back vessels heading to Australia illegally.

The situation is not precisely analogous, but Australian officials have said in private since the beginning of the current European crisis that this is the way in which Europe will have to deal with its crisis at some point anyway. With the political will and financial incentive there is no reason why European governments could not institute arrangements with various North African governments to set up facilities on their territory. A process of 'leasing' territory in Libya is not impossible at some stage. It would certainly be feasible in Tunisia and Morocco, and the French government could help persuade the Algerians to cooperate in a similar manner. Egypt could also be incentivised as part of its European cooperation packages. Processing claimants in North Africa would not only have a disincentivising effect, as it has had in the Australian case, it would also give the European asylum system a chance to catch its breath.

Another solution would be a concerted Europe-wide effort to organise the deportation of all those found to have no asylum claim. This is easier said than done: millions of people who are currently in

Europe have no legal right to be here. Some might welcome assistance to return home, having found themselves working for gangs or otherwise finding life in Europe less appealing than they had expected. Still, this would be a monumental task to undertake. But it would be better to do it than to pretend – as members of the German and Swedish governments did in recent years – to do it while having no real intention of doing so. To 'include' some people in a society necessarily means 'excluding' others. Governments found it very easy to dwell on the sympathetic language of 'inclusion', but their publics – including legitimate asylum seekers – need also to hear the language of exclusion.

Another policy that would assist in a sensible migration policy and help restore public confidence would be a system of temporary asylum. If during the crucial months of 2015 Chancellor Merkel had called on European countries to take in a certain number of legitimate and properly vetted refugees from Syria until such a time as Syria returned to stability, there may have been significantly more public and political support. The fact that there was not – and the reason why the public as well as governments remained so opposed to Merkel's quota system – was because those countries knew that asylum is nearly always for good. It is hard to convince the Swedish public that Syrian migrants are going to remain in their country only until Syria stabilizes when Sweden still has tens of thousands of asylum seekers from the Balkans, which has been at peace for two decades.

The nature of temporary asylum obviously has its own problems. People's lives continue once they migrate. Their children enter the school system and other aspects of normalisation occur which make the return of whole families to their country of origin ever harder. But that is a reason why European governments would have to be strict with such a policy. If people apply for asylum and are given it, then they must recognise that the arrangement is benevolent but not permanent. Much confidence in the asylum system and the migration issue as a whole could be reclaimed if such a policy were implemented.

In order to bring an end to the ongoing migration problem and turn around the challenge that already exists, it would also be necessary for Europe's political leaders to acknowledge where they have gone wrong in the past. They might, for instance, acknowledge that if Europe is concerned about an ageing population there are more sensible policies than importing the next generation of Europeans from Africa. They might concede that while diversity may be advantageous in small numbers, in large numbers it would irrevocably end society as we know it. They might then stress that they do not actually want to fundamentally change our societies. This would be a painful concession for the political class, but it would have overwhelming support from the European publics.

In recent years those publics have been exceptionally accepting of immigrants while opposed to mass immigration. Long before their political leaders told them that it was acceptable to have concerns about immigration, they knew this. Before the sociologists proved it, they knew that immigration weakened all sense of societal 'trust'. And before the politicians admitted it, the public were struggling to get their children into over-subscribed local schools. It was the public who were told that health-tourism was not a problem, even as they queued for appointments in waiting rooms filled with people from other countries.

The public also knew long before their political leaders that the benefits the migrants undoubtedly brought were not endless, and they sensed long before it became acceptable to say it that migration on such a scale would fundamentally change their countries. They noticed that some of the major battles of the twentieth century over rights were having to be refought again in the twenty-first century because of a growing number of opponents. They intimated that when it came to social liberalism Islam was simply the slowest child in the class. Just one result of which was that in the early twenty-first century, when Europe had hoped to have settled many of these issues – not least the separation of religion from politics and the law – the whole of society was having to go at the speed of this slowest child in the class. Thus, the increasing discussions about whether women should cover their faces in public, or be taken by their husband to their own special type of court if they happened to be of a particular faith.

The first arrivals benefited Europe by bringing a different culture, their vibrancy and their cuisine. But what did the ten millionth bring that was different from all those before? The European public was far ahead of the politicians in recognising that the benefits were not endless. Long before the politicians noticed, the public already knew that a continent which imports the world's people will also import the world's problems. And contrary to the race-relations industry, it turned out that the immigrants into Europe often exhibited far more differences than similarities to the resident populations and towards each other, and that the larger the numbers the greater the dissimilarities.

For the problems that exist are not just between minorities and their adopted country but between various minorities in their adopted country. Despite the much-vaunted horror of 'Islamophobia' trailed by 'anti-racists' and others in Britain, those who have actually killed Muslims in Britain have been overwhelmingly other Muslims murdering them for doctrinal reasons. There has been one case of a Ukrainian neo-Nazi who was in the United Kingdom for a matter of hours before killing his Muslim victim. Otherwise, the most serious attacks on Muslims have been carried out by other Muslims. Many Muslims from the minority Ahmadiyya sect came to Britain because they are so persecuted in their native Pakistan. But it was a Sunni Muslim from Bradford who travelled up to Glasgow before Easter 2016 to stab the Muslim Ahmadiyya shopkeeper Asad Shah repeatedly in the head for what his killer regarded as apostasy and heresy. And it was not knuckle-dragging white racists but other members of the Muslim communities in Scotland who caused the family of the murdered shopkeeper to flee the country in the wake of that murder. Today in Britain it is rarely white racists who openly advocate the murder of minorities, but clerics from Pakistan who tour the United Kingdom preaching to thousands of British citizens the necessity of murdering other Muslims who disagree with them. Such problems within minorities are a foretaste of the intolerance to come.

Of even greater concern to the majority is the observation that many of those who come to Europe – even when they have no desire to hurt or kill anyone – seem happy about transforming European societies. Politicians cannot address this because they have colluded in it or helped cover it over. But it cannot go unnoticed when a Muslim of Syrian background such as Lamya Kaddor, for instance, goes on German television at the height of the migration crisis and tells the nation that in the future being German will not mean having 'blue eyes and blond hair', but will instead be about having a 'migration background'. Only in Germany would such a sentiment continue, for the time being, to get applause. But most Europeans do not appreciate this common glee over radical changes to their society, and it would be wise for mainstream political figures to acknowledge this fact and concede that the resulting fears are not unfounded.

As part of that concession it would also be wise to extend the parameters of what is acceptable in mainstream politics. Parties of the centre right and centre left have found it enormously useful in recent decades to portray people who do not sign up to their narrow consensus as racist, fascist or Nazi, even when they know that they are no such thing. They have been able to position themselves as centrists and anti-fascists whilst smearing all opponents with the crimes of the last century. The complex situation in Europe, of course, is that there are parties which had fascist or racist origins. Belgium's Vlaams Belang, France's Front National and the Sweden Democrats all have histories that have included racism. In different ways all have changed to some extent in recent decades. The political mainstream finds it useful to pretend that such parties are the only ones on our continent who do not change, or are incapable of changing, or lie and conceal their true nature even after years of changing. However, at some point people have to allow the political far-right to moderate, in the same way that many socialist and far-left parties were allowed to enter the mainstream and moderated their views in the process. These nationalist parties should be allowed to occupy a place in the political debate without being forever charged with the sins of their pasts.

The move from Jean-Marie Le Pen to his daughter Marine Le Pen, for instance, is clearly a move of significance. A true devotee of racist nationalist politics would find it harder to join today's Front National than they would have done the party of Marine's father. There are of course serious questions all around the edges. Still, these parties have problems with people trying to get involved who hold to Holocaust denial and similarly extreme views. This is in part – as with the EDL in England and Pegida in Germany – a result of the entire media and political class telling people that this is what such parties stand for and effectively sending any true extremists to join them. It is also true that these parties include people with rancid political views. But so too, it must be noted, do mainstream parties of the political left and right. It is not possible to regard parties that often poll ahead of other mainstream parties as being wholly Nazi, fascist or racist, since it should be obvious to any politician with experience of the public in any of these countries that they are not largely Nazi, fascist or racist.

In other words, it will be necessary to broaden the political consensus and to accept thoughtful and clearly non-fascist parties once described as 'far right' at the political table. Not only would it be unwise to continue to marginalise people who have spent years warning about events just as those warnings are coming true, it would also be unwise to continue a situation which would mean that any truly fascist parties emerging in the years ahead (such as Jobbik in Hungary, Ataka in Bulgaria or Golden Dawn in Greece) can be identified accurately and without the accusation that this label had been used about almost everybody. Europeans have been deflating the language of anti-fascism ahead of a time when they might need it. Warnings of fascism should be used exceptionally carefully in Europe. In recent years they have been worn down and become so commonplace as to be rendered almost meaninglessness. Finally, it would be an unsustainable position for the political and media elites of Europe to continue to pretend that the views of the majority of the public are unacceptable whilst the pro-mass migration views of a comparatively small and extreme fringe are the only legitimate views for the mainstream in European politics.

It may be the case that the issue of racism has to adapt in other ways. One way to defang the constant frivolous uses of the term would be to ensure that the cost in social terms for making the charge falsely becomes at least as serious as being guilty of the charge. Or it may be that Europeans become so mired in accusations and counter-accusations from and towards every direction in the years ahead that there is an implicit agreement that unpleasant as racism is, it is one of a number of nasty facets to which some people are prone and not the basis for all political and cultural positioning.

Any solution to our crisis would also involve not only a fresh attitude towards our future but a more balanced attitude towards our past. It is not possible for a society to survive if it routinely suppresses and otherwise fights against its own origins. Just as a nation could not thrive if it forbade any criticism of its past, so no nation can survive if it suppresses everything that is positive about its past. Europe has reason to feel tired and worn down by its past, but it could also approach its past with an air of self-forgiveness as much as self-reproach. At the very least Europe needs to continue to engage with the glories as well as the pains of its past. It is not possible to give a comprehensive answer to this difficult problem here, but for my own part I cannot help feeling that much of the future of Europe will be decided on what our attitude is towards the church buildings and other great cultural buildings of our heritage standing in our midst. Around the questions of whether we hate them, ignore them, engage with them or revere them, a huge amount will depend.

Again it is worth pondering the question of what would happen if the bubble were to pop and the next generations of Europeans suddenly experienced a decline in living standards because people in the rest of the world were to catch up with them, or because the debts accumulated through Europe's expectations of 'normal' living standards piled up beyond acceptable limits. Enjoyable as it might be while it lasts, it probably goes without saying that the life of a mere consumer lacks any real meaning and purpose. Instead, it reveals a gap in human experience that every society in history has attempted to address and which something else will try to fill if our own societies do not apply themselves to it. A society that sells itself solely on its pleasures is one that can swiftly lose its attractions. That post-nightclub convert had experienced the pleasures but then came to the realisation they were not enough. A society that says we are defined exclusively by the bar and the nightclub, by self-indulgence and our sense of entitlement, cannot be said to have deep roots or much likelihood of survival. But a society which holds that our culture consists of the cathedral, the playhouse and the playing field, the shopping mall and Shakespeare, has a chance.

Still, there remains the unwillingness to confront these deeper issues. And each time it seems to come down to a sense of fatalism – in particular the sense that we have tried all of these things before. Why would we do all that again? This must be one of the reasons why appeals to Europeans to recapture their faith – even by Church leaders – are made not in the admonitory tones of the past but in a spirit of impeachment or even partial defeat. When Pope Benedict implored Europeans to behave 'as though God exists', he was acknowledging something that his predecessors were rarely able to accept: that some people today cannot believe and that the Church ought nevertheless to have some approach to them. Indeed, it was this appeal, more than anything else, that made the dying Oriana Fallaci a believer in Pope Benedict even whilst not being a believer in God. Elsewhere, the Pope appealed for the great gulf between religion and philosophy to be breached, specifically appealing that rather than being enemies, religion and philosophy must at least be in dialogue with each other.[3]

At the root of such appeals is an awareness that Europeans are unlikely to simply find or come up with another culture or a better culture. And also an acknowledgement that modern Europeans from school upwards are currently doing a very poor job of celebrating a culture that has nurtured believers and doubters of previous generations and may nurture believers and doubters in this generation too. A growing number of both believers and non-believers have begun to realise that during the potentially huge upheavals in the years ahead it will not be enough to face them by first stripping ourselves absolutely bare. That practice is of course a particular part of the French tradition and the reason why when the country seeks to circumscribe the wearing of the Islamic headscarf, or burka, it has to excuse it by circumscribing the wearing of Jewish and Christian symbols as well. While many people will see the sense in this, it also risks a game of strip-poker in which you begin stripped down to nothing whereas your opposite number has come fully clothed. It is possible that Islamic radicals will remain in France despite the ban on the wearing of the headscarf in certain public buildings while it is also possible that Jews – caught between the Islamists and the stricter secularisation they have provoked – will leave. Neither would be a desirable outcome.

If the culture that shaped Western Europe has no part in its future, then there are other cultures and traditions that will surely step in to take its place. To re-inject our own culture with some sense of a deeper purpose need not be a proselytising mission, but simply an aspiration of which we should be aware. Of course, it is always possible that the tide of faith that began its long, withdrawing roar of retreat in the nineteenth century will come back in again. But whether it does or not a mending of the culture will be impossible if the religious think that those who have split off from the same tree are their greatest problem, while those on the secular branch try to saw themselves off from the tree as a whole. Many people can sense the pain of that separation and the resulting want of meaning that arises from the shallows. A split has occurred in our culture that it will take the work of a generation to mend.

19

What will be

It is also worth considering what – on the current performance of Europe's politicians and the attitudes of its populations – are more likely scenarios than the one set out in the last chapter. For instance, it would seem far more likely that rather than massive U-turns occurring, politics across Europe will instead continue in the coming decades much as it was up until now. There has been little meaningful acknowledgement among the political class that what it has done during the decades of mass immigration is in any way regrettable. There is no evidence that they would wish to reverse that policy. And there is a great deal of evidence to suggest that they could not do so even if they wished to. The events of 2015 onwards have merely sped up a process that had long been underway.

Every new migrant to Western Europe becomes harder to eject the longer they are settled, and most of us do not want to eject most or many of them in any case. But with every new arrival the balance of Europe's future attitudes shifts. Those arriving have children who will remember their roots and are more likely than the rest of the population to oppose further restrictions on immigration. An ever larger number of people who are themselves of immigrant background will be ever less likely to support any political party proposing limits on immigration. They will feel suspicious of those parties, even where their agendas are comparatively modest. Aside from worrying for themselves, it is hard for somebody who has come to Europe from elsewhere to reason why other people like them should not come in their wake. The line between legal and illegal immigration will continue to blur ever further. So with each passing day it will become harder to find a large enough portion of the population opposed to mass immigration in order to push for a policy that would reverse or at least prevent the continuation of it. And so in time, during the present century, in the major cities first and then across whole countries, our societies will finally become those 'nations of immigrants' that we pretended for a period we always were.

Politicians willing to argue against such a dwindling position will continue to be deterred by the unique price they must pay to make their case. In Holland, Denmark and other countries across Europe, politicians who oppose mass immigration – and the influx of certain communities in particular – exist in a state of permanent police protection, change their sleeping arrangements most nights and sometimes live on army bases. Even if someone was willing to take the risk of career-damaging name-calling, how many will continue to come forward to argue the case of the European people when such a life has become one inevitable consequence? And in a situation that will only get worse? For the time being most politicians will continue to find the short-term benefits of taking the 'compassionate', 'generous' and 'open' course of action to be personally preferable, even if it leads to long-term national problems. They will continue to believe, as they have done for decades, that it is better to put these difficult matters off so that their successors have to deal with the consequences instead.

So they will continue to ensure that Europe is the only place in the world that belongs to the world. It is already clear what type of society will result. By the middle of this century, while China will probably still look like China, India will probably still look like India, Russia like Russia, and Eastern Europe like Eastern Europe, Western Europe will at best resemble a large-scale version of the United Nations. Many people will welcome this, and it will have its pleasures of course. Certainly not everything about it will be a catastrophe. Many people will enjoy living in such a Europe. They will continue to enjoy cheap services, at least for a time, as incomers compete with those already here to do work for less and less money. There will be an endless influx of new neighbours and staff, and there will be many interesting conversations to be had. This place where international cities develop into something resembling international countries will be many things. But it will not be Europe anymore.

Perhaps the European lifestyle, culture and outlook will survive in small pockets. A pattern that is already underway will mean that there will be some rural areas where immigrant communities choose not to live and towards which non-immigrants retreat. Those who have the resources will – as is already the case – be able to sustain a recognisably similar lifestyle for a while longer. The less well off will have to accept that they do not live in a place that is their home but in one that is a home for the world. And whilst incomers will be encouraged to pursue their traditions and lifestyles, Europeans whose families have been here for generations will most likely continue to be told that theirs is an oppressive, outdated tradition, even as they constitute a smaller and smaller minority of the population. This is not science fiction. It is simply what the current situation looks like in much of Western Europe and what the demographic projections show the continent's future to be.

For although our societies integrated people better than some people feared, we are not after all such great melting pots that anything and anyone can be endlessly poured in with the results always coming out the same. To return to the analogy of the ship of Theseus, the ship can only be said to remain the ship if it remains recognisable. For that to happen, when the ship needs mending it needs to be repaired using recognisable parts that fit in with the whole. But European society today is ever less recognisable, and what chances it had to sustain the whole were lost when it chose to wage a war on its own design. The pieces of the ship that were added were not carefully selected and did not fit the old shapes. Rather, by government design and incompetence the ship was pulled apart and anything at all that stood in its place was crow-barred in and still called Europe.

Nonetheless, the political leadership of Europe will go around and around the same failed and contradictory ideas and repeat the same mistake. Which is why the analogy presented to me in the Bundestag mattered. My German interlocutor's analogy presented Europe as a room into which a person in mortal danger in the corridor outside must be allowed to come and join us. Politicians from Britain to Sweden sometimes like to proclaim that our room is a large territory that we could easily concrete over in order to house the world's needy. But our societies are not like that. Any sensible policy on immigration and integration would have taken into account that although this ship of Europe may occasionally save people in distress from the seas around us, there is a point – when we take too many people on board, take them on too quickly, or take on those with bad intent – at which we will capsize the only vessel that we, the peoples of Europe, have.

During the migration crisis it was not only 'open borders' activists who believed that bringing the whole world on board was a sensible policy. It was members of the Greek government and of governing parties across Europe. Some believed it as ideology. Others simply could find no reasonable moral way to deny entry to the world's inhabitants. Others flailed around for an excuse. After the British vote to leave the EU, Daniel Korski, the former deputy director of David Cameron's Policy Unit, recalled how before the vote Britain's European counterparts tried to persuade the country to take in more migrants, using the argument – among others – that migrants paid more in taxes than they consumed in public services. Even at this point – at the height of the crisis – the continent relied on old and disproven lies. What made it worse was that Korski claimed, 'We were never able to counter these arguments', claiming that although they looked, 'There was no hard evidence.'[1] The evidence – had they looked properly – was all around them. They could have gone to the schools in their local area, the A&E wards of any local hospital, and wondered how all these incomers could possibly have paid their way already. That was what the British people were wondering. Only their representatives remained unbothered, incurious or in denial.

And so the policies that had already made the native British a minority in their own capital city ineluctably sped up a change in the demographics of the entire continent. The 'dark specialism' of the French turned out to be the dark discovery of Europe. Promised throughout their lifetimes that the changes were temporary, that the changes were not real, or that the changes did not signify anything, Europeans discovered that in the lifespan of people now alive they would become minorities in their own countries. And it did not much matter whether the country had a reputation for liberalism or a reputation for fire-breathing conservatism, the direction of travel was the same. When the Vienna Institute of Demography confirmed that by the middle of this century a majority of Austrians under the age of 15 would be Muslims, the Austrian people were – like everybody else in Europe – simply expected to ignore or wish away their own cultural end point. The dark Brechtian joke appeared after all to be true: the political elites had found their publics wanting and had solved the problem by dissolving the people and appointing another people in their place.

What is more, it had all been done on the laughable presumption that while all cultures are equal, European cultures are less equal than others. And that a person who favoured the culture of Germany over that of Eritrea had, in the most gracious interpretation, an out-of-date or ill-informed opinion, and in the more common view was simply an out-and-out racist. That all this was done in the name of a diversity that became less and less diverse by the year should have been the clearest possible warning sign.

For if there was any chance at all of this working it would be that the new Europeans from Africa or anywhere else in the world would swiftly learn to be as European as any Europeans in the past. Perhaps there has been some official nervousness about this. For some years in Britain the annual list of most popular babies' names cited in the Office for National Statistics was a subject of contention. Again and again variants of the name 'Mohammed' climbed higher and higher up the lists. Officials defended their practice of listing the 'Mohammeds' separately from the 'Muhammads' and other variant spellings of the same name. Only in 2016 did it become clear that this was immaterial because the name in all its variants had indeed become the most popular boy's name in England and Wales. At which point the official line changed to 'And so what?' It was implied that the Mohammeds of tomorrow will be as English or as Welsh as the Harrys or Dafydds of the generations before. In other words, Britain will remain British even when most of the men are called Mohammed, in the same way that Austria will remain Austria even when most of the men are called Mohammed. That this is unlikely hardly needs saying.

Indeed, nearly all the evidence appears to be pointing the opposite way. Anyone in doubt about this might simply consider the minorities within the minorities. Who, for instance, are the Muslims in Europe who are most under threat. Are they the radicals? Do the Salafists and Khomeinists and Muslim Brotherhood and Hamas leaders in Europe live under any threat or ever have to worry even about their reputations? There is no evidence to suggest they do. Even groups whose graduates go on to behead Europeans are taken on their own estimation inside Europe to be 'human rights' groups, intent merely on tackling the injustices endemic in our racist and patriarchal society. This is why by 2015 more British Muslims were fighting for Isis than for the British armed forces.

The people who are at risk and the people who are most criticised both from within Muslim communities in Europe and among the wider population are in fact the people who fell hardest for the integration promises of liberal Europe. It was not the Muslim and non-Muslim persecutors of Ayaan Hirsi Ali who left the Netherlands, but Hirsi Ali herself. In twenty-first-century Holland she believed in the principles of the Enlightenment more than the Dutch any longer did. In Germany it is not the Salafists who live under police protection, but their critics like Hamed Abdel-Samad whose life is in danger simply for exercising his democratic rights in a free and secular society. And in Britain it is not those who preach the murder of apostates to packed mosques up and down the country who draw British Muslim ire and who consequently have to be careful about their security. Instead, it is a progressive British Muslim of Pakistani heritage like Maajid Nawaz, an activist and columnist, whose only mistake was in believing Britain when it presented itself as a society that still wanted legal equality and one law for all. In France a writer of Algerian origin – Kamel Daoud – publishes an article in *Le Monde*[2] speaking frankly about the sex attacks in Cologne, and is then criticised by a cohort of sociologists, historians and others who call him an 'Islamophobe' and claim he is speaking 'as the European far right'. In every Western European country it is the Muslims who have come here or been born here and stood up for our own ideals – including our ideals of free speech – who have been castigated by their co-religionists and carefully dropped by what was once 'polite' European society. To say that in the long run this heralds the makings of a societal catastrophe is to understate matters.

Nothing here is possible to predict. But everywhere in Europe new things have already started to happen that signal a direction of travel. In terms of foreign policy, for years Europe has found itself incapable of expressing a coordinated strategic view. And now thanks to our immigration policies international politics has also become domestic politics, making Europe all but incapable of acting discriminatingly on the world stage with either soft or hard power. In June 2016, when the UN accused the Eritrean government of committing crimes against humanity, thousands of Eritreans protested outside the UN building in Geneva.[3] The Swiss people had been told, like everyone else in Europe, that here were people who had come to Switzerland because they were fleeing a government they could not live under. Yet thousands of them turned out to support that same government when someone in Europe criticised them. In 2014 a leaked report from Britain's Ministry of Defence revealed that military planners believed that 'an increasingly multicultural Britain' and 'increasingly diverse nation' meant that British military intervention in foreign countries was becoming impossible. The government would gain less and less public support for British troops being deployed in countries 'from which UK citizens, or their families, come'.[4]

Domestically, the situation has the potential to become infinitely worse. Just one consequence of having 'diversity' and 'difference' rather than 'colour blindness' and proper integration as a goal is that Europe in the twenty-first century is obsessed with race. Rather than diminishing, the subject grows larger by the day. It is the same story in politics, sport and even television, where not a single reality-TV programme seems immune from the endless obsession with race. If a non-white, non-European does well he or she is hailed as an example to everyone and a model of successful integration. If that person is voted out there is yet another national debate about racism and whether the individual was voted out because of their ethnicity. On a more serious level, nobody has any idea long term where any of this will go.

For instance, in Britain it might have been thought that since the 1980s at least, racial divisions have significantly diminished. Yet thanks to the internationalising of societies, nobody can predict the consequences of events happening anywhere in the world and their effect on domestic politics. For example, the Black Lives Matter movement that started in the United States in 2012, as a result of a number of killings by police of unarmed black men, eventually spread to Britain and other European countries. Whatever the rights and wrongs of the BLM movement in America, almost none of the circumstances for such a movement exist in Britain. In 2016 I watched a BLM protest of several thousand people marching through the centre of London giving black-power salutes and chanting, among other BLM themes, 'Hands up, don't shoot'. All the while they were escorted along the route of their march by British police officers, who of course do not carry guns. Whatever was comedic about this evaporated weeks later when on one of the hottest nights of the year a large crowd chanting BLM slogans met in Hyde Park. By the end of the evening one police officer had been stabbed and four other officers injured. Elsewhere the protest spilled over into one of London's busiest streets where a man was set upon by three men armed with a machete. It was the most serious violence in the capital for years.

Nobody can have any idea where future movements of such a kind will come from. But if you have many people from various parts of the whole world living in close proximity, who come to entertain various degrees of resentment, it is probable that various of the world's problems will descend on those communities at some time. And the world will always have problems. In the meantime it is not certain that the European publics will forever cease to resist the issue of race. If every other group and movement in society is able to identify race and talk explicitly about it, why not the Europeans? In the same way that it is not inevitable that Europeans will forever be persuaded of our historical and hereditary iniquity, so it is possible that we might eventually say that racial politics cannot be for everyone else but not for us.

For the time being it seems that things will continue as they are. Even now the onus still remains on Europeans to solve the world's problems by bringing in people from many parts of the world. Only we, when we say 'enough', are castigated and then troubled by such castigation: a response that many other nations and despotisms remain happy to encourage. No Western European country has played a major role in destabilizing the regime in Syria or prolonging the ensuing civil war. But those countries that have done so – for instance Qatar and the United Arab Emirates – pay no humanitarian price. Iran – whose Hezbollah among other militias have been fighting for Iranian interests in Syria since 2011 – has even berated Europe for not doing more to help the refugees. In September 2015 Iran's President Rouhani had the gall to lecture the Hungarian ambassador to Iran over Hungary's alleged 'shortcomings' in the refugee crisis. Likewise Saudi Arabia, which has spent the period since the beginning of the Syrian civil war backing its preferred sides inside the country. Not only has Saudi Arabia not made one Syrian into a Saudi citizen, it has also refused to allow the use of 100,000 air-conditioned tents that are erected for only five days a year by pilgrims on the Hajj. At the height of the 2015 crisis the single offer the Saudis did make was to build 200 new mosques in Germany for the benefit of the country's new arrivals.

Other than European goodwill continuing to be taken advantage of, one further thing can be predicted with some certainty: public sentiment among Europeans will continue to sour. Although recent history shows that politicians certainly can go on ignoring majority public opinion for decades, it is not inevitable that such a situation will continue indefinitely. A typical poll carried out in 2014 found that a mere 11 per cent of the British public wanted the population of their country to increase.[5] Yet in the two years that followed the population grew enormously. Since 2010 the number of those in the United Kingdom who were born outside it has grown by 1.4 million. During the same period 940,000 children were born in Britain to foreign-born mothers. And this is in a country that has avoided the worst consequences of the 2015 crisis.

Can governments continue to dodge the consequences of their own actions and inactions? Perhaps in some countries they will. Others may cynically switch track in a second. During this crisis I spoke with one French politician of the centre right who could hardly locate any remaining differences between his own party's immigration policies and those of the Front National. Asked how he would deal with a particular set of challenges to do with people who were already nationals, he replied with remarkable nonchalance that it would 'probably be necessary to change some bits of the constitution'. Perhaps cynical land-grabs for political ground will become commonplace. In lieu of any more meaningful policies German politicians have already suggested that citizens with dual nationality who fight with foreign terrorist groups should lose their German citizenship. Denmark has introduced a law allowing authorities to seize valuables from migrants in order to cover the cost of their presence in the country. And everywhere the question of what to do with people who subvert the state is going through various iterations of a debate. Currently, all countries refuse to break international law by making people stateless, but the sense prevails that Europe is not much more than one terrorist attack away from the rules of the game changing completely. At which point Europeans may choose to name almost anyone as their umpire.

Perhaps in one European country in the near future a party of the kind previously described as 'far right' will come to power. Perhaps a party even further to the right will then come to power at some point later. One thing is certain, which is that if the politics are to turn bad it will be because the ideas turned increasingly bad. And if the ideas turn bad it will be because the rhetoric became increasingly bad. In the wake of Cologne and other similar attacks one could hear the language deteriorate around the fringes. Street movements began to talk of all arrivals into Europe as 'rapefugees'. In Paris I met an elected official who referred to all migrants as 'refu-jihadists'. These were unamusing as well as insulting terms for anybody who knew first hand that some at least of the people who had come were fleeing rape or escaping jihad. But such deterioration in the language seems inevitable after a period of dishonesty from the other direction. If you pretend for long enough, in the face of clear evidence, that all the arrivals into the continent are asylum seekers, you will eventually spawn a movement that believes none of them are.

In some ways it is amazing that such a movement has not kicked off in earnest already. All the while public opinion continues to progress ineluctably in one direction. In 2010 the German political class had worried in the loudest way they could about public opinion polls showing 47 per cent of Germans didn't think Islam belonged in Germany. By 2015 the number of Muslims in Germany had gone up again, but so had the number of people who believed that Islam did not belong there. In 2015 that figure had risen to 60 per cent. By the following year almost two-thirds of Germans said that Islam did not belong in Germany, with only 22 per cent of the population saying the religion was integral to German society.[6] In February 2017, after a new American President attempted to pass temporary travel restrictions on citizens from seven unstable Muslim-majority countries, Chatham House released a survey of European opinion. The London think tank had asked 10,000 people across ten European countries whether they agreed or disagreed with the statement, 'All further migration from mainly Muslim countries should be stopped'. The majority of the public in eight out of the ten countries surveyed – including

Germany – agreed with the statement. Britain was one of only two European countries where a desire to halt all further Muslim migration into the country remained a minority opinion. In Britain only 47% of the public agreed with the statement.[7]

Europeans are left in the position of not believing sufficiently in their own story and being distrustful of their past whilst knowing that there are other stories moving in that they do not want. Everywhere a feeling is growing of all options being closed off. All routes out seem to have been tried before and appear impossible to venture into again. Perhaps the only country in Europe that could lead the continent out of such stagnation would be Germany. Yet even before the last century Europeans had every reason to fear the notion of German leadership. Today, younger Germans tend to fear this even more than their parents. And so the sense of general drift and leaderlessness continues.

In the meantime elected officials and bureaucrats continue to do everything they can to make the situation as bad as possible as fast as possible. In October 2015 there was a public meeting in the small city of Kassel in the state of Hesse. Eight hundred immigrants were due to arrive in the following days and concerned residents had a meeting to ask questions of their representatives. As a video recording of the meeting shows, citizens were calm, polite but concerned. Then at a certain point their district president, one Walter Lübcke, calmly informs them that anybody who does not agree with the policy is 'free to leave Germany'. You can see and hear on the tape the intake of breath, amazed laughter, hoots and finally shouts of anger.[8] Whole new populations are being brought into their country and they are being told that if they don't like this they are always free to leave? Do no politicians in Europe realise what could happen if they continue to treat the European people like this?

Apparently not. Nor do all of the arrivals. In October 2016 *Der Freitag* and *Huffington Post Deutschland* both published an article by an 18-year-old Syrian migrant called Aras Bacho. In the piece he complained that the migrants in Germany were 'fed up' with the 'angry' German people who 'insult and agitate' and are 'unemployed racists'. Among other imprecations he continued, 'We refugees ... do not want to live in the same country with you. You can, and I think you should, leave Germany. Germany does not fit you, why do you live here? ... Look for a new home.'⁹

On New Year's Eve 2016, on the first anniversary of the Cologne rape attacks, there were similar sex attacks in a number of European cities, including Innsbruck and Augsburg. Police in Cologne were heavily criticised by MPs from the SPD and Green parties, among others, for allegedly 'racially profiling' those seeking access to the city's main square in an attempt to prevent a repeat of the previous year's atrocities. One year after Germany had awoken to part of its new reality, the censors had returned and resumed control. On the same night in France just under 1,000 cars were set alight – a 17% rise on the same night one year before. The French Interior Ministry described the night as having gone off 'without any major incident.'

Day by day the continent of Europe is not only changing but is losing any possibility of a soft landing in response to such change. An entire political class have failed to appreciate that many of us who live in Europe love the Europe that was ours. We do not want our politicians, through weakness, self-hatred, malice, tiredness or abandonment to change our home into an utterly different place. And while Europeans may be almost endlessly compassionate, we may not be boundlessly so. The public may want many contradictory things, but they will not forgive politicians if – whether by accident or design – they change our continent completely. If they do so change it then many of us will regret this quietly. Others will regret it less quietly. Prisoners of the past and of the present, for Europeans there seem finally to be no decent answers to the future. Which is how the fatal blow will finally land.

AFTERWORD

The Strange Death of Europe came out in the UK on 4 May 2017. Six weeks earlier, on 22 March, a 52-year-old British-born convert to Islam, Khalid Masood, ploughed his car across Westminster Bridge, killing an American tourist, a Romanian tourist and two British nationals. Dozens more were injured as they scattered from the car's trajectory, some falling into the River Thames below. Crashing into the railings of the Houses of Parliament, Masood then ran out of the hired vehicle and through the front gates of the British Parliament. There he stabbed to death one of the policemen on duty, PC Keith Palmer, before himself being shot and killed by armed police. Masood's last phone messages revealed that he believed he was 'waging jihad.'

In the immediate aftermath the British press fell back on the routine clichés. In a much-forwarded piece one prominent British journalist took to the pages of the *New York Times* to insist that by the morning after the attack 'London was, if not quite back to normal, then certainly back in business. As I travelled through the south of the city, up to Chelsea and later over to King's Cross, Londoners really were going about their lives as on any other day.' He went on, 'This behaviour reflects something deeper than conscious defiance, I think. It would simply not occur to the 8.6 million citizens of this megalopolis to allow one man to send them into hiding. As they say in the East End, you're having a laugh, aren't you?'[1] One wonders when the author last went into the East End of London and found a pub filled with cockneys uttering such phrases? Perhaps they were singing 'Roll out the barrel' as well.

Two weeks after the Westminster attack, and before PC Palmer's funeral, there was a national 'Service of Hope' at Westminster Abbey, just across from where the policeman had been stabbed to death.

In his sermon at the inter-faith service the Dean of Westminster, the Very Reverend John Hall, spoke for a nation that he described as 'bewildered'. He asked, 'What could possibly motivate a man to hire a car and take it from Birmingham to Brighton to London, and then drive it fast at people he had never met, couldn't possibly know, against whom he had no personal grudge, no reason to hate them and then run at the gates of the Palace of Westminster to cause another death? It seems likely that we shall never know.' More bewildering events swiftly followed.

On Monday 22 May thousands of young women were leaving a concert by the American pop singer Ariana Grande at Manchester Arena. Waiting for them as they streamed out was Salman Abedi, a 22-year-old whose Libyan parents had arrived in the UK in the 1990s after fleeing the Gadaffi regime. In the foyer Abedi detonated a bomb he was carrying which was packed with nuts, bolts and other shrapnel. 22 people – children and parents – were killed instantly. Hundreds more were injured and many suffered life-changing injuries. ISIS claimed Abedi as one of their soldiers.

In the wake of Manchester there was a twist on the new European tradition of featuring John Lennon's 'Imagine' after any terrorist attack ('Imagine there's no countries / It isn't hard to do/ Nothing to kill or die for / And no religion, too'). A Mancunian take on this developed when members of a crowd at a memorial shortly after the attack sang the 1990s Oasis hit 'Don't look back in anger'. This seemed to perfectly fit the mood that politicians and press wished to encourage. Soon the stories of the dead and maimed disappeared. Broadcasters didn't seem to wish to focus on young women having bits of nails and bolts pulled from their heads and spines. Instead, within a little over 24 hours of the attack the main theme of the response to Manchester was, 'Don't look back in anger.'

Almost nobody asked, 'Why not? Why shouldn't people look back in anger when their daughters have been blown up just because they went to see their favourite pop singer on a Monday evening?' Why shouldn't people be angry that the young Abedi killed 22 people, one for each year of life their country had given him?

A fortnight after the attack in Manchester Ariana Grande returned to the city and with a line-up of other pop stars including Justin Bieber performed a 'One Love' concert. There was observation of the tragedy and then the party started and people began to enjoy themselves again. Some observers lauded this as a demonstration of resilience in the face of terror. Few noted that, as with the previous month's 'Service of Hope', the dead still hadn't been buried before everybody else 'moved on'.

In what began to seem a remorseless set of events, the night before the 'One Love' concert in Manchester it was London's turn again. On the evening of Saturday 3 June three men drove a van into pedestrians as they crossed London Bridge. They then leaped out of the van and began slashing at the throats and bodies of pedestrians, appearing to target women in particular. Then they ran, slashing at the crowds of tourists and Londoners alike, through the pubs and streets of Borough Market. Among their shouts was 'This is for Allah'. Eight people were killed and many more seriously injured before armed police shot the three men dead. They were later identified as Youssef Zaghba (22), Khuram Butt (27) and Rachid Redouane (30). Both Zaghba and Redouane had been born in Morocco. A subsequent inquest heard that Redouane had entered Britain using a false name, claiming to be Libyan and was actually five years older than he had pretended. He had been refused asylum under his false Libyan identity, exhausted his further appeals, absconded and lived under his Moroccan identity instead. Khuram Butt, meanwhile, had been born in Pakistan and was described as having arrived in the UK as a 'child refugee' in 1998, his family having moved to the UK to claim asylum based on 'political oppression'.[2]

In the aftermath of the killing spree these men took part in, and while securing the area, Londoners who had been enjoying a night out were ordered to put their hands on their heads and exit the area in single file with armed police training guns on them in case of further attackers. Though the theme of London's resilience was constantly raised, the public that night looked more like a defeated people being marched into captivity than anything else. In the days that followed even more protective barriers, walls and bollards were put up around landmarks and vulnerable infrastructure points around Britain. A traditional cry of the 'open borders' movement for years had been 'build bridges, not walls'. Such people should go to London today. By the end of 2017 all of London's bridges were covered in walls.

Nevertheless the theme of 'resilience' before terror was stressed by the British Prime Minister, Theresa May, as well as other political leaders. Happening as it did on the eve of a general election, the Labour opposition managed to make some political capital out of these attacks by claiming that they were at least in part the result of police cuts. The Prime Minister announced on the steps of Downing Street that there had been too much tolerance of extremism in the UK and that after this third attack 'enough is enough'. She did not elaborate on this, beyond promising to appoint a commissioner to look into the issue of extremism.

Otherwise the emphasis was on 'Keep Calm and Carry On', Blitz spirit and much more. It was struck even more hollowly once again in September when (on the 15th of the month), Ahmed Hassan got on the London Underground's District line and left a bomb on the carriage during rush hour. The 18-year-old Iraqi turned out to have arrived in the UK illegally in 2015 and lived with foster parents since then. Indeed he had built the bomb he took onto the morning rush hour train in his foster parents' house. Fortunately for the many schoolchildren and others on the tube the detonator exploded without managing to ignite the device itself, leading to a stampede from the carriage and several dozen people with minor burns and other injuries, rather than dozens of corpses being taken away in body bags.

Of course there is no reason why Londoners should have much or any residual 'Blitz spirit'. As the 2011 census showed, the families of most people now in London weren't even in Britain at the time of the Blitz. There is no reason why people imbibe the memories of a previous generation just because they happen to inhabit the same bit of territory as those earlier people did.

As if to emphasise the fact that Blitz spirit isn't just imbibed in the London water, in November of the year that all these terrorist attacks occurred – and many others were thwarted – in the UK an event unfolded which was lingered over even less than the dead from the terrorist attacks. Early in the evening on Friday 24 November there were reports of shots having been fired at Oxford Circus station. A crowd stampede ensued, with hundreds of people fleeing in terror through some of the busiest streets in London. Terrified pedestrians barricaded themselves inside major department stores. A singer and celebrity called Olly Murs tweeted to his nearly 8 million followers that he was inside Selfridges. 'F**k everyone get out of Selfridges now gun shots!! I'm inside'. Even more unwisely this Tweet was followed with 'Really not sure what's happened! I'm in the back office … but people screaming and running towards exits!' The British police announced that they were responding to events as a terrorist incident, and on social media and in prominent papers online stories emerged of a vehicle having ploughed into pedestrians on Oxford Street, of blood and bodies lying everywhere.

Within an hour all this turned out to be nonsense. There had been no vehicle attack, no gunmen, no bodies and no blood. It is true that 16 people had been injured – one seriously – but this had been in the stampede out of Oxford Circus station and the surrounding area. There were reports that the whole incident had been sparked by a gang fight. This too turned out to be untrue. The day after the incident two men who feared that they might have been responsible for involuntarily causing the panic handed themselves into a police station but were released shortly afterwards without charge. On 26 December a similar incident occurred. Another stampede took place in Oxford Street when false reports of shots being fired caused Boxing Day shoppers to run screaming in panic into stores and down the adjoining streets.

Of course incidents like these – like similar panics after the November 2015 attacks in Paris – swiftly disappear from the news and nobody writes about them. They are passed over with embarrassment. Yet they suggest that the public are not as stoical as opinion writers and politicians like to claim. Rather, they are so jumpy that a minor disagreement can cause a mass stampede, and terrified celebrities and public alike start running from wholly imagined horrors.

The only event around this time that bucked any of these trends came as a result of an attack near Finsbury Park mosque on 19 June. That evening Darren Osborne, a 47-year-old father of four from Cardiff drove a van into crowds of people in the area of the mosque and the nearby Muslim Welfare House. One man, who had earlier collapsed, died at the scene and almost a dozen more were injured. There were a number of striking aspects to this attack. Most obviously the fear that perhaps the much-vaunted 'backlash' might in fact have become a reality. But most striking was that the condemnation which people were so keen to keep as precise and non-sweeping as possible after any and every Islamist attack was wholly absent here. In the aftermath of the attack near the mosque in Finsbury Park, Islamic organisations and some mainstream media were allowed to spread the blame for the attack as widely as possible. Against whole communities, against individuals who had nothing to do with the attack and had never advocated any such thing, and against any individual against whom they had a grudge. 'Don't look back in anger' was not a theme that was adopted very widely after the Finsbury Park attack.

While we may all agree that most Muslims are law-abiding, decent citizens, the same presumption does not appear to be able to be levelled at the rest of the population who are still judged as though only one step away from pogrom-mode. Perhaps it is because of such different standards of presumption of innocence that movements such as the so-called 'Identitarians' have begun to spring up in Europe. It is too early to judge what such movements currently consist of, let alone where they might go. On everybody's minds is a fear that their ideas and actions could in time justify precisely the reaction against which they ostensibly sprang up.

As it happened, when the first of 2017's attacks in the UK was taking place I was trudging along one of the new border fences that had recently gone up in central Europe. The flows of people had diminished but the preparedness of the authorities was on a very different level to that in 2015. Guards at the Hungarian-Serbian border demonstrated the new drone camera technology they were using and described their round-the-clock efforts to keep the borders of their own country secure. Of course no border would have kept Khalid Masood out. The Westminster Bridge attacker had been born in the UK. But the need for borders – or at least a workable and efficient asylum policy – continued to be a political battleground. Like the streets of an increasing number of European cities.

On 7 April it was Stockholm's turn. That afternoon a failed asylum seeker from Uzbekistan hijacked a truck and drove it into the crowds shopping on one of Sweden's busiest streets. Reports said that the driver seemed to be deliberately aiming the truck at families. Five people were killed and many more injured. The perpetrator had arrived in Sweden in 2014, claiming asylum, though the Swedish authorities swiftly found that he had no legitimate asylum claim. He was ordered to leave the country in late 2016, but had stayed.

On 17 August it was Spain's turn again. 14 people were killed and more than a hundred injured after Younes Abouyaaqoub, a 22-year-old Moroccan, drove a van into the crowds walking down the sidewalk of the popular La Rambla in Barcelona. He killed another person as he attempted to steal their car to escape. The perpetrator turned out to be part of a terror cell, members of which later ploughed a vehicle into pedestrians in nearby Cambrils, killing one woman and injuring six others. Other members of the cell had been killed the night before while they were preparing a bomb in a house in Alcanar. It was later reported that the cell had been planning far more spectacular attacks, including the blowing up of Antoni Gaudi's masterpiece, the Sagrada Familia Cathedral. A month later, in a separate incident, anti-terrorist police stormed the cathedral, evacuated it and shut down the entire surrounding area after reports of a 'suspicious' van nearby.

The day after the Barcelona attack two Finnish women were stabbed to death and eight others injured by an attacker in Turku, Finland shouting 'Allahu Akbar'. The attacker – who had deliberately targeted women – again turned out to be from that largest contingent of recent migrants to Europe: a person who had no more right to be in Europe than anyone else in the world. Abderrahman Bouanane had arrived in Finland in 2016 under a false name, claiming to be a child refugee. He turned out to be a 22-year-old from the perfectly peaceful country of Morocco. Despite being denied asylum and adopting different, false, identities, he was not removed from the country. And so another set of families had their lives changed forever.

Yet it appeared that little or nothing could be done to prevent such attacks. All that could be relied upon was policing, intelligence work, and the erection of ever more bollards in all European cities. About the larger issues nobody seemed to want to get out ahead of the belligerent political consensus.

In December 2017 Dimitris Avramopoulos, the European commissioner for migration, home affairs and citizenship summed up the ongoing policy of the political mainstream in an article titled 'Europe's migrants are here to stay'. 'It's time to face the truth,' he insisted. 'We cannot and will never be able to stop migration'. He boasted that 'The EU has granted protection to more than 700,000 people last year', something he argued was not only 'a moral imperative' but also 'an economic and social imperative for our ageing continent.' 'At the end of the day,' he wrote, 'we all need to be ready to accept migration, mobility and diversity as the new norm and tailor our policies accordingly. The only way to make our asylum and migration policies future-proof, is to collectively change our way of thinking first.' Avramopoulos did recognise failures, however, acknowledging that 'Of course, a lot still remains to be done in the European Union. We need to deliver on our promises to evacuate thousands of migrants from Libya either through resettlement or assisted voluntary return in the coming months.'[3]

The Italian government soon after promised to rectify this failing in the EU's migration policy. That same month for the first time it began flying migrants from Libya to Rome, with the country's interior minister promising to bring another 10,000 people by plane in the coming year in order to save them from people traffickers. Marco Minniti even went to meet the first migrants to be flown in from Libya himself, announcing 'This is a historic moment because we have created the first humanitarian corridor to save migrants given refugee status by the UN from the clutches of criminals'. In order to help migrants avoid the treacherous crossings on the Mediterranean the new policy was to get around the smuggling gangs by the EU doing their work for them, using airplanes instead of boats. In the year before this announcement the Italian authorities had gained proof (through undercover work) that a number of NGOs were actively co-operating with the smuggling networks, arranging meeting points and times, and even handing boats back to the networks. The Italian public responded to these discoveries with anger but not surprise.

Of course Minniti and others among the Italian authorities claimed that their new scheme would allow only genuine refugees to arrive in Italy. But the track record of all European countries suggested that this – as with so much else – would prove to be a fantasy. Minniti boasted that migrants who should not be in Italy would be deported at a greater rate. But this is another claim that the publics of Europe have reason to be skeptical about. Indeed figures released in the UK at the same time as Minniti's announcement revealed that only one in five lone child migrants who lie about their age in a bid to stay in the country are ever deported. A study by the national forensic medicine agency (Rättsmedicinalverket) in Sweden sought to discover the age of almost 8,000 people who had recently arrived in Sweden claiming to be 'child refugees'. The checks – carried out in cases where there were doubts as to the age – found that 6,600 of the 8,000 people tested were in fact over the age of 18. That is more than 82%.[4] What will happen to them? The same thing that happens with very nearly everybody: they will stay.

If the European authorities had been lax about who they let in, time and the consequences of being this lax – and thinking so little about the long-term consequences – made itself felt in the ugliest ways. Above all one irreversible fact kept asserting itself: that if you import the world's people you also import the world's problems, with perhaps some new ones. Events that happened anywhere else in the world now had an impact inside Europe.

In December 2017 the US President announced that he was planning to move the US Embassy in Israel from Tel Aviv to Jerusalem. Pundits and opponents of the President immediately warned that this would lead to the 'Arab street' rising up. In fact the Arab world remained remarkably quiet. At the Damascus Gate the Friday after the President's announcement a disappointed BBC journalist admitted that there were more press gathered than there were Palestinian protestors. But to the extent that the fabled 'Arab Street' did rise up it rose up in Europe.

In the wake of the President's announcement crowds of Muslims gathered outside the American embassy in London and among other things chanted, 'Khaybar Khaybar, ya yahud, Jaish Muhammad, sa yahud'. That is, 'Jews, remember Khaybar, the army of Muhammad is returning.' A chant which recalls the slaughter of the Jewish community near Medina by the armies of Mohammed in the seventh century. In Amsterdam a man with a Palestinian flag and a *keffiyah* smashed in the windows of a kosher restaurant in a Jewish quarter of the city. Up in Sweden things got even nastier. In Malmo the crowds chanted 'We're going to shoot the Jews', while in Gothenburg a crowd of around 20 masked men attacked the local synagogue, hurling Molotov cocktails at it. The crowd of 20–30 young Jews inside the adjacent community centre managed to escape unharmed. Two days later two fire bombs were found outside the Jewish burial chapel in Malmo. In Stockholm, as in Berlin, crowds burned the Star of David and a speaker called Jews 'apes and pigs'. Promises of martyrdom were made. A spokesman for the remaining Jewish community in Malmo put it starkly: you 'don't want to display the Star of David around your neck. It's a constant battle to live a normal life.'[5]

In the year since this book was published further details about the fateful decisions described have come to light. A journalist from *Die Welt* relayed some of Merkel's reasoning in August 2015, not least her fear that photographs would go around the world showing German border guards repelling migrants.[6] 'Meanwhile one former European government official has described the conversation at the emergency meeting in Brussels in October 2015. He quotes Merkel sighing '*Wir saufen ab'* ('We are drowning'), going on, 'We are getting so many refugees from Austria today. Imagine tomorrow.' She then apparently noted that she came from a country where they once had to live with walls and said that she did not want to have in her biography that she had built new walls.[7]

On the political level the policies of the latest generation of European politicians began to have some expected consequences. In the Dutch elections in March the reigning VVD (Liberal) party managed to remain the largest party, defying pre-election polls which predicted Geert Wilders's party to be the winner and the VVD coming second. A new party – Forum for Democracy – ate into some of Wilders's support. But more striking was that as polling day approached the VVD's campaign rhetoric became more and more indistinguishable from that of Wilders. In one advert, published in the Dutch papers, Prime Minister Mark Rutte – who was campaigning for re-election – warned immigrants, 'Act normal, or leave'. Then in the days before the election, there was a remarkable stand-off between the Turkish and Dutch governments. A number of Turkish politicians, including ministers, were due to arrive in the Netherlands to campaign for a 'yes' vote in the Turkish referendum designed to congregate further powers around President Erdogan. The Dutch authorities took a stand against Turkish politicians campaigning in their country, forbidding the Turkish Foreign Minister's plane from even landing and expelling another Turkish minister from the country. The moment of perceived toughness paid off and Wilders's party became only the second largest in the Dutch Parliament.

In France the following month Marine Le Pen managed to get down to the last two in the Presidential race. The following month she was beaten to the Presidency by Emmanuel Macron who had broken through an unusual election season without even having the support or structure of one of the mainstream parties. Perhaps his opponents' chances had always been talked up. Perhaps he was just lucky to be facing a member of the Le Pen family in a popular vote. But the election of Macron suggested to some people that the whole landscape of European politics could perhaps remain with the status quo. Amid the celebrations few people seemed to keep in mind the long-term trajectory. In the Presidential run-off in France in 2002 Marine Le Pen's father had managed to get only 17.8 per cent of the vote. In 2017 his daughter managed to get 33.9 per cent.

The German elections in September silenced anyone who still thought that European centrist politics could continue as normal. Before the elections even a centrist such as Merkel's interior minister, Thomas de Maiziere, used the pages of *Bild-Zeitung* to try to play the same game that the Dutch VVD had used to stay in power. 'We are not Burka' was one of the things he said, in a desperate hope of emulating the tactics and success of Prime Minister Rutte. Despite such efforts, September 2017 – two years after her fateful borders decision – was the month that the German electorate seriously humbled their Chancellor. It was the worst result for her party since 1949. And although the CDU remained the largest party, the German electorate shook their nation's politics by making the four-year old Alternative für Deutschland (AfD) into the third largest party in the Bundestag, with 94 seats. That is a party whose joint leader, Alexander Gauland, declared an hour after the results that he would 'hunt down the government, Mrs Merkel, and get our country and people back.' Merkel's sister party in Bavaria, the CSU, found the Chancellor unwilling to accept their demands for a tougher line on immigration. And, having suffered an electoral catastrophe of their own the SPD refused to go back into coalition with Merkel. When coalition talks failed in November there was talk of another election but nobody could see how it could turn up particularly different results. Finally in February 2018, almost half a year after the election, the parties of the old 'Grand Coalition' (or 'GroKo') agreed to come back together once more. The move left the AfD as the main opposition party to the German government.

Amid much talk of the 'humiliation' of Angela Merkel there was little demonstration of any actual backtracking. The words were often there of course, as they had been so many times before. On the first anniversary of the Berlin marketplace attack the Chancellor promised that she would 'guarantee security' for the German people. But these were hollow words. The attacker a year earlier had been a Tunisian asylum seeker. Neither Merkel nor any other European leader had instituted any policy or system to ensure that such a person would not get in or stay in Europe. All they had done was continue providing opportunities for the bollard-making industry, and made every Christmas market across Europe for the foreseeable future become an armed-police and ring-fenced security nightmare. Mark Steyn summed up the curiosity of all this by asking, 'If free countries have to have unsightly security controls, why don't they have them around the national borders rather than around every single thing inside those borders?'[8]

In a way even more striking than the German election was the shift that occurred next door in Austria the months after the election. The country's young former Foreign Minister, Sebastian Kurz, managed to ensure his Austrian People's Party became the largest party by making a stand on issues of immigration and integration in the run-up to the election. His party won 62 seats, and after a short period of negotiation formed a government with the Freedom Party of Austria which had won 51 seats. The acceptance of a party generally termed 'far-right' back into government in Austria attracted significant international attention. But the election proved two things. Firstly that the Austrian public wanted a government that was tougher on immigration and issues of identity. Secondly that at the political level it was possible for a mainstream party to bring in a non-mainstream party to help it govern. For the future of European politics the Austrian election and coalition may be the most important of the post-2015 era so far. If this new arrangement works it could provide an example for the political mainstream in the rest of Europe. If it goes even minimally wrong it could prove a klaxon call.

For their part the Central and Eastern European states continued in their stand-off with Berlin and Brussels. The 'Visegrad' group of four nations (the Czech Republic, Hungary, Poland and Slovakia) found some strength in numbers. Continuing to refuse migrant quotas or in any way to green light in retrospect or in the future the policies that had led to the catastrophe of 2015, Brussels became increasingly threatening. In December 2017 the European Commission announced that it was suing Poland, Hungary and the Czech Republic at the European

Court of Justice over their refusal to take in the migrants that Brussels and Berlin had invited. Sanctions and heavy fines are threatened down the line. Yet at the time of writing these countries are holding out against the European Commission's threats.

In conversations in these countries since *The Strange Death of Europe* came out I have been struck by the number of officials who have brought my attention to the crunch that is at some point going to occur. Strong majorities of the public in these countries are in favour of membership of the EU. But strong majorities are also consistently in favour of their national governments' attitudes of hostility towards the demands over migrants being made by Brussels. And they object to the bullying. Saying 'something has got to give' is not true. Often things just rub along badly for a very long time. But a Commission which sought to unify rather than divide Europe would not seek to blackmail member states for refusing to pick up the tab for Berlin's mistakes. Especially when Berlin has shown no significant remorse and every sign that those mistakes will remain unacknowledged. In essence the Central and Eastern European states look at what is happening in Western Europe and do not want to become like them. They see demonstrations by residents of Malmo calling on the Swedish government to do more to prosecute the increasing number of rapes in the city.[9] They see that on New Year's Eve in Berlin in 2017 the city has to arrange a 'safe zone' for women by the Brandenburg Gate so that they might celebrate New Year's without the fear of rape. And they see the reports confirming what everybody knew but nobody would admit. In January 2018 figures were released showing that the recent rise in violent crime in Germany had a particular cause. It was, as only officialdom in Germany would have been able to try to deny, because of the recent influx of migrants. Indeed the study, which used data from Lower Saxony, showed that more than 90% of the rise in violent crime was attributable to young male migrants.[10] Who would want these problems, or tolerate them if they did not already have them?

****

From the moment it was published in the UK *The Strange Death of Europe* went into the bestseller lists. It remained in the *Sunday Times* top 10 non-fiction bestsellers for almost 20 weeks and became one of the bestselling books of the year. For most authors such an event would be an unmitigated joy. This was not the case on this occasion. I learned that the book had reached number 1 on the *Sunday Times* bestseller lists whilst in France. At the same time I began to receive calls from concerned friends and colleagues in London caught up in the terrorist attacks on London Bridge and Borough Market.

The book was received well by the critics as well as by the public. But most striking was the number of politicians and serving and former political leaders who admitted to having read the book and admitted, what is more, to heartily agreeing with it. Indeed the reception from high-ranking political leaders was such that it did make me several times wonder why if there was so much agreement this had gone so wrong in the first place. All of it went to show what I had long suspected, which is that it is simply easier to let the status quo roll along and then complain about it than it is to take a short term political hit for the long-term well-being of your society. The book was also well received by publics in other countries, especially the USA and Australia. In both of these countries readers and politicians often said to me 'It's about us, isn't it?' The answer to which is 'Yes, of course.'

I suppose it is inevitable in a book of this length that some errors will be found. After the hardback edition came out I expected that various people would claim that the statistics and figures herein (factual and correct though they are) were in some way erroneous. I expected people to contest the numbers Europe has taken in, the numbers affected by the decisions or the numbers expected in the years ahead. I expected them to claim I had 'cherry-picked' their speeches or even 'quoted out of context'.

Yet none of the many facts in this book were able to be refuted and nobody of any consequence has even tried to contest or deny them. The only minor individual mentioned in the book who I know to have objected to the descriptions of himself here is Jonathan Portes, one of the figures glancingly mentioned for his role in lubricating the open-door policies of the post-1997 UK Labour government – a policy that his superiors have long since expressed regret over. Via his social media outlet from his post at King's College London, Portes let it be known that the description of him and his involvement in that deeply damaging policy was riddled with errors. He neither contested the facts nor refuted the political disaster. Instead he objected to his coupling with Sarah Spencer as an 'academic', stating that although he was in academia before that role and although he has been in academia since that role, he was not in academia at the time. Secondly, he objected that rather than being 'noted' for his views on immigration like Sarah Spencer he in fact 'had never worked on immigration' until the British government invited him to help formulate its stance on the matter. Accordingly, I withdraw my accusation that he is an academic or any kind of expert in these areas. The evidence of his work should have been enough.

There are still people who try to pretend that all we are going through – and all that we are going to go through in the years ahead – is normal. Or not going on. Only occasionally do the places which push this lie make any concession to the reality that the European people can see all around them. In November the Pew Research Center released a striking new study which vindicated the claims made in this book and added more alarm for anyone who could cope with it. The study showed the extent to which Europe's Muslim population was due to increase even without any massive upsurge in migration of the kind that had occurred in recent years. It also showed it in other scenarios so that for instance Sweden (with an 8 per cent Muslim population in 2016) would have an 11 per cent Muslim population in 2050 if there was no more migration at all, a 21 per cent Muslim population if there was a 'regular' flow, and a 31 per cent Muslim population if recent migration was kept up.[11] Even the *Guardian* in Britain covered this story, under the headline 'Muslim population in some EU countries could triple, report says.'[12] The paper's readers must have found this a shock. Before wondering why their favourite left-wing paper had (by its own lights) become so inflammatorily racist.

As this book suggests, there is an ongoing effort to make the European publics not believe the evidence of their own lives. The point of this book is in part to point out that there is no point in this pretence – no point in pretending that everything going on does not constitute the most significant change possible in a culture. Sweden in 1950 was an ethnically homogenous society with almost no migration. A century on it will look an almost entirely different place. And within the life-spans of many of us it is fair to say that such a country – like most other countries in Western Europe – will become unrecognisable even to fairly recent inhabitants. Perhaps it will all be fine. Perhaps the people who remember what Sweden was, what France was, what Britain and what the rest of Europe was will just die out. Perhaps then all the problems, not least the problem of identifying the problem, will cease. Perhaps. Or perhaps a whole new world of problems is being born.

Douglas Murray

April 2018

NOTES

INTRODUCTION

1 Stefan Zweig, *The World of Yesterday*, Pushkin Press, 2014, p. 425.
2 'Merkel confronts Facebook's Zuckerberg over policing hate-posts', *Bloomberg*, 26 September 2015.
3 Pope John Paul II, *Ecclesia in Europa*, 28 June 2003.
4 Chancellor Helmut Kohl, speech at the Catholic University of Louvain, Belgium, 5 February 1996.
5 For an interesting discussion of many of these issues, see Samuel Moyn, *The Last Utopia: Human Rights in History*, Harvard University Press, 2012.

THE BEGINNING

1 Hansard, 2 December 2002. Blunkett was talking about the *Times* journalist Anthony Browne.
2 Office for National Statistics (hereafter ONS), 2011 Census. Available at: https://www.ons.gov.uk/census/2011census.
3 Guy Goodwin from the ONS quoted in 'Census shows rise in foreign-born', BBC News, 11 December 2012.
4 Ken Livingstone in 'World civilisation or clash of civilisations?' conference, London, 20 January 2007.
5 See David Miles, *The Tribes of Britain*, Weidenfeld & Nicolson, 2005, p. 236.
6 Simon Heffer, *Like the Roman: The Life of Enoch Powell*, Weidenfeld & Nicolson, 1998, pp. 467–8.
7 Full text in *Reflections of a Statesman: The Writings and Speeches of Enoch Powell*, Bellew Publishing, 1991, pp. 373–9.
8 Ibid.
9 See the 2008 BBC documentary, 'Rivers of Blood'.

10 For instance in the Commonwealth Immigrants Act, 1962.

11 In the wake of the 1977 Franks Report.

12 See 'Ray Honeyford: Racist or right?', BBC, 10 February 2012.

13 Andrew Neather, 'Don't listen to the whingers – London needs immigrants', *Evening Standard*, 22 October 2009.

14 Tom Bower, *Broken Vows: Tony Blair and the Tragedy of Power*, Faber & Faber, 2016, pp. 171–8.

15 Hugh Muir, 'Hideously diverse Britain: The immigration "conspiracy"', *The Guardian*, 2 March 2011.

16 Bower, *Broken Vows*, pp. 175–6.

17 ONS figures.

18 Ibid., Migration Statistics Quarterly Report, November 2015.

HOW WE GOT HOOKED ON IMMIGRATION

1 This conversation from March 1959 was recalled by his colleague and confidant Alain Peyrefitte in *C'était de Gaulle* (1994) and is the subject of some contention.

2 Boris Johnson, 'Let's not dwell on immigration but sow the seeds of integration', *The Telegraph*, 17 December 2012.

3 Sunder Katwala quoted in 'Census shows rise in foreign-born', BBC News, 11 December 2012.

4 YouGov poll for *The Sunday Times*. Fieldwork 13–14th December 2012. Available at http://cdn.yougov.com/cumulus_uploads/document/wohvkihpjg/YG-Archive-Pol-Sunday-Times-results-14-161212.pdf.

5 BBC Newsnight, 11 December 2012.

6 The Louise Casey review into Rotherham borough council, 4 February 2015.

7 Robert Winder, *Bloody Foreigners: The Story of Immigration to Britain*, Little Brown, 2004, pp. x and 2.

8 Barbara Roche speaking at TEDxEastEnd, uploaded 3 October 2011, 'The British story of migration' [https://www.youtube.com/watch?v=_fMpxkHJRtk].

9 BBC Question Time, 13 December 2012.

10 Principal Projections (PP) of the ONS, based on 2014 figures.

11 See David Coleman, 'Uncontrolled migration means Finis Britanniae', *Standpoint*, June 2016, issue 83.

THE EXCUSES WE TOLD OURSELVES

1 'Migration: an economic and social analysis', Home Office Economics and Resource Analysis Unit and the Cabinet Office Performance and Innovation Unit, November 2000 (https://www.gov.uk/government/uploads/system/uploads/attachment_data/file/61131/migrationreportnov2000.pdf).
2 Peter Sutherland and Cecilia Malmström, 'Europe's migration challenge', Project Syndicate, 20 July 2012.
3 See for instance BBC News, 'Recent immigrants to UK "make net contribution"', 5 November 2013.
4 Professor Christian Dustmann and Dr Tommaso Frattini, 'The fiscal effects of immigration to the UK', University College London, Centre for Research and Analysis of Migration, 27 November 2013.
5 Dustmann and Frattini, 'The fiscal effects of immigration to the UK', *The Economic Journal*, vol. 124, issue 580, November 2014. See especially Table 5.
6 Sutherland and Malmström, 'Europe's migration challenge'.
7 For this and other information on fertility rates, see Eurostat, 'Total fertility rate, 1960–2014 (live births per woman' [http://ec.europa.eu/eurostat/statistics-explained/index.php/File:Total_fertility_rate,_1960%E2%80%932014_(live_births_per_woman)_YB16.png].
8 Eurostat.
9 Population Trends, Summer 2002, ONS.
10 ONS, 'Average age of retirement rises as people work longer', 16 February 2012.
11 'Merkel warns on cost of welfare', *The Financial Times*, 16 December 2012.
12 Richard Reed, in *The Daily Express* debate, 3 June 2016.
13 Sarah Spencer (ed.), *Strangers and Citizens: A Positive Approach to Migrants and Refugees*, Paul and Company, 1994, p. 340.
14 Ibid., p. 109.
15 Sarah Spencer, *Migrants, Refugees and the Boundaries of Citizenship*, IPPR pamphlet, 1995.
16 Sarah Spencer (ed.), *The Politics of Migration*, Blackwell, 2003 p. 6.
17 'Muslims in Britain have zero tolerance of homosexuality, says poll', *The Guardian*, 7 May 2009.

18 ICM poll reported in 'Half of all British Muslims think homosexuality should be illegal, poll finds', *The Guardian*, 11 April 2016.

19 YouGov survey, fieldwork, 23–24 February 2015.

20 Professor Alexis Jay, Independent Inquiry into Child Sexual Exploitation in Rotherham (1997–2013).

21 For instance, outside the Old Bailey in London after the Operation Bullfinch trial.

22 Mohammed Shafiq of the Ramadhan Foundation.

23 'Innvandrere bak alle anmeldte overfallsvoldtekter i Oslo', *Dagbladet*, 15 April 2009.

24 'Norway offers migrants a lesson in how to treat women', *The New York Times*, 19 December 2015.

25 Tom Bower, *Broken Vows: Tony Blair and the Tragedy of Power*, Faber & Faber, 2016, p. 175.

'WELCOME TO EUROPE'

1 IOM, 'IOM applauds Italy's life-saving Mare Nostrum operation: "Not a migrant pull factor"', press release, 31 October 2014.

2 *The New York Times*, 'Aliens find a European gateway at Spain's coast', report by Alan Riding, 18 October 1992.

3 Ibid.

4 This case actually came to trial in Spain two years later. See 'Muslim migrant boat captain faces murder charges for pushing Christians overboard', *Daily Telegraph*, 19 September 2016.

'WE HAVE SEEN EVERYTHING'

1 Neujahrsansprache von Bundeskanzlerin Angela Merkel, Die Bundesregierung, 31 December 2014.

2 Sommerpressekonferenz von Bundeskanzlerin Merkel, Die Bundesregierung, 31 August 2015.

3 *The Economist*, 5 September 2015.

MULTICULTURALISM

1 See Paul Scheffer, *Het Land van Aankomst*, De Bezige Bij, 2007.

2 'Merkel says German multicultural society has failed', BBC News, 17 October 2010.

3 Friedrich Ebert Foundation study, October 2010.

4 David Cameron speech at the Munich Security Conference, 5 February 2011.

5 *Le Figaro*, 'Sarkozy: le multiculturalisme, "un chec"', 10 February 2011.

6 For one of the best discussions of the idea of multiculturalism as an ideology, see Rumy Hassan, *Multiculturalism: Some Inconvenient Truths*, Methuen, 2010.

7 BBC News, 'Sharia law in UK is unavoidable', 7 February 2007.

8 Samuel P. Huntington, *Who Are We?*, Free Press, p. 171.

9 In his 1996 essay 'Multikultureller Werte-Relativismus und Werte-Verlust'.

10 Quoted in an opinion piece by Karen Jespersen in *Berlingske Tidende*, 19 February 2005.

11 Hege Storhaug, *But the Greatest of These is Freedom* (originally published in Norwegian by Kagge Forlag, 2006), 2011 pp. 282–3.

12 Edward Gibbon, *The Decline and Fall of the Roman Empire*, John Murray, 1855, vol. 6, ch. 52, p. 387.

13 For instance, Nicholas Sarkozy in his book *Tout pour La France*, Plon, 2016.

14 Bernard-Henri Lévy in conversation with the author, 12 July 2016.

15 Jean Raspail, 1982 Afterword to *The Camp of the Saints*.

16 Ibid., pp. 9–13.

17 Jean Raspail, *The Camp of the Saints*, trans Norman Shapiro, The Social Contract Press, 1995, p. 34.

18 Matthew Connelly and Paul Kennedy, 'Must it be the West against the Rest?', *The Atlantic*, December 1994.

19 *Le Figaro* magazine, 26 October 1985.

20 'French article sets off furor on immigrants', *The New York Times*, 3 November 1985.

21 OFPRA (Office français de protection des réfugiés et apatrides).

22 INSEE (Institut national de la statistique et des études économiques).

23 Raspail, *The Camp of the Saints*, 1995, 'Author's Introduction to the 1985 French Edition', p. xiii.

24 'Le tabou des statistiques ethniques', *Le Point*, 18 February 2016.

25 Ipsos poll carried out for Le Centre National de la Recherche Scientifique and Sciences Po Grenoble.

THEY ARE HERE

1 Bundesamt für Migration und Flüchtlinge, Aktuelle Zahlen zu Asyl, December 2013.

2 ONS, Migration Statistics Quarterly Report, November 2015.

3 'Get rid of the immigrants? No, we can't get enough of them, says German Mayor', *The Guardian*, 6 August 2015.

4 Eugenio Ambrosi, 'Europe can cope with the influx of migrants', *The Wall Street Journal*, 25 August 2015.

5 The video of this conference can be viewed online here: https://www.youtube.com/watch?v=YNXECcltt9U.

6 Quoted in Kenan Malik, *From Fatwa to Jihad*, Atlantic Books, 2009, p. 8.

7 Salman Rushdie, *Joseph Anton: A Memoir*, Jonathan Cape, 2012, p. 143.

8 The comments were made on the BBC programme 'Hypotheticals', broadcast in May 1989, moderated by Geoffrey Robertson QC. Clips from the programme intermittently appear and disappear from the internet, but the relevant clip can still currently be viewed on YouTube.

9 Hugh Trevor-Roper (Lord Dacre) quoted in *The Independent*, 10 June 1989.

10 Rushdie, *Joseph Anton*, p. 252.

11 Ibid., p. 152.

12 Ibid., p. 186.

13 Correspondence between Salman Rushdie, John le Carré and others in *The Guardian*, 18–22 November 1997.

14 Tony Benn, *The Benn Diaries*, ed. Ruth Winstone, Arrow Books, 1996, entry for 15 February 1989, pp. 616–17.

15 Rushdie, *Joseph Anton*, p. 147.

16 Fay Weldon, *Sacred Cows: A portrait of Britain, post-Rushdie, pre-Utopia*, Chatto & Windus, CounterBlasts, no. 4, 1989, p. 7.

17 Ziauddin Sardar, *Desperately Seeking Paradise: Journeys of a Sceptical Muslim*, Granta Books, 2004, p. 285.

18 Cited in Christopher Hitchens, *Hitch-22: A Memoir*, Atlantic Books, 2010, p. 271.

19 Malik, *From Fatwa to Jihad*, p. 197.

20 There is an interesting discussion of this episode in Malise Ruthven, *A Satanic Affair: Salman Rushdie and the Rage of Islam*, Chatto & Windus, 1990, esp. pp. 68ff and p. 107.

21 Shikha Dalmia, 'The Iconoclast', an interview with Salman Rushdie, *Reason*, 1 August 2005.

PROPHETS WITHOUT HONOUR

1   See Frits Bolkestein, 'On the collapse of the Soviet Union', a speech at the Liberal International Conference in Lucerne, Switzerland, 6 October 1991; and Frits Bolkestein, 'De integratie von minderheden', *De Volkskrant*, 12 October 1991.

2   See Frits Bolkestein, *Breakthrough: From Innovation to Impact*, ed. Henk van den Breemen, Owls Foundation 2014, p. 221.

3   Paul Scheffer, 'Het multiculturele drama', NRC Handelsblad, 29 January 2000.

4   Survey carried out in 1998 by Paul M. Sniderman and Louk Hagendoorn and included in their book *When Ways of Life Collide: Multiculturalism and its Discontents in the Netherlands*, Princeton University Press, 2007, p. 22.

5   *De Islamisering van onze cultuur: Nederlandse Identitieit als Fundament*, Pim Fortuyn, Karakter Uitgevers BV, 2001 edn.

6   This famous debate is available to watch on YouTube [https://www.youtube.com/watch?v=tMxS_xSKujU].

7   Heard by Jort Kelder; reported in Ian Buruma, *Murder In Amsterdam*, Atlantic, 2006, p. 100.

8   Conversation between the author and Hans Teeuwen, Amsterdam, 12 March 2016.

9   Ayaan Hirsi Ali, *The Caged Virgin*, The Free Press, 2006, p. ix.

10   Ibid., p. 76.

11   Ayaan Hirsi Ali, *Infidel*, The Free Press, 2007, p. 32.

12   Ibid., p. 287.

13   Ibid., p. xii.

14   'Germany investigating Imam who urged God to "destroy the Zionist Jews"', Haaretz, 23 July 2014.

15   See Oriana Fallaci, *Interviews with History and Conversations with Power*, Rizzoli, 2011.

16   See, for instance, Riccardo Nencini, *Oriana Fallaci: I'll Die Standing on My Feet*, Edizioni Polistampa, 2008, pp. 18 and 28.

17   For a discussion of this trend at an earlier stage of her life, the content of *Oriana Fallaci* by her exasperated would-be biographer Santo L. Arico, Southern Illinois University Press, 1998, is instructive.

18   Oriana Fallaci, *The Rage and the Pride*, Rizzoli, 2002, p. 22.

19   Ibid., p. 57.

20   Ibid., p. 85.

21   See, for instance, ibid., p. 116.

22   Ibid., p. 129.

23   Ibid., p. 98.

24   Ibid., pp. 137–8.

25   See Fallaci's own unapologetic discussion of this in *The Force of Reason*, Rizzoli, 2006, p. 53.

26   'Brigitte Bardot unleashes colourful diatribe against Muslims and modern France', *Agence France Presse*, 12 May 2003.

27   'Calling Islam stupid lands author in court', *The Guardian*, 18 September 2002.

28   See Fallaci, *The Force of Reason*, p. 287.

29   Ibid., p. 56.

30   *Oriana Fallaci intervista Oriana Fallaci*, Rizzoli, 2004.

31   Pope Benedict XVI's address to the University of Regensburg, 12 September 2006.

EARLY-WARNING SIRENS

1   See especially Bruce Bawer, *While Europe Slept*, Doubleday, 2006, and *Surrender*, Doubleday, 2009.

2   Jeffrey Goldberg, 'Is it time for the Jews to leave Europe?', *The Atlantic*, April 2015.

3   'Tories attack Islamic terrorism "rebranding"', *The Daily Telegraph*, 18 January 2008, http://www.telegraph.co.uk/news/uknews/1575925/Tories-attack-Islamic-terrorism-rebranding.html.

4   David Cameron, 'Statement on Woolwich incident', 23 May 2013, https://www.gov.uk/government/speeches/statement-on-woolwich-incident.

5   David Cameron, 'Statement on the killing of David Haines', 14 September 2014, http://www.bbc.co.uk/news/uk-29198128.

6   Fraser Nelson, 'Woolwich was a case study in the banality – and the idiocy – of evil', *The Daily Telegraph*, 23 May 2013.

7   Dan Hodges, 'Woolwich attack: confusing, horrific, bizarre – the horror that made literally no sense', *The Daily Telegraph*, blogs, 23 May 2013.

8   Simon Jenkins, 'Woolwich attack: This echo chamber of mass hysteria only aids terrorists', *The Guardian*, 23 May 2013.

9   Salman Rushdie and Sam Harris, 'Abandoned to fanatics', *The Los Angeles Times*, 9 October 2007.

10 'Turkish Prime Minister says "assimilation is a crime against humanity"', *The Local*, 11 February 2008.

THE TYRANNY OF GUILT

1   France 24 Arabic TV, 17 March 2015.

2   Anon., 'Swedes will compare this to the Holocaust', *The Local*, 20 April 2015.

3   'Migrant crisis: British student drives Syrians to Munich', BBC News, 6 September 2015.

4   'Refugee crisis: Danish yachtswoman smuggles refugee on her boat from Copenhagen to Malmo', *The Independent*, 8 September 2015.

5   For a rigorous counter-argument to the prevailing opinion on the 'stolen generation', see Keith Windschuttle, *The Fabrication of Aboriginal History, Volume 3: The Stolen Generations 1881–2008*, Macleay Press, 2009.

6   See, for instance, Prime Minister Kevin Rudd's 'Apology to Australia's indigenous peoples', Australian Parliament, 13 February 2008.

7   Ashraf H. A. Rushdy, *A Guilted Age: Apologies for the Past*, Temple University Press, 2015, p. xi.

8   Prime Minister Stephen Harper's 'Apology on behalf of Canadians for the Indian Residential Schools system', 11 June 2008.

9   Chantal Delsol is especially interesting on this point. See especially 'Historical forgiveness in question', *Hungarian Review*, vol. 3, no. 3, pp. 72–80.

10 See for examples Roger Sandall's book *The Culture Cult*, Westview Press, 2001.

11 Consider the statue in the centre of Columbus Circle in New York.

12 David Stannard, *American Holocaust: Columbus and the Conquest of the New World*, Oxford University Press, 1992, p. 246.

13 Kirkpatrick Sale, *The Conquest of Paradise: Christopher Columbus and the Columbian Legacy*, Alfred A. Knopf, 1991, p. 369.

14 'More cities celebrating "Indigenous Peoples Day" amid effort to abolish Columbus Day', *Washington Post*, 12 October 2015.

15 Ta-Nehisi Coates, 'The case for reparations', *The Atlantic*, June 2014.

16 Consider the Intelligence Squared debate in London, 'We should not be reluctant to assert the superiority of Western values', 9 October 2007, where this claim was made by the authors Charles Glass and William Dalrymple (video available on YouTube).

17 See David Cameron's response to question by Kenneth Clarke, House of Commons Hansard, 19 October 2015.

18 'His blood be on us, and on our children'. King James Bible, Matthew 27:25.

19 Pope Paul VI, 'Nostra Aetate'.

20 See Pascal Bruckner, *La Tyrannie de la penitence: essai sur le masochisme occidental*, Grasset & Fasquelle, 2006.

21 Andy Beckett, 'Heirs to the slavers', *The Guardian*, 2 December 2006.

22 'My ancestor traded in human misery', BBC News, 23 June 2006.

23 Karsten Nordal Hauken, 'Jeg ble voldtatt av en mann', *NRK*, 6 April 2016.

THE PRETENCE OF REPATRIATION

1 Immanuel Kant, *Perpetual Peace: A Philosophical Essay* (1795), George Allen & Unwin, 1903, pp. 155–6.

2 'Orbán accuses Soros of stoking refugee wave to weaken Europe', *Bloomberg*, 30 October 2015.

3 *The Atlantic*, December 1994.

LEARNING TO LIVE WITH IT

1 'Swallow fears and shop, Parisians told', *The Times* (London), 21 November 2015.

2 'Norway offers migrants a lesson in how to treat women', *The New York Times*, 19 December 2015.

3 'Polizei fühlt sich bei Migranten-Kriminalität gegängelt', *Die Welt*, 24 January 2016.

4 https://linksjugendbhvcux.wordpress.com/2016/02/24/kein-pegida-shit-in-bremerhaven-2-0.

5 'Attivista stuprata da un migrante "Gli altri mi chiesero di tacere"', Corriere Della Sera, 25 September 2015.

6 https://www.facebook.com/ob.boris.palmer/posts/1223835707655959.

7   Ipsos Mori migration and refugees poll, 11 August 2016, https://
    www.ipsos-mori.com/researchpublications/researcharchive/3771/
    Global-study-shows-many-around-the-world-uncomfortable-with-
    levels-of-immigration.aspx.

8   'Aliens find a European gateway at Spain's coast', *The New York Times*,
    18 October 1992.

9   Tom Bower, *Broken Vows: Tony Blair and the Tragedy of Power*, Faber
    & Faber, 2016, p. 173.

10 'Terror suspect protected', *The Sun*, 8 August 2016.

11 'Müssen wir Angst vor dem Islam haben, Frau Merkel?', *Bild*,
    10 September 2015. Original TV clip via Swiss television on http://
    www.srf.ch/play/tv/news-clip/video/merkel-ueber-die-angst-vor-eine
    r-islamisierung?id=18886c54-51e4-469b-8a98-45f1a817219b.

TIREDNESS

1   See, among many other works, Byung-Chul Han's *Müdigkeitsgesellschaft*
    (2010).

2   Friedrich Nietzsche, *Writings from the Late Notebooks*, Cambridge
    Texts in the History of Philosophy, ed. Rudiger Bittner, trans. Kate
    Sturge, Cambridge University Press, 2003, p. 267.

3   H. P. Liddon, *The Life of Edward Bouverie Pusey*, Longmans, 1893,
    vol. I, pp. 73–7.

4   Richard Dawkins, 'Why Darwin Matters', *The Guardian*, 9 February
    2008.

5   Don Cupitt, *The Meaning of the West: An Apologia for Secular
    Christianity*, SCM, 2008, p. 67.

6   Ibid.

7   Consider for instance John Locke, 'A Letter Concerning Toleration', in
    Two Treatises of Government and A Letter Concerning Toleration, ed.
    Ian Shapiro, Yale University Press, 2003, p. 219.

8   Stephen Spender, 8 September 1939, in *New Selected Journals
    1939–1995*, ed. Lara Feigel and John Sutherland with Natasha Spender,
    Faber & Faber, 2012, p. 13.

9   Choruses from 'The Rock', VI.

10 Jean-François Revel, *Without Marx or Jesus*, MacGibbon & Kee, 1972,
    p. 17.

11 Chantal Delsol, trans. Robin Dick, *Icarus Fallen: The Search for Meaning in an Uncertain World*, ISI Books, 2003, p. 46.

12 Interview with Ayaan Hirsi Ali by Giulio Meotti, *Il Foglio*, 31 January 2016.

13 'Fico: EU's migration policy is "ritual suicide"', EurActiv, 26 January 2016.

14 Chantal Delsol, preface to the English edition of Dick, *Icarus Fallen*, p. xx.

15 'Fico sieht keinen Platz für Islam in der Slowakei', *Der Standard*, 27 May 2016.

16 'Refugees and migrants stuck in Italy open up new route', *The Daily Telegraph*, 22 July 2016.

WE'RE STUCK WITH THIS

1 'Blaming policy, not Islam, for Belgium's radicalised youth', *The New York Times*, 7 April 2016.

2 National Opinion Poll, commissioned by Channel 4, August 2006.

3 ComRes poll for BBC Radio 4 'Today', 25 February 2015.

4 ComRes, BBC 'Young People and Prejudice' survey published 24 September 2013. http://comres.co.uk/wp-content/themes/comres/poll/BBC_Radio_1_Newsbeat_Discrimination_Poll_September_2013.pdf.

5 The original letter is available at http://www.bbc.co.uk/news/uk-25298580.

6 'Muslim project aims to break down barriers and educate youngsters on the human side of Islam', *Daily Record*, 27 November 2013, http://www.dailyrecord.co.uk/news/real-life/muslim-project-aims-break-down-2856192.

7 The poll was commissioned by the PVV party and conducted by the research bureau of Maurice de Hond in June 2013, http://www.geertwilders.nl./images/Reactie_op_Islam_in_Nederland.pdf.

8 Harris Interactive, 'Le Regard des Français sur la religion musulmane', April 2013, http://www.harrisinteractive.fr/news/2013/Results_HIFR_PAI_16042013.pdf.

9 'Les crispations alarmantes de la société française', *Le Monde*, 24 January 2013, http://www.lemonde.fr/politique/article/2013/01/24/les-crispations-alarmantes-de-la-societe-francaise_1821655_823448.html.

10 Harris Interactive, 'Le Regard des Français'.

11 Survation poll (fieldwork carried out April 2015), http://survation.com/british-muslims-is-the-divide-increasing.

12 YouGov Cambridge poll (fieldwork conducted in March 2015), http://cdn.yougov.com/cumulus_uploads/document/0gqzisd2xq/Islam%20and%20British%20values.pdf.

13 Institut fur Demoskopie Allensbach, November 2012, http://www.ifd-allensbach.de/uploads/tx_reportsndocs/November12_Islam_01.pdf.

14 'Für fast zwei Drittel der Bürger gehört der Islam nicht zu Deutschland', *WDR*, 12 May 2016.

15 See interview with Tommy Robinson by the current author, *The Spectator*, 19 October 2013.

16 Author interview with Wilders, March 2008.

17 Author interview with Robinson, *The Spectator*, 19 October 2013. Also see Tommy Robinson, *Enemy of the State*, The Press News, 2015.

CONTROLLING THE BACKLASH

1 Mark Steyn, 'Gay professors on the march', *The Daily Telegraph*, 11 May 2002.

2 *de Volkskrant*, 4 June 2016.

3 Eva Jacobsson, 'Boverket: Bristen ännu värre än väntat', *Hem & Hyra*, 1 April 2015.

4 Study by the Department of Journalism, Media and Communication at the University of Gothenburg, 2011.

5 Figures from the Swedish National Council for Crime Prevention (Brottsförebyggande rådet – Brå).

6 Frederic Morenius, 'Våldtäkt och förövarens nationella bakgrund', 12 August 2016, at https://fredricmorenius.wordpress.com/2016/08/12/valdtakt-och-forovarens-nationella-bakgrund.

7 Erico Matias Tavares, 'Sweden on the brink? – An Interview with Dr. Tino Sanandaji', 21 February 2016, at https://www.linkedin.com/pulse/sweden-brink-interview-dr-tino-sanandaji-erico-matias-tavares.

8 'Thousands of migrants rescued off Libya', BBC News, 30 August 2016.

9 'Bye bye, Willkommenskultur', *Die Zeit*, 7 July 2016.

10 Poll carried out for the German broadcaster ARD.

THE FEELING THAT THE STORY HAS RUN OUT

1 Jurgen Habermas et al., *An Awareness of what is Missing: Faith and Reason in a Post-Secular Age*, trans. Ciaran Cronin, Polity Press, 2010, p. 15.

2 E.W. Böckenförde, 'Die Entstehung des Staates als Vorgang der Sakularisation' (1967), in *Recht, Staat, Freiheit*, Frankfurt am Main, 1991, p. 112.

3 Eric Kaufmann, *Shall the Religious Inherit the Earth?*, Profile Books, 2010, p. 182.

4 Morten Storm with Paul Cruickshank and Tim Lister, *Agent Storm: My Life inside al-Qaeda*, Viking, 2014, pp. 117–19.

5 Benedetto Croce, 'Why we cannot help calling ourselves Christians', in *My Philosophy*, George Allen & Unwin, 1949; Marcello Pera, *Why We Should Call Ourselves Christians*, Encounter Books, 2011.

6 See Dietmar Eger, *Gerhard Richter, Catalogue Raisonné, Vol. I, 1962–1968*, Hatje Cantz, 2011: *Onkel Rudi*, p. 208; *Herr Heyde*, p. 233; *Familie Liechti*, p. 249.

7 See Richard Davey, Kathleen Soriano and Christian Weikop, *Anselm Kiefer*, Royal Academy, 2014: 'Interior', p. 144; 'Ages of the World', pp. 172–3.

THE END

1 'Tödliche Schüsse in Berliner Flüchtlingsheim', *Die Welt*, 29 September 2016.

2 'European Jews are too afraid to go to synagogue on religious holidays due to fears of anti-Semitic attacks', *The Daily Mail*, 20 September 2016.

3 'Merkel admits she would turn back the clock on refugee policy', *The Financial Times*, 19 September 2016.

4 'Trump wants border wall, but Britain is building one in France', NBC News, 12 September 2016.

WHAT MIGHT HAVE BEEN

1 Paul Collier, *Exodus: Immigration and Multiculturalism in the 21st Century*, Allen Lane, 2013; David Goodhart, *The British Dream: Successes and Failures of Post-war Migration*, Atlantic Books, 2013.

2   Erico Matias Tavares, 'Sweden on the brink? – An Interview with Dr. Tino Sanandaji', 21 February 2016, at https://www.linkedin.com/pulse/ sweden-brink-interview-dr-tino-sanandaji-erico-matias-tavares.

3   See, in particular, Joseph Ratzinger and Marcello Pera, *Without Roots: The West, Relativism, Christianity and Islam*, Basic Books, 2006; Jürgen Habermas and Joseph Ratzinger, *The Dialectics of Secularization: On Reason and Religion*, Ignatius Press, 2006.

WHAT WILL BE

1   Daniel Korski, 'Why we lost the Brexit vote', *Politico*, 20 October 2016.

2   *Le Monde*, 31 January 2016.

3   'It's bad in Eritrea, but not that bad', *The New York Times*, 23 June 2016.

4   'Multicultural Britain rejecting foreign conflict, MoD admits', *The Guardian*, 23 January 2014.

5   YouGov poll for Population Matters, May 2014.

6   'Umfrage zeigt: Das denken die Deutschen wirklich über den Islam', *Focus*, 5 May 2016.

7   'What do Europeans think about Muslim immigration?', Chatham House, 7 February 2017.

8   The video is available on YouTube under the title 'Erstaufnahme Asyl RP Lübke Kassel Lohfelden 14.10.2015'.

9   'Die Wutbürger sollten Deutschland verlassen', *Der Freitag*, 12 October 2016.

AFTERWORD

1   Matthew d'Ancona, 'London Pride, Undaunted', *New York Times*, 23 March 2017.

2   'Attacks in London and Manchester, March-June 2017', Independent Assessment of MI5 and Police Internal Reviews (Unclassified) by David Anderson QC, December 2017.

3   Dimitris Avramopoulos, 'Europe's migrants are here to stay', Politico, 18 December 2017.

4   'Impact of Sweden's asylum age assessment tests revealed' *The Local*, 4 December 2017.

5   Paulina Neuding, 'The uncomfortable truth about Swedish anti-Semitism', *New York Times*, 14 December 2017.

6   See Robin Alexander's *Die Getriebenen* (*The Driven Ones*), *Siedler Verlag*, 2017.

7   Bruno Maçães, *The Dawn of Eurasia: On the Trail of the New World Order*, Allen Lane, 2018, pp. 247-8.

8   Mark Steyn, 'Market Forces', www.steynonline.com, 19 December 2016.

9   'Demonstrators call for Swedish government to do more to combat rape', *The Local*, 20 December 2017.

10 'Germany: migrants "may have fuelled violent crime rise"', BBC News website, 3 January 2018.

11 'Europe's growing Muslim population', Pew Research Center, 29 November 2017.

12 'Muslim population in some EU countries could triple, report says', *Guardian*, 29 November 2017.

ACKNOWLEDGEMENTS

I would like to thank Robin Baird-Smith and Jamie Birkett at Bloomsbury. Also my agent Matthew Hamilton at Aitken Alexander Associates. This book was commissioned under Matthew's predecessor, Gillon Aitken and was one of the last book deals he did. As well as being a legendary agent, Gillon was a wonderful and wise friend who is very much missed.

Many people have been exceptionally kind and helpful during the years in which I have been exploring the themes of this book. I could not possibly name them all, as they cross several continents. But I would particularly like to thank the editors of all the publications which have allowed me to explore the issues raised in this book as well as all the friends, family, antagonists and colleagues who have been willing to discuss aspects of it.

And I would like to dedicate this book to one guide and friend in particular – Stanley.

INDEX

A NOTE ON THE AUTHOR

Douglas Murray is Associate Editor of the *Spectator* and writes frequently for a variety of other publications, including the *Sunday Times* and *Wall Street Journal*. An experienced debater, Douglas has spoken on a variety of prominent platforms, including at the British and European Parliaments and at the White House.

His previous books include *Bloody Sunday: Truth, Lies and the Saville Inquiry* (joint winner of the 2011-12 Christopher Ewart-Biggs Memorial Prize for advancing peace and understanding), *Neoconservatism: Why We Need It* and *Bosie: A Biography of Lord Alfred Douglas*.

A NOTE ON THE TYPE

The text of this book is set in Minion, a digital typeface designed by Robert Slimbach in 1990 for Adobe Systems. The name comes from the traditional naming system for type sizes, in which minion is between nonpareil and brevier. It is inspired by late Renaissance-era type.